FOLGER Shakespeare Library

The Tragedy of

Richard II

By
WILLIAM SHAKESPEARE

AN UPDATED EDITION

EDITED BY BARBARA A. MOWAT
AND PAUL WERSTINE

SIMON & SCHUSTER PAPERBACKS
NEW YORK LONDON TORONTO SYDNEY

Simon & Schuster Paperbacks
An Imprint of Simon & Schuster
1230 Avenue of the Americas
New York, NY 10020

This book is a work of fiction. Any references to historical events, real people, or real places are used fictitiously. Other names, characters, places, and events are products of the author's imagination, and any resemblance to actual events or places or persons, living or dead, is entirely coincidental.

This Simon & Schuster paperback edition January 2017

SIMON & SCHUSTER PAPERBACKS and colophon are registered trademarks of Simon & Schuster, Inc.

For information about special discounts for bulk purchases, please contact Simon & Schuster Special Sales at 1-866-506-1949 or business@simonandschuster.com.

The Simon & Schuster Speakers Bureau can bring authors to your live event. For more information or to book an event, contact the Simon & Schuster Speakers Bureau at 1-866-248-3049 or visit our website at www.simonspeakers.com.

Manufactured in the United States of America

19   18   17   16   15   14   13   12

ISBN 978-0-7434-8491-6
ISBN 978-1-5011-2886-8 (ebook)

THE NEW FOLGER LIBRARY SHAKESPEARE

Designed to make Shakespeare's great plays available to all readers, the New Folger Library edition of Shakespeare's plays provides accurate texts in modern spelling and punctuation, as well as scene-by-scene action summaries, full explanatory notes, many pictures clarifying Shakespeare's language, and notes recording all significant departures from the early printed versions. Each play is prefaced by a brief introduction, by a guide to reading Shakespeare's language, and by accounts of his life and theater. Each play is followed by an annotated list of further readings and by a "Modern Perspective" written by an expert on that particular play.

Barbara A. Mowat is Director of Research *emerita* at the Folger Shakespeare Library, Consulting Editor of *Shakespeare Quarterly*, and author of *The Dramaturgy of Shakespeare's Romances* and of essays on Shakespeare's plays and their editing.

Paul Werstine is Professor of English at the Graduate School and at King's University College at Western University. He is a general editor of the New Variorum Shakespeare and author of *Early Modern Playhouse Manuscripts and the Editing of Shakespeare* and of many papers and articles on the printing and editing of Shakespeare's plays.

Folger Shakespeare Library

The Folger Shakespeare Library in Washington, D.C., is a privately funded research library dedicated to Shakespeare and the civilization of early modern Europe. It was founded in 1932 by Henry Clay and Emily Jordan Folger, and incorporated as part of Amherst College in Amherst, Massachusetts, one of the nation's oldest liberal arts colleges, from which Henry Folger had graduated in 1879. In addition to its role as the world's preeminent Shakespeare collection and its emergence as a leading center for Renaissance studies, the Folger Shakespeare Library offers a wide array of cultural and educational programs and services for the general public.

EDITORS

BARBARA A. MOWAT
Director of Research emerita
Folger Shakespeare Library

PAUL WERSTINE
Professor of English
King's University College
at Western University, Canada

From the Director of the Folger Shakespeare Library

It is hard to imagine a world without Shakespeare. Since their composition more than four hundred years ago, Shakespeare's plays and poems have traveled the globe, inviting those who see and read his works to make them their own.

Readers of the New Folger Editions are part of this ongoing process of "taking up Shakespeare," finding our own thoughts and feelings in language that strikes us as old or unusual and, for that very reason, new. We still struggle to keep up with a writer who could think a mile a minute, whose words paint pictures that shift like clouds. These expertly edited texts, presented here with accompanying explanatory notes and up-to-date critical essays, are distinctive because of what they do: they allow readers not simply to keep up, but to engage deeply with a writer whose works invite us to think, and think again.

These New Folger Editions of Shakespeare's plays are also special because of where they come from. The Folger Shakespeare Library in Washington, D.C., where the Editions are produced, is the single greatest documentary source of Shakespeare's works. An unparalleled collection of early modern books, manuscripts, and artwork connected to Shakespeare, the Folger's holdings have been consulted extensively in the preparation of these texts. The Editions also reflect the expertise gained through the regular performance of Shakespeare's works in the Folger's Elizabethan Theater.

I want to express my deep thanks to editors Barbara Mowat and Paul Werstine for creating these indispensable editions of Shakespeare's works, which incorporate the best of textual scholarship with a richness of commentary that is both inspired and engaging. Readers who want to know more about Shakespeare and his plays can follow the paths these distinguished scholars have tread by visiting the Folger itself, where a range of physical and digital resources (available online) exist to supplement the material in these texts. I commend to you these words, and hope that they inspire.

Michael Witmore
Director, Folger Shakespeare Library

Contents

Contents

Editors' Preface

In recent years, ways of dealing with Shakespeare's texts and with the interpretation of his plays have been undergoing significant change. This edition, while retaining many of the features that have always made the Folger Shakespeare so attractive to the general reader, at the same time reflects these current ways of thinking about Shakespeare. For example, modern readers, actors, and teachers have become interested in the differences between, on the one hand, the early forms in which Shakespeare's plays were first published and, on the other hand, the forms in which editors through the centuries have presented them. In response to this interest, we have based our edition on what we consider the best early printed version of a particular play (explaining our rationale in a section called "An Introduction to This Text") and have marked our changes in the text—unobtrusively, we hope, but in such a way that the curious reader can be aware that a change has been made and can consult the "Textual Notes" to discover what appeared in the early printed version.

Current ways of looking at the plays are reflected in our brief introductions, in many of the commentary notes, in the annotated lists of "Further Reading," and especially in each play's "Modern Perspective," an essay written by an outstanding scholar who brings to the reader his or her fresh assessment of the play in the light of today's interests and concerns.

As in the Folger Library General Reader's Shakespeare, which the New Folger Library Shakespeare replaces, we include explanatory notes designed to help make Shakespeare's language clearer to a modern reader, and we place the notes on the page facing the text that they explain. We also follow the earlier edition in including illustrations—of objects, of clothing, of mythological figures—from books and manuscripts in the Folger Shakespeare Library collection. We provide fresh accounts of the life of Shakespeare, of the publishing of his plays, and of the theaters in which his plays were performed, as well as an introduction to the text itself. We also include a section called "Reading Shakespeare's Language," in which we try to help readers learn to "break the code" of Elizabethan poetic language.

For each section of each volume, we are indebted to a host of generous experts and fellow scholars. The "Reading Shakespeare's Language" sections, for example, could not have been written had not Arthur King, of Brigham Young University, and Randal Robinson, author of *Unlocking Shakespeare's Language*, led the way in untangling Shakespearean language puzzles and shared their insights and methodologies generously with us. "Shakespeare's Life" profited by the careful reading given it by S. Schoenbaum; "Shakespeare's Theater" was read and strengthened by Andrew Gurr, John Astington, and William Ingram; and "The Publication of Shakespeare's Plays" is indebted to the comments of Peter W. M. Blayney. We, as editors, take sole responsibility for any errors in our editions.

We are grateful to the authors of the "Modern Perspectives"; to Leeds Barroll and David Bevington for their generous encouragement; to the Huntington and Newberry Libraries for fellowship support; to King's University College for the grants it has provided to Paul Werstine; to the Social Sciences and Humanities Research Council of Canada, which provided him with Research Time Stipends; to R. J. Shroyer of Western University for essential computer support; and to the

Folger Institute's Center for Shakespeare Studies for its fortuitous sponsorship of a workshop on "Shakespeare's Texts for Students and Teachers" (funded by the National Endowment for the Humanities and led by Richard Knowles of the University of Wisconsin), a workshop from which we learned an enormous amount about what is wanted by college and high-school teachers of Shakespeare today.

In preparing this preface for the publication of *Richard II* in 1996, we wrote: "Our biggest debt is to the Folger Shakespeare Library—to Werner Gundersheimer, Director of the Library, who made possible our edition; to Deborah Curren-Aquino, who provides extensive editorial and production support; to Jean Miller, the Library's Art Curator, who combs the Library holdings for illustrations, and to Julie Ainsworth, Head of the Photography Department, who carefully photographs them; to Peggy O'Brien, former Director of Education at the Folger and now Director of Education Programs at the Corporation for Public Broadcasting, and her assistant at the Folger, Molly Haws, who gave us expert advice about the needs being expressed by Shakespeare teachers and students (and to Martha Christian and other 'master teachers' who used our texts in manuscript in their classrooms); to Jessica Hymowitz, who provides expert computer support; to the staff of the Academic Programs Division, especially Mary Tonkinson, Lena Cowen Orlin, Amy Adler, Kathleen Lynch, and Carol Brobeck; and, finally, to the staff of the Library Reading Room, whose patience and support are invaluable."

As we revise the play for publication in 2016, we add to the above our gratitude to Michael Witmore, Director of the Folger Shakespeare Library, who brings to our work a gratifying enthusiasm and vision; to Gail Kern Paster, Director of the Library from 2002 until

July 2011, whose interest and support have been unfailing and whose scholarly expertise continues to be an invaluable resource; to Jonathan Evans and Alysha Bullock, our production editors at Simon & Schuster, whose expertise, attention to detail, and wisdom are essential to this project; to the Folger's Photography Department; to Deborah Curren-Aquino for continuing superb editorial assistance and for her exceptionally fine Further Reading annotations; to Alice Falk for her expert copyediting; to Michael Poston for unfailing computer support; to Cecelia Lewin for commentary-note assistance; to Anna Levine; and to Rebecca Niles (whose help is crucial). Among the editions we consulted, we found Anthony B. Dawson and Paul Yachnin's 2011 Oxford World Classics edition especially useful. Finally, we once again express our thanks to Stephen Llano for twenty-five years of support as our invaluable production editor, to the late Jean Miller for the wonderful images she unearthed, and to the ever-supportive staff of the Library Reading Room.

Barbara A. Mowat and Paul Werstine
2016

Shakespeare's *Richard II*

Shakespeare's *Richard II* represents a momentous struggle in English history, the struggle between King Richard II and his cousin Henry Bolingbroke. Richard is apparently secure on his throne at the beginning of the play. He is, beyond any question, the legitimate heir to the crown of England, which is normally passed from the father to the eldest son. Richard's father was Edward, the Black Prince, the eldest son of the reigning monarch and a great military hero, who predeceased his own father, King Edward III. Thus Richard, as the Black Prince's only son, properly inherited the crown directly from Edward III, his grandfather. As rightful monarch, Richard authorizes his rule by invoking in a particularly strong way a tradition of belief that the king is God's deputy and is accountable to God alone. Challenges to the king's rule are thus made to appear not only high treason but also blasphemy. Bolingbroke, who is openly mistreated by Richard, seems powerless to oppose Richard's will.

When the play opens, Richard is seen by many as a tyrant, the opposite of a true monarch. He is believed to have arranged the assassination of his own uncle. He seems to toy with his subjects, exiling one, Thomas Mowbray, for life, and another, Henry Bolingbroke himself, for ten years—reduced, minutes after the banishment is announced, to six years. Richard is blamed for placing his subjects at the mercy of his friends, who grow wealthy at the cost of the people of England. Finally, when he seizes the title and property that Henry Bolingbroke should have inherited, Richard is perceived as a threat to the very structure of the kingdom.

Despite Richard's tyrannical behavior, he is elo-

Richard II.
From William Martyn, *The historie and lives of the kings of England . . .* (1638).

quently defended, by himself and others, as God's chosen ruler, immune from punishment by any subject. If the crown were to be taken from him by force, then the kingdom, it is said, would be threatened by endless civil war as others entered the bloody competition for the kingship. In the face of this belief in the king's sanctity, Bolingbroke seizes the occasion of Richard's invasion of Ireland to return from exile with an army. Bolingbroke's announced cause is the restoration of his title and property, though he is suspected, with good reason, of aiming at the crown itself. Nobles and commons, thinking themselves oppressed by Richard, rally to Bolingbroke's cause. Richard's supporters disperse; his deputy reaches an accommodation with Bolingbroke. The stage is set for a final confrontation between the powerful army commanded by an increasingly unsympathetic Bolingbroke, who summarily executes friends of Richard, and the tradition of sacred kingship that supports the now isolated but more sympathetic Richard in his rule.

After you have read the play, we invite you to turn to the back of the book and read "*Richard II:* A Modern Perspective" by Professor Harry Berger, Jr. of the University of California, Santa Cruz.

Reading Shakespeare's Language: *Richard II*

For many people today, reading Shakespeare's language can be a problem—but it is a problem that can be solved. Those who have studied Latin (or even French or German or Spanish) and those who are used to reading poetry will have little difficulty understanding the language of Shakespeare's poetic drama. Others, however, need to develop the skills of untangling unusual sentence structures and of recognizing and understanding poetic compressions, omissions, and wordplay. And even those skilled in reading unusual sentence structures may have occasional trouble with Shakespeare's words. More than four hundred years of "static"—caused by changes in language and life—intervene between his speaking and our hearing. Most of his immense vocabulary is still in use, but a few of his words are no longer used, and many of his words now have meanings quite different from those they had in the sixteenth century. In the theater, most of these difficulties are solved for us by actors who study the language and articulate it for us so that the essential meaning is heard—or, when combined with stage action, is at least *felt*. When reading on one's own, one must do what each actor does: go over the lines (often with a dictionary close at hand) until the puzzles are solved and the lines yield up their poetry and the characters speak in words and phrases that are, suddenly, rewarding and wonderfully memorable.

St. George and the dragon. (1.3.84)

From [Jacobus de Varagine,] *Here begynneth the legende named in latyn legenda aurea . . .* (1493).

Shakespeare's Words

As you begin to read the opening scenes of a Shakespeare play, you may notice occasional unfamiliar words. Some are unfamiliar simply because we no longer use them. In the opening scenes of *Richard II*, for example, you will find the words *complotted* (i.e., conspired), *exclaims* (i.e., outcries), *cheerly* (i.e., heartily), *sprightfully* (i.e., full of spirit), *regreet* (i.e., salute or greet), *determinate* (i.e., put an end to), and *underbearing* (i.e., endurance). Words of this kind are explained in notes to the text and will become familiar the more of Shakespeare's plays you read.

In *Richard II*, as in all of Shakespeare's writing, more problematic are the words that are still in use but that now have different meanings. Such words abound in *Richard II*. In the opening scenes, for example, the word *eager* is used where we would say "sharp" or "acid," *inhabitable* where we would say "not habitable, unfit for human habitation," the word *ill* where we would say "evil," *consequently* where we would say "subsequently," *envy* where we would say "hatred" or "malice," *champions* where we would say "combatants," and *baffled* where we would say "subjected to public disgrace." Such words will be explained in the notes to the text, but they, too, will become familiar as you continue to read Shakespeare's language.

Some words are strange not because of the "static" introduced by changes in language over the past centuries but because these are words that Shakespeare is using to build a dramatic world that has its own space, time, history, and background mythology. In *Richard II* Shakespeare creates the courtly and military world of late fourteenth-century England. This is a world inhabited by *Lancaster* and *Gloucester* and *Hereford*, with castles named *Flint* and *Bristow* and *Pomfret* and houses

An Irish kern in a mantle. (2.1.164)
From John Derricke, *The image of Irelande, with a discouerie of woodkarne* . . . (1883 facsimile).

called *Plashy* and *Ely House;* it is a world of *warders,* *gages,* and *pawns;* of *boist'rous appeals* (violent accusations), of *careers* (charges or encounters), and of *royal* *lists* (arenas set up for trials by combat supervised by the king). In this world a character *plated in habiliments* *of war* (i.e., dressed in armor) might call another a *recreant* (i.e., someone who breaks allegiance) or a *slander of his blood* (i.e., disgrace to his family line), might forbid another to *impeach my height* (i.e., disgrace my noble standing), or might invoke *my scepter's awe* (i.e., the power of my scepter to inspire dread or fear). References to *lions* and *leopards* bring into the play traditional hierarchies in the natural world that mirror the social world (the so-called great chain of being) as well as reminders of heraldic emblems on royal and noble shields, and allusions to *Saint George* (patron saint of England) and *Mars* (the Roman god of war) give mythological ballast to the play's military context.

Shakespeare's Sentences

In an English sentence, meaning is quite dependent on the place given each word. "The dog bit the boy" and "The boy bit the dog" mean very different things, even though the individual words are the same. Because English places such importance on the positions of words in sentences, on the way words are arranged, unusual arrangements can puzzle a reader. Shakespeare frequently shifts his sentences away from "normal" English arrangements—often in order to create the rhythm he seeks, sometimes in order to use a line's poetic rhythm to emphasize a particular word, sometimes in order to give a character his or her own speech patterns or to allow the character to speak in a special way. When we attend a good performance of a play, the actors will have worked out the sentence structures and will articulate the sentences so that the meaning is clear. When reading the play, we need to do as the actor does; that is, when puzzled by a character's speech, check to see if words are being presented in an unusual sequence.

Shakespeare often rearranges subjects and verbs (e.g., instead of "He goes," we find "Goes he," or instead of "He did go," we find "Did he go"). In *Richard II*, we find such a construction when Bolingbroke says (1.1.36) "Now, Thomas Mowbray, *do I turn* to thee" (instead of ". . . I do turn to thee") and again (at 1.1.78) when he says "*Will I* make good against thee."

Such inversions rarely cause much confusion. More problematic is Shakespeare's frequent placing of the object or the predicate adjective before the subject and verb or between the subject and verb (e.g., instead of "I hit him" we might find "Him I hit," or instead of "It is black" we might find "Black it is"). Richard's "impartial are our eyes and ears" (1.1.119) is an example of such an inversion (the normal order would be "Our eyes and ears are impartial"), as is his "Free speech and fearless I to thee allow" (1.1.127), where "free speech and fearless" is the object of the verb "allow." Mowbray's "My life thou shalt command, but not my shame" (1.1.171) is another example of a sentence in which the object ("My life") is placed before the verb ("shalt command"). Often in *Richard II* this kind of inversion appears in combination with subject-verb inversions, as when Mowbray says (at 1.1.54) "Yet can I not of such tame patience boast," where the normal order would read "Yet I cannot boast of such tame patience."

Inversions are not the only unusual sentence structures in Shakespeare's language. Often in his sentences words that would normally appear together are separated from each other. (Again, this is often done to create a particular rhythm or to stress a particular word.) The play opens, for example, with a sentence that sepa-

rates the basic sentence elements from each other with
several intervening words, phrases, and clauses:

> *Old John of Gaunt*, time-honored Lancaster,
> *Hast thou*, according to thy oath and band,
> *Brought hither Henry Hereford*, thy bold son,
> Here *to make good the* boist'rous late *appeal*,
> Which then our leisure would not let us hear,
> *Against the Duke of Norfolk*, Thomas Mowbray?
>   (1.1.1–6)

Here the intervening words are bits of narrative information that an audience can absorb as it moves from
element to element of King Richard's basic question:
"Old John of Gaunt, hast thou brought hither Henry
Hereford to make good the appeal against the Duke of
Norfolk?" Later in the same scene, Bolingbroke speaks
in a similar kind of interrupted sentence:

> *Further I say*, and further will maintain
> Upon his bad life to make all this good,
> *That he did plot the Duke of Gloucester's death*,
> *Suggest his soon-believing adversaries*,
> *And consequently*, like a traitor coward,
> *Sluiced out his innocent soul through streams of*
>   *blood*,
> *Which blood*, like sacrificing Abel's, *cries*
> Even from the tongueless caverns of the Earth
> *To me for justice and rough chastisement.*
>   (1.1.101–10)

In order to create sentences that seem more like the
English of everyday speech, you can rearrange the
words, putting together the word clusters ("consequently sluiced out," "which blood cries to me"). The
result will usually be an increase in clarity but a loss of
rhythm or a shift in emphasis.

Locating and if necessary rearranging words that "belong together" is especially helpful in passages with long delaying or expanding interruptions. Such interrupted sentences are often used to catch the audience up in the narrative or are used as a characterizing device. In *Richard II*, Bolingbroke uses such an interrupted construction when he says to King Richard at 1.1.94–100

> *Besides I say*, and will in battle prove,
> Or here or elsewhere to the furthest verge
> That ever was surveyed by English eye,
> *That all the treasons for these eighteen years*
> *Complotted and contrivèd in this land*
> *Fetch from false Mowbray their first head and spring.*

The Duchess of Gloucester uses a similar construction when she says to her brother-in-law, John of Gaunt, at 1.2.16–21,

> *But Thomas*, my dear lord, my life, my Gloucester,
> One vial full of Edward's sacred blood,
> One flourishing branch of his most royal root,
> *Is cracked* and all the precious liquor spilt,
> *Is hacked down*, and his summer leaves all faded,
> *By envy's hand and murder's bloody ax.*

The complexity of the language of *Richard II* is illustrated in this example, where the subject ("Thomas") becomes so absorbed into the intervening phrases that its verbs seem more closely connected to the nouns *vial* and *branch* than to the word *Thomas*, their actual grammatical subject.

Occasionally, rather than separating basic sentence elements, Shakespeare simply holds them back, delaying them until subordinate material has been given.

Bolingbroke uses this kind of delaying structure when he says, at 1.1.31–35,

> First—heaven be the record to my speech!—
> In the devotion of a subject's love,
> Tend'ring the precious safety of my prince,
> And free from other misbegotten hate,
> *Come I appellant to this princely presence.*

Here the basic sentence elements "Come I [i.e., I come] appellant to this princely presence" are held back until four lines of self-presentation are delivered.

Finally, in *Richard II*, as in other of Shakespeare's plays, sentences are sometimes complicated not because of unusual structures or interruptions or delays but because he omits words and parts of words that English sentences normally require. (In conversation, we, too, often omit words. We say "Heard from him yet?" and our hearer supplies the missing "Have you.") Frequent reading of Shakespeare—and of other poets— trains us to supply such missing words. In plays written ten years or so after *Richard II*, Shakespeare uses omissions both of verbs and of nouns to great dramatic effect. In *Richard II* omissions are few and seem primarily a function of the formal, public language of this extremely rhetorical play. For example, Bolingbroke challenges Mowbray at 1.1.71–73 with the lines "Pale trembling coward, there I throw my gage, / Disclaiming here the kindred of the King, / And lay aside my high blood's royalty." The third line of this formal challenge omits the pronoun *I* before "lay," creating along the way an ambiguity that makes the line seem simultaneously a statement about the speaker (". . . I lay aside . . .") and an order to Mowbray (". . . lay aside . . ."). Later in the same scene (1.1.169) King Richard omits a word (or words) in his order to Mowbray, duke of Norfolk, to throw down the gage he has picked up: "Norfolk, throw down, we bid; there is no boot." (The full sentence might have read "throw it down" or "throw down his gage.") Richard's cryptic sentence allows Mowbray a powerful answer: "Myself I throw, dread sovereign, at thy foot"—a line that completes a rhyming couplet and, with Mowbray's gesture of kneeling at Richard's feet, moves the scene into high drama.

Shakespearean Wordplay

Shakespeare plays with language so often and so variously that entire books are written on the topic. Here we will mention only two kinds of wordplay, puns and metaphors. A pun is a play on words that sound the same but that have different meanings. Some of Shakespeare's plays use puns routinely; in *Richard II* they are used very sparingly but complexly. At 1.3.277, for example, when Bolingbroke expresses his dismay at the sentence of banishment passed on him by King Richard, he does so at one point through elaborate puns:

> Must I not serve a long apprenticehood
> To foreign passages, and in the end,
> Having my freedom, boast of nothing else
> But that I was a journeyman to grief?

These lines pun on the words *passages* (which meant, in Shakespeare's day, both "experiences" and "journeys"), *journeyman* (which means one who has finished his apprenticeship and works for daily hire, but which here also plays with the sense of "journey-man" as "a man who journeys"), and *freedom* (which here means freedom from his sentence of exile, but which also alludes to the word's technical meaning as the right to follow a trade or to become part of a guild once one has completed one's contract as an apprentice).

Again, at 5.2.54–55, puns are used complexly as York warns his son about how to behave under the new king:

> Well, bear you well in this new spring of time,
> Lest you be cropped before you come to prime.

The phrase *bear you* means "conduct yourself," but it carries a pun on *bear* (i.e., "bring forth leaves or fruit") that, together with the words *cropped* (i.e., "cut") and *prime* (i.e., "full bloom"), creates a larger image of the young courtier as a plant vulnerable to the gardener's shears in this new political springtime.

In all of Shakespeare's plays, one must be aware of the sounds of words and the possibility of double meanings. In *Richard II*, however, it is more important to stay alert for metaphors. A metaphor is a play on words in which one object or idea is expressed as if it were something else, something with which it is said to share common features. *Richard II* is rich in metaphoric language, often used as a kind of rhetorical flourish. When Mowbray, for example, wants to say that King Richard's presence prevents him from calling Bolingbroke (Richard's cousin) a traitor, Mowbray dresses that statement in metaphoric language, using the words *curbs*, *reins*, *spurs*, and *post* to talk about speech as if it were a horse he was riding:

> First, the fair reverence of your Highness curbs me
> From giving reins and spurs to my free speech,
> Which else would post until it had returned
> These terms of treason doubled down his throat.
>   (1.1.56–59)

Later in the same scene (156–61), Richard too uses metaphoric language as a rhetorical flourish when he urges Bolingbroke and Mowbray to make peace:

> Wrath-kindled gentlemen, be ruled by me.
> Let's purge this choler without letting blood.
> This we prescribe, though no physician.
> Deep malice makes too deep incision.
> Forget, forgive; conclude and be agreed.
> Our doctors say this is no month to bleed.

The speech says, in effect, let's cure this anger without bloodshed, but, as we point out in our explanatory notes, Richard's language plays with the idea of bloodletting as a medical cure, or *purge*, for *choler*— biliousness, anger, or other signs of an excess of bile. Richard's wordplay culminates in a pun on *bleed*—i.e., (1) to draw blood from the body to remove such excess fluid, and (2) to spill blood.

Often in *Richard II*, metaphor is used not to dress up a speech but as a potent vehicle for conveying meaning. Indeed, some metaphors seem almost to embody the major movements of the play's narrative. To take a single example: throughout the play, the king is to England as the sun is to the Earth. In the first half of the play, Richard is the sun. He describes himself as "the searching eye of heaven" that "darts his light through every guilty hole"; his absence from England he sees as having allowed Bolingbroke to "revel in the night," and under "the cloak of night" to "range abroad unseen / In murders and in outrage." However, he predicts,

> . . . when this thief, this traitor Bolingbroke,
> Who all this while hath reveled in the night
> Whilst we were wand'ring with the Antipodes,
> Shall see us rising in our throne, the east,
> His treasons will sit blushing in his face,
> Not able to endure the sight of day,
> But self-affrighted, tremble at his sin.
>
>   (3.2.48–54)

As Richard's fortunes begin to fall, Richard becomes "the setting sun"(2.1.15) and then "the blushing discontented sun" (3.3.65). When Richard sends his followers "from Richard's night to Bolingbroke's fair day" (3.2.226), the sun image begins its transfer to Bolingbroke. It is as Phaëton disastrously piloting the chariot of the sun that Richard subsequently descends, at Bolingbroke's command, to the base court of Flint Castle (3.3.183–85). By the time Richard is deposed, the transfer is complete, and he imagines himself as a "mockery king of snow" melting "before the sun of Bolingbroke" (4.1.271–73).

Other metaphors—e.g., Richard as lion, England as garden—have a similar controlling power within the play's narrative, and they, too, strongly affect audience response to the story.

Implied Stage Action

Finally, in reading Shakespeare's plays we should always remember that what we are reading is a performance script. The dialogue is written to be spoken by actors who, at the same time, are moving, gesturing, picking up objects, weeping, shaking their fists. Some stage action is described in what are called "stage directions"; some is suggested within the dialogue itself. We must learn to be alert to such signals as we stage the play in our imaginations. This is especially true in reading *Richard II* since stage action is so often correlated with the play's metaphors. Richard's metaphoric descent as Phaëton at Flint Castle, for example, is enacted onstage with an actual descent from "the walls" of the castle to its "base court." His metaphorical interrogating of his identity in the "Deposition Scene" in 4.1 is enacted onstage as he calls for a looking glass, examines his face in the glass, and then shatters the glass on the stage floor.

Stage action also correlates with character positions in the play's narrative, as Richard's and Bolingbroke's relative positions on the stage shift in the course of the play. In early scenes Richard is placed above and Bolingbroke below (with Richard descending to embrace Bolingbroke in 1.3); in midplay Richard comes down from "the walls" to Bolingbroke's level, Bolingbroke kneels, and Richard raises him up (all of these stage actions accompanied by descriptive dialogue). Finally, Bolingbroke (as King Henry) ends the play seated above on the throne with Richard in a coffin at his feet. Because in this play stage action so closely mirrors and reinforces language and narrative threads, we need to be especially alert to all signals for gesture, movement, and character positioning.

It is immensely rewarding to work carefully with Shakespeare's language—with the words, the sentences, the wordplay, and the implied stage action—as readers for the past four centuries have discovered. It may be more pleasurable to attend a good performance of a play—though not everyone has thought so. But the joy of being able to stage one of Shakespeare's plays in one's imagination, to return to passages that continue to yield further meanings (or further questions) the more one reads them—these are pleasures that, for many, rival (or at least augment) those of the performed text, and certainly make it worth considerable effort to "break the code" of Elizabethan poetic drama and let free the remarkable language that makes up a Shakespeare text.

Shakespeare's Life

Surviving documents that give us glimpses into the life of William Shakespeare show us a playwright, poet, and actor who grew up in the market town of Stratford-upon-Avon, spent his professional life in London, and returned to Stratford a wealthy landowner. He was born in April 1564, died in April 1616, and is buried inside the chancel of Holy Trinity Church in Stratford.

We wish we could know more about the life of the world's greatest dramatist. His plays and poems are testaments to his wide reading—especially to his knowledge of Virgil, Ovid, Plutarch, Holinshed's *Chronicles*, and the Bible—and to his mastery of the English language, but we can only speculate about his education. We know that the King's New School in Stratford-upon-Avon was considered excellent. The school was one of the English "grammar schools" established to educate young men, primarily in Latin grammar and literature. As in other schools of the time, students began their studies at the age of four or five in the attached "petty school," and there learned to read and write in English, studying primarily the catechism from the Book of Common Prayer. After two years in the petty school, students entered the lower form (grade) of the grammar school, where they began the serious study of Latin grammar and Latin texts that would occupy most of the remainder of their school days. (Several Latin texts that Shakespeare used repeatedly in writing his plays and poems were texts that schoolboys memorized and recited.) Latin comedies were introduced early in the lower form; in the upper form, which the boys entered at age ten or eleven, students wrote their own Latin orations and declamations, studied Latin

Title page of a 1573 Latin and Greek catechism for children.
From Alexander Nowell, *Catechismus paruus pueris
primum Latine . . .* (1573).

historians and rhetoricians, and began the study of Greek using the Greek New Testament.

Since the records of the Stratford "grammar school" do not survive, we cannot prove that William Shakespeare attended the school; however, every indication (his father's position as an alderman and bailiff of Stratford, the playwright's own knowledge of the Latin classics, scenes in the plays that recall grammar-school experiences—for example, *The Merry Wives of Windsor*, 4.1) suggests that he did. We also lack generally accepted documentation about Shakespeare's life after his schooling ended and his professional life in London began. His marriage in 1582 (at age eighteen) to Anne Hathaway and the subsequent births of his daughter Susanna (1583) and the twins Judith and Hamnet (1585) are recorded, but how he supported himself and where he lived are not known. Nor do we know when and why he left Stratford for the London theatrical world, nor how he rose to be the important figure in that world that he had become by the early 1590s.

We do know that by 1592 he had achieved some prominence in London as both an actor and a playwright. In that year was published a book by the playwright Robert Greene attacking an actor who had the audacity to write blank-verse drama and who was "in his own conceit [i.e., opinion] the only Shake-scene in a country." Since Greene's attack includes a parody of a line from one of Shakespeare's early plays, there is little doubt that it is Shakespeare to whom he refers, a "Shake-scene" who had aroused Greene's fury by successfully competing with university-educated dramatists like Greene himself. It was in 1593 that Shakespeare became a published poet. In that year he published his long narrative poem *Venus and Adonis*; in 1594, he followed it with *Lucrece*. Both poems were dedicated to the young earl of Southampton (Henry

Wriothesley), who may have become Shakespeare's patron.

It seems no coincidence that Shakespeare wrote these narrative poems at a time when the theaters were closed because of the plague, a contagious epidemic disease that devastated the population of London. When the theaters reopened in 1594, Shakespeare apparently resumed his double career of actor and playwright and began his long (and seemingly profitable) service as an acting-company shareholder. Records for December of 1594 show him to be a leading member of the Lord Chamberlain's Men. It was this company of actors, later named the King's Men, for whom he would be a principal actor, dramatist, and shareholder for the rest of his career.

So far as we can tell, that career spanned about twenty years. In the 1590s, he wrote his plays on English history as well as several comedies and at least two tragedies (*Titus Andronicus* and *Romeo and Juliet*). These histories, comedies, and tragedies are the plays credited to him in 1598 in a work, *Palladis Tamia*, that in one chapter compares English writers with "Greek, Latin, and Italian Poets." There the author, Francis Meres, claims that Shakespeare is comparable to the Latin dramatists Seneca for tragedy and Plautus for comedy, and calls him "the most excellent in both kinds for the stage." He also names him "Mellifluous and honey-tongued Shakespeare": "I say," writes Meres, "that the Muses would speak with Shakespeare's fine filed phrase, if they would speak English." Since Meres also mentions Shakespeare's "sugared sonnets among his private friends," it is assumed that many of Shakespeare's sonnets (not published until 1609) were also written in the 1590s.

In 1599, Shakespeare's company built a theater for themselves across the river from London, naming it the Globe. The plays that are considered by many to be Shakespeare's major tragedies (*Hamlet, Othello, King Lear*, and *Macbeth*) were written while the company was resident in this theater, as were such comedies as *Twelfth Night* and *Measure for Measure*. Many of Shakespeare's plays were performed at court (both for Queen Elizabeth I and, after her death in 1603, for King James I), some were presented at the Inns of Court (the residences of London's legal societies), and some were doubtless performed in other towns, at the universities, and at great houses when the King's Men went on tour; otherwise, his plays from 1599 to 1608 were, so far as we know, performed only at the Globe. Between 1608 and 1612, Shakespeare wrote several plays—among them *The Winter's Tale* and *The Tempest*—presumably for the company's new indoor Blackfriars theater, though the plays were performed also at the Globe and at court. Surviving documents describe a performance of *The Winter's Tale* in 1611 at the Globe, for example, and performances of *The Tempest* in 1611 and 1613 at the royal palace of Whitehall.

Shakespeare seems to have written very little after 1612, the year in which he probably wrote *King Henry VIII*. (It was at a performance of *Henry VIII* in 1613 that the Globe caught fire and burned to the ground.) Sometime between 1610 and 1613, according to many biographers, he returned to live in Stratford-upon-Avon, where he owned a large house and considerable property, and where his wife and his two daughters lived. (His son Hamnet had died in 1596.) However, other biographers suggest that Shakespeare did not leave London for good until much closer to the time of his death. During his professional years in London, Shakespeare had presumably derived income from the acting company's profits as well as from his own career as an actor, from the sale of his play manuscripts to

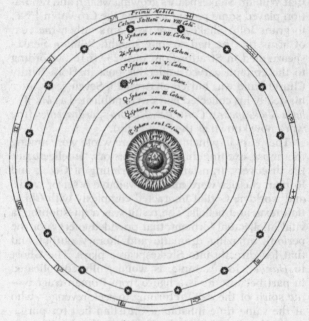

Ptolemaic universe.
From Marcus Manilius, *The sphere of . . .* (1675).

the acting company, and, after 1599, from his shares as an owner of the Globe. It was presumably that income, carefully invested in land and other property, that made him the wealthy man that surviving documents show him to have become. It is also assumed that William Shakespeare's growing wealth and reputation played some part in inclining the Crown, in 1596, to grant John Shakespeare, William's father, the coat of arms that he had so long sought. William Shakespeare died in Stratford on April 23, 1616 (according to the epitaph carved under his bust in Holy Trinity Church) and was buried on April 25. Seven years after his death, his collected plays were published as *Mr. William Shakespeares Comedies, Histories, & Tragedies* (the work now known as the First Folio).

The years in which Shakespeare wrote were among the most exciting in English history. Intellectually, the discovery, translation, and printing of Greek and Roman classics were making available a set of works and worldviews that interacted complexly with Christian texts and beliefs. The result was a questioning, a vital intellectual ferment, that provided energy for the period's amazing dramatic and literary output and that fed directly into Shakespeare's plays. The Ghost in *Hamlet*, for example, is wonderfully complicated in part because he is a figure from Roman tragedy—the spirit of the dead returning to seek revenge—who at the same time inhabits a Christian hell (or purgatory); Hamlet's description of humankind reflects at one moment the Neoplatonic wonderment at mankind ("What a piece of work is a man!") and, at the next, the Christian view of the human condition ("And yet, to me, what is this quintessence of dust?").

As intellectual horizons expanded, so also did geographical and cosmological horizons. New worlds—both North and South America—were explored, and in them were found human beings who lived and worshiped in ways radically different from those of Renaissance Europeans and Englishmen. The universe during these years also seemed to shift and expand. Copernicus had earlier theorized that the Earth was not the center of the cosmos but revolved as a planet around the sun. Galileo's telescope, created in 1609, allowed scientists to see that Copernicus had been correct: the universe was not organized with the Earth at the center, nor was it so nicely circumscribed as people had, until that time, thought. In terms of expanding horizons, the impact of these discoveries on people's beliefs—religious, scientific, and philosophical—cannot be overstated.

London, too, rapidly expanded and changed during the years (from the early 1590s to 1610 or somewhat later) that Shakespeare lived there. London—the center of England's government, its economy, its royal court, its overseas trade—was, during these years, becoming an exciting metropolis, drawing to it thousands of new citizens every year. Troubled by overcrowding, by poverty, by recurring epidemics of the plague, London was also a mecca for the wealthy and the aristocratic, and for those who sought advancement at court, or power in government or finance or trade. One hears in Shakespeare's plays the voices of London—the struggles for power, the fear of venereal disease, the language of buying and selling. One hears as well the voices of Stratford-upon-Avon—references to the nearby Forest of Arden, to sheepherding, to small-town gossip, to village fairs and markets. Part of the richness of Shakespeare's work is the influence felt there of the various worlds in which he lived: the world of metropolitan London, the world of small-town and rural England, the world of the theater, and the worlds of craftsmen and shepherds.

That Shakespeare inhabited such worlds we know

from surviving London and Stratford documents, as well as from the evidence of the plays and poems themselves. From such records we can sketch the dramatist's life. We know from his works that he was a voracious reader. We know from legal and business documents that he was a multifaceted theater man who became a wealthy landowner. We know a bit about his family life and a fair amount about his legal and financial dealings. Most scholars today depend upon such evidence as they draw their picture of the world's greatest playwright. Such, however, has not always been the case. Until the late eighteenth century, the William Shakespeare who lived in most biographies was the creation of legend and tradition. This was the Shakespeare who was supposedly caught poaching deer at Charlecote, the estate of Sir Thomas Lucy close by Stratford; this was the Shakespeare who fled from Sir Thomas's vengeance and made his way in London by taking care of horses outside a playhouse; this was the Shakespeare who reportedly could barely read, but whose natural gifts were extraordinary, whose father was a butcher who allowed his gifted son sometimes to help in the butcher shop, where William supposedly killed calves "in a high style," making a speech for the occasion. It was this legendary William Shakespeare whose Falstaff (in *1* and *2 Henry IV*) so pleased Queen Elizabeth that she demanded a play about Falstaff in love, and demanded that it be written in fourteen days (hence the existence of *The Merry Wives of Windsor*). It was this legendary Shakespeare who reached the top of his acting career in the roles of the Ghost in *Hamlet* and old Adam in *As You Like It*—and who died of a fever contracted by drinking too hard at "a merry meeting" with the poets Michael Drayton and Ben Jonson. This legendary Shakespeare is a rambunctious, undisciplined man, as attractively "wild" as his plays were seen by earlier generations to be. Unfortunately, there is no trace of evidence to support these wonderful stories.

Perhaps in response to the disreputable Shakespeare of legend—or perhaps in response to the fragmentary and, for some, all-too-ordinary Shakespeare documented by surviving records—some people since the mid-nineteenth century have argued that William Shakespeare could not have written the plays that bear his name. These persons have put forward some dozen names as more likely authors, among them Queen Elizabeth, Sir Francis Bacon, Edward de Vere (earl of Oxford), and Christopher Marlowe. Such attempts to find what for these people is a more believable author of the plays is a tribute to the regard in which the plays are held. Unfortunately for their claims, the documents that exist that provide evidence for the facts of Shakespeare's life tie him inextricably to the body of plays and poems that bear his name. Unlikely as it seems to those who want the works to have been written by an aristocrat, a university graduate, or an "important" person, the plays and poems seem clearly to have been produced by a man from Stratford-upon-Avon with a very good "grammar-school" education and a life of experience in London and in the world of the London theater. How this particular man produced the works that dominate the cultures of much of the world four hundred years after his death is one of life's mysteries—and one that will continue to tease our imaginations as we continue to delight in his plays and poems.

A stylized representation of the Globe theater.
From Claes Jansz Visscher, *Londinum florentissima
Britanniae urbs* . . . [c. 1625].

Shakespeare's Theater

The actors of Shakespeare's time are known to have performed plays in a great variety of locations. They played at court (that is, in the great halls of such royal residences as Whitehall, Hampton Court, and Greenwich); they played in halls at the universities of Oxford and Cambridge, and at the Inns of Court (the residences in London of the legal societies); and they also played in the private houses of great lords and civic officials. Sometimes acting companies went on tour from London into the provinces, often (but not only) when outbreaks of bubonic plague in the capital forced the closing of theaters to reduce the possibility of contagion in crowded audiences. In the provinces the actors usually staged their plays in churches (until around 1600), in guildhalls, or in the great houses of individual patrons. While surviving records show only a handful of occasions when actors played at inns while on tour, London inns were important playing places up until the 1590s.

The building of theaters in London had begun only shortly before Shakespeare wrote his first plays in the 1590s. These theaters were of two kinds: outdoor or public playhouses that could accommodate large numbers of playgoers, and indoor or private theaters for much smaller audiences. What is usually regarded as the first London outdoor public playhouse was called simply the Theatre. James Burbage—the father of Richard Burbage, who was perhaps the most famous actor in Shakespeare's company—built it in 1576 in an area north of the city of London called Shoreditch. Among the more famous of the other public playhouses that capitalized on the new fashion were the Curtain and the Fortune (both also built north of the city), the Rose, the Swan, the Globe, and the Hope (all located on the Bankside, a region just across the Thames south of the city of London). All these playhouses had to be built outside the jurisdiction of the city of London because many civic officials were hostile to the performance of drama and repeatedly petitioned the royal council to abolish it.

The theaters erected on the Bankside (a region under the authority of the Church of England, whose head was the monarch) shared the neighborhood with houses of prostitution and with the Paris Garden, where the blood sports of bearbaiting and bullbaiting were carried on. There may have been no clear distinction between playhouses and buildings for such sports, for we know that the Hope was used for both plays and baiting and that Philip Henslowe, owner of the Rose and, later, partner in the ownership of the Fortune, was also a partner in a monopoly on baiting. All these forms of entertainment were easily accessible to Londoners by boat across the Thames or over London Bridge.

Evidently Shakespeare's company prospered on the Bankside. They moved there in 1599. Threatened by difficulties in renewing the lease on the land where their first theater (the Theatre) had been built, Shakespeare's company took advantage of the Christmas holiday in 1598 to dismantle the Theatre and transport its timbers across the Thames to the Bankside, where, in 1599, these timbers were used in the building of the Globe. The weather in late December 1598 is recorded as having been especially harsh. It was so cold that the Thames was "nigh [nearly] frozen," and there was heavy snow. Perhaps the weather aided Shakespeare's company in eluding their landlord, the snow hiding their activity and the freezing of the Thames allowing them to slide the timbers across to the Bankside without paying tolls for repeated trips over London

Bridge. Attractive as this narrative is, it remains just as likely that the heavy snow hampered transport of the timbers in wagons through the London streets to the river. It also must be remembered that the Thames was, according to report, only "nigh frozen," and therefore did not necessarily provide solid footing. Whatever the precise circumstances of this fascinating event in English theater history, Shakespeare's company was able to begin playing at their new Globe theater on the Bankside in 1599. After this theater burned down in 1613 during the staging of Shakespeare's *Henry VIII* (its thatch roof was set alight by cannon fire called for in performance), Shakespeare's company immediately rebuilt on the same location. The second Globe seems to have been a grander structure than its predecessor. It remained in use until the beginning of the English Civil War in 1642, when Parliament officially closed the theaters. Soon thereafter it was pulled down.

The public theaters of Shakespeare's time were very different buildings from our theaters today. First of all, they were open-air playhouses. As recent excavations of the Rose and the Globe confirm, some were polygonal or roughly circular in shape; the Fortune, however, was square. The most recent estimates of their size put the diameter of these buildings at 72 feet (the Rose) to 100 feet (the Globe), but we know that they held vast audiences of two or three thousand, who must have been squeezed together quite tightly. Some of these spectators paid extra to sit or stand in the two or three levels of roofed galleries that extended, on the upper levels, all the way around the theater and surrounded an open space. In this space were the stage and, perhaps, the tiring house (what we would call dressing rooms), as well as the so-called yard. In the yard stood the spectators who chose to pay less, the ones whom Hamlet contemptuously called "groundlings." For a roof they had only the sky, and so they were exposed to all kinds of weather. They stood on a floor that was sometimes made of mortar and sometimes of ash mixed with the shells of hazelnuts, which, it has recently been discovered, were standard flooring material in the period.

Unlike the yard, the stage itself was covered by a roof. Its ceiling, called "the heavens," is thought to have been elaborately painted to depict the sun, moon, stars, and planets. The exact size of the stage remains hard to determine. We have a single sketch of part of the interior of the Swan. A Dutchman named Johannes de Witt visited this theater around 1596 and sent a sketch of it back to his friend, Arend van Buchel. Because van Buchel found de Witt's letter and sketch of interest, he copied both into a book. It is van Buchel's copy, adapted, it seems, to the shape and size of the page in his book, that survives. In this sketch, the stage appears to be a large rectangular platform that thrusts far out into the yard, perhaps even as far as the center of the circle formed by the surrounding galleries. This drawing, combined with the specifications for the size of the stage in the building contract for the Fortune, has led scholars to conjecture that the stage on which Shakespeare's plays were performed must have measured approximately 43 feet in width and 27 feet in depth, a vast acting area. But the digging up of a large part of the Rose by late twentieth-century archaeologists has provided evidence of a quite different stage design. The Rose stage was a platform tapered at the corners and much shallower than what seems to be depicted in the van Buchel sketch. Indeed, its measurements seem to be about 37.5 feet across at its widest point and only 15.5 feet deep. Because the surviving indications of stage size and design differ from each other so much, it is possible that the stages in other theaters, like the Theatre, the Curtain, and the Globe (the outdoor playhouses where we know that Shakespeare's plays were performed), were different from those at both the Swan and the Rose.

After about 1608 Shakespeare's plays were staged not only at the Globe but also at an indoor or private playhouse in Blackfriars. This theater had been constructed in 1596 by James Burbage in an upper hall of a former Dominican priory or monastic house. Although Henry VIII had dissolved all English monasteries in the 1530s (shortly after he had founded the Church of England), the area remained under church, rather than hostile civic, control. The hall that Burbage had purchased and renovated was a large one in which Parliament had once met. In the private theater that he constructed, the stage, lit by candles, was built across the narrow end of the hall, with boxes flanking it. The rest of the hall offered seating room only. Because there was no provision for standing room, the largest audience it could hold was less than a thousand, or about a quarter of what the Globe could accommodate. Admission to Blackfriars was correspondingly more expensive. Instead of a penny to stand in the yard at the Globe, it cost a minimum of sixpence to get into Blackfriars. The best seats at the Globe (in the Lords' Room in the gallery above and behind the stage) cost sixpence; but the boxes flanking the stage at Blackfriars were half a crown, or five times sixpence. Some spectators who were particularly interested in displaying themselves paid even more to sit on stools on the Blackfriars stage.

Whether in the outdoor or indoor playhouses, the stages of Shakespeare's time were different from ours. They were not separated from the audience by the dropping of a curtain between acts and scenes. Therefore the playwrights of the time had to find other ways of signaling to the audience that one scene (to be imagined as occurring in one location at a given time) had ended and the next (to be imagined at perhaps a different location at a later time) had begun. The customary way used by Shakespeare and many of his contemporaries was to have everyone on stage exit at the end of one scene and have one or more different characters enter to begin the next. In a few cases, where characters remain onstage from one scene to another, the dialogue or stage action makes the change of location clear, and the characters are generally to be imagined as having moved from one place to another. For example, in *Romeo and Juliet*, Romeo and his friends remain onstage in Act 1 from scene 4 to scene 5, but they are represented as having moved between scenes from the street that leads to Capulet's house into Capulet's house itself. The new location is signaled in part by the appearance onstage of Capulet's servingmen carrying table napkins, something they would not take into the streets. Playwrights had to be quite resourceful in the use of hand properties, like the napkin, or in the use of dialogue to specify where the action was taking place in their plays because, in contrast to most of today's theaters, the playhouses of Shakespeare's time did not fill the stage with scenery to make the setting precise. A consequence of this difference was that the playwrights of Shakespeare's time did not have to specify exactly where the action of their plays was set when they did not choose to do so, and much of the action of their plays is tied to no specific place.

Usually Shakespeare's stage is referred to as a "bare stage," to distinguish it from the stages of the last two or three centuries with their elaborate sets. But the stage in Shakespeare's time was not completely bare. Philip Henslowe, owner of the Rose, lists in his inventory of stage properties a rock, three tombs, and two mossy banks. Stage directions in plays of the time also call for such things as thrones (or "states"), banquets (presumably tables with plaster replicas of food on them), and beds and tombs to be pushed onto the stage. Thus the stage often held more than the actors.

The actors did not limit their performing to the stage alone. Occasionally they went beneath the stage, as the Ghost appears to do in the first act of *Hamlet*. From there they could emerge onto the stage through a trapdoor. They could retire behind the hanging across the back of the stage, as, for example, the actor playing Polonius does when he hides behind the arras. Sometimes the hangings could be drawn back during a performance to "discover" one or more actors behind them. When performance required that an actor appear "above," as when Juliet is imagined to stand at the window of her chamber in the famous and misnamed "balcony scene," then the actor probably climbed the stairs to the gallery over the back of the stage and temporarily shared it with some of the spectators. The stage was also provided with ropes and winches so that actors could descend from, and reascend to, the "heavens."

Perhaps the greatest difference between dramatic performances in Shakespeare's time and ours was that in Shakespeare's England the roles of women were played by boys. (Some of these boys grew up to take male roles in their maturity.) There were no women in the acting companies. It was not so in Europe, and it had not always been so in the history of the English stage. There are records of women on English stages in the thirteenth and fourteenth centuries, two hundred years before Shakespeare's plays were performed. After the accession of James I in 1603, the queen of England and her ladies took part in entertainments at court called masques, and with the reopening of the theaters in 1660 at the restoration of Charles II, women again took their place on the public stage.

The chief competitors of such acting companies as the one to which Shakespeare belonged and for which he wrote were companies of exclusively boy actors. The competition was most intense in the early 1600s. There were then two principal children's companies: the Children of Paul's (the choirboys from St. Paul's Cathedral, whose private playhouse was near the cathedral); and the Children of the Chapel Royal (the choirboys from the monarch's private chapel, who performed at the Blackfriars theater built by Burbage in 1596). In *Hamlet* Shakespeare writes of "an aerie [nest] of children, little eyases [hawks], that cry out on the top of question and are most tyrannically clapped for 't. These are now the fashion and . . . berattle the common stages [attack the public theaters]." In the long run, the adult actors prevailed. The Children of Paul's dissolved around 1606. By about 1608 the Children of the Chapel Royal had been forced to stop playing at the Blackfriars theater, which was then taken over by the King's Men, Shakespeare's own troupe.

Acting companies and theaters of Shakespeare's time seem to have been organized in various ways. For example, with the building of the Globe, Shakespeare's company apparently managed itself, with the principal actors, Shakespeare among them, having the status of "sharers" and the right to a share in the takings, as well as the responsibility for a part of the expenses. Five of the sharers, including Shakespeare, owned the Globe. As actor, as sharer in an acting company and in ownership of theaters, and as playwright, Shakespeare was about as involved in the theatrical industry as one could imagine. Although Shakespeare and his fellows prospered, their status under the law was conditional upon the protection of powerful patrons. "Common players"—those who did not have patrons or masters—were classed in the language of the law with "vagabonds and sturdy beggars." So the actors had to secure for themselves the official rank of servants of patrons. Among the patrons under whose protection Shakespeare's company worked were the lord chamberlain and, after the accession of King James in 1603, the king himself.

In the early 1990s we began to learn a great deal more about the theaters in which Shakespeare and his contemporaries performed—or, at least, began to open up new questions about them. At that time about 70 percent of the Rose had been excavated, as had about 10 percent of the second Globe, the one built in 1614. Excavation was halted at that point, but London has come to value the sites of its early playhouses, and takes what opportunities it can to explore them more deeply, both on the Bankside and in Shoreditch. Information about the playhouses of Shakespeare's London is therefore a constantly changing resource.

The Publication of Shakespeare's Plays

Eighteen of Shakespeare's plays found their way into print during the playwright's lifetime, but there is nothing to suggest that he took any interest in their publication. These eighteen appeared separately in editions in quarto or, in the case of *Henry VI, Part 3*, octavo format. The quarto pages are not much larger than a modern mass-market paperback book, and the octavo pages are even smaller; these little books were sold unbound for a few pence. The earliest of the quartos that still survive were printed in 1594, the year that both *Titus Andronicus* and a version of the play now called *Henry VI, Part 2* became available. While almost every one of these early quartos displays on its title page the name of the acting company that performed the play, only about half provide the name of the playwright, Shakespeare. The first quarto edition to bear the name Shakespeare on its title page is *Love's Labor's Lost* of 1598. A few of the quartos were popular with the book-buying public of Shakespeare's lifetime; for example, quarto *Richard II* went through five editions between 1597 and 1615. But most of the quartos were far from best sellers; *Love's Labor's Lost* (1598), for instance, was not reprinted in quarto until 1631. After Shakespeare's death, two more of his plays appeared in quarto format: *Othello* in 1622 and *The Two Noble Kinsmen*, coauthored with John Fletcher, in 1634.

In 1623, seven years after Shakespeare's death, *Mr. William Shakespeares Comedies, Histories, & Tragedies* was published. This printing offered readers in a single book thirty-six of the thirty-eight plays now thought to have been written by Shakespeare, including eighteen that had never been printed before. And it offered them in a style that was then reserved for serious literature and scholarship. The plays were arranged in double columns on pages nearly a foot high. This large page size is called "folio," as opposed to the smaller "quarto," and the 1623 volume is usually called the Shakespeare First Folio. It is reputed to have sold for the lordly price of a pound. (One copy at the Folger Shakespeare Library is marked fifteen shillings—that is, three-quarters of a pound.)

In a preface to the First Folio entitled "To the great Variety of Readers," two of Shakespeare's former fellow actors in the King's Men, John Heminge and Henry Condell, wrote that they themselves had collected their dead companion's plays. They suggested that they had seen his own papers: "we have scarce received from him a blot in his papers." The title page of the Folio declared that the plays within it had been printed "according to the True Original Copies." Comparing the Folio to the quartos, Heminge and Condell disparaged the quartos, advising their readers that "before you were abused with divers stolen and surreptitious copies, maimed, and deformed by the frauds and stealths of injurious impostors." Many Shakespeareans of the eighteenth and nineteenth centuries believed Heminge and Condell and regarded the Folio plays as superior to anything in the quartos.

Once we begin to examine the Folio plays in detail, it becomes less easy to take at face value the word of Heminge and Condell about the superiority of the Folio texts. For example, of the first nine plays in the Folio (one-quarter of the entire collection), four were essentially reprinted from earlier quarto printings that Heminge and Condell had disparaged, and four have now been identified as printed from copies written in

the hand of a professional scribe of the 1620s named
Ralph Crane; the ninth, *The Comedy of Errors*, was
apparently also printed from a manuscript, but one
whose origin cannot be readily identified. Evidently,
then, eight of the first nine plays in the First Folio
were not printed, in spite of what the Folio title page
announces, "according to the True Original Copies," or
Shakespeare's own papers, and the source of the ninth
is unknown. Since today's editors have been forced to
treat Heminge and Condell's pronouncements with
skepticism, they must choose whether to base their
own editions upon quartos or the Folio on grounds
other than Heminge and Condell's story of where the
quarto and Folio versions originated.

Editors have often fashioned their own narratives to
explain what lies behind the quartos and Folio. They
have said that Heminge and Condell meant to criti-
cize only a few of the early quartos, the ones that offer
much shorter and sometimes quite different, often gar-
bled, versions of plays. Among the examples of these
are the 1600 quarto of *Henry V* (the Folio offers a much
fuller version) or the 1603 *Hamlet* quarto. (In 1604 a
different, much longer form of the play got into print
as a quarto.) Early twentieth-century editors and some
scholars in the present century have speculated that
these questionable texts were produced when someone in the audience took notes from the plays' dialogue during performances and then employed "hack
poets" to fill out the notes. The poor results were then
sold to a publisher and presented in print as Shakespeare's plays. For much of the twentieth century this
story gave way to another in which the shorter versions
are said to be re-creations from memory of Shakespeare's plays by actors who wanted to stage them in
the provinces but lacked manuscript copies. Most of
the quartos offer much better texts than these so-called

bad quartos. Indeed, in most of the quartos we find texts that are at least equal to or better than what is printed in the Folio. Many Shakespeare enthusiasts persuaded themselves that most of the quartos were set into type directly from Shakespeare's own papers, although there is nothing on which to base this conclusion except the desire for it to be true. Thus speculation continues about how the Shakespeare plays got to be printed. All that we have are the printed texts.

The book collector who was most successful in bringing together copies of the quartos and the First Folio was Henry Clay Folger, founder of the Folger Shakespeare Library in Washington, D.C. While it is estimated that there survive around the world only about 230 copies of the First Folio, Mr. Folger was able to acquire more than seventy-five copies, as well as a large number of fragments, for the library that bears his name. He also amassed a substantial number of quartos. For example, only fourteen copies of the First Quarto of *Love's Labor's Lost* are known to exist, and three are at the Folger Shakespeare Library. As a consequence of Mr. Folger's labors, scholars visiting the Folger Shakespeare Library have been able to learn a great deal about sixteenth- and seventeenth-century printing and, particularly, about the printing of Shakespeare's plays. And Mr. Folger did not stop at the First Folio, but collected many copies of later editions of Shakespeare, beginning with the Second Folio (1632), the Third (1663–64), and the Fourth (1685). Each of these later folios was based on its immediate predecessor and was edited anonymously. The first editor of Shakespeare whose name we know was Nicholas Rowe, whose first edition came out in 1709. Mr. Folger collected this edition and many, many more by Rowe's successors, and the collecting and scholarship continue.

An Introduction to This Text

Richard II was first printed in 1597 as a quarto (Q1). The present edition is based directly on this printing of the play, except for a passage in 4.1 that the quarto does not print.* *Richard II* was a popular book; it went through four more editions in quarto before its appearance in the First Folio of 1623. The Second Quarto (Q2) simply reprints Q1, and, in turn, the Third Quarto (Q3) reprints Q2. The Fourth Quarto (Q4) in the main reprints Q3, but Q4 adds about 160 lines (the so-called Deposition Scene) in 4.1. These lines, which appear in no earlier extant quarto, would seem then to have been printed from manuscript copy. (When the "Deposition Scene" was printed in the 1623 Folio, it seems to have been printed from yet a different manuscript, since the passage in Q4 differs considerably from the lines printed in the Folio. The differences between the Q4 and Folio versions of the "Deposition Scene" will be described below.) Finally, the Fifth Quarto (Q5) simply reprints Q4. (For our comment on the "Deposition Scene," see longer note to 4.1.160–331, page 226, below.)

For the most part, the Folio text of 1623 was printed from an edited copy of one of the later quartos, most likely the Fifth Quarto of 1615.† There are, however,

---

*We have also consulted the computerized text of the First Quarto provided by the Text Archive of the Oxford University Computing Centre, to which we are grateful. The First Quarto presents unusual challenges to the reader to discern the difference between some of its commas and its periods because these punctuation marks look so much alike.

†It has been suggested more than once that the Third Quarto of 1598 was used as Folio printer's copy, but because there are errors

quite a number of significant differences between the Folio version of *Richard II* and what one finds in the later quartos like Q5. (1) The Folio restores many Q1 readings that had been corrupted in the printing of the later quartos (though it reproduces as much of this corruption as it corrects). (2) It omits passages that total fifty-one lines; some omissions seem to be rough cuts whose edges are difficult to join. (3) The Folio supplements the meager stage directions of the quartos. (4) The Folio offers the fuller, and better, version of the "Deposition Scene." (The Q4 version lacks several lines and part-lines found in the Folio, and the Q4 verse is very badly divided. Some editors have argued that the Q4 version is a memorial reconstruction of the F version, but the differences between the versions hardly resemble the kinds of differences attributed to memorial reconstruction in other texts to which this theory has been affixed.) (5) Finally, the Folio version is divided into acts and scenes.

Editors have tried to imagine from what source this array of changes could have arisen. Their speculation has favored a theatrical manuscript, which they see as having been compared in a rather perfunctory way to the printed quarto used by the Folio printers as their copy.[*] In support of this suggestion, these editors point to the many necessary entrances and exits that appear for the first time in print in the Folio, as well as directions for trumpets, drums, and colors (banners) that would be relevant and necessary to theatrical produc-

---

in the Folio that are identical to some first made in the course of printing Q5, this suggestion needs to be supplemented by further speculation about how the text of Q5 may have influenced Folio printers when they were allegedly using Q3 as their copy. The more speculation, the less attractive the hypothesis.

[*]It has been argued—although not persuasively, it seems to us— that the Folio version is Shakespeare's revision of the Q1 version.

tion. (They instance, for example, the exit of Gaunt
in 1.1, discussed in our longer note to 1.1.201.) One
difficulty with the supposition that the changes came
in by way of a theatrical manuscript is that some of
the Folio's additions to Q's stage directions contradict
theatrical practice of Shakespeare's time. For example,
when Richard enters in 3.3 "on the walls," in the theater he would actually appear in the gallery above the
stage—that is, among the best seats in the house, from
which the actors would be loath to displace paying
patrons. In Q1 Richard appears there with Aumerle,
with whom he converses, but the Folio entrance sur-
rounds him with a silent crowd of actors, "*Carlile, . . .
Scroop, Salisbury,*" who would have no place in an
actual theater gallery. The addition of these extra,
nonspeaking characters seems more literary than theatrical, since a reader who noticed that the dialogue
has described Carlisle, Scroop, and Salisbury as having accompanied Richard to Flint Castle might expect
them to appear with him on the castle walls. There
are thus difficulties with the view that the Folio's stage
directions trace back to a manuscript from the theater.
Nonetheless, the Folio stage directions can often be
useful to readers in imagining the play onstage, and
where they seem useful we have included them in our
edition. We also follow the Folio act and scene division
(with one exception near the end of Act 5), and follow the Folio printing of the "Deposition Scene." With
these exceptions, this edition is based directly on Q1.

For the convenience of the reader, we have modernized the punctuation and the spelling of the quarto.
Sometimes we go so far as to modernize certain old
forms of words; for example, when *a* means "he," we
change it to *he;* we change *mo* to *more* and *ye* to *you.*
But it is not our practice in editing any of the plays to
modernize words that sound distinctly different from

modern forms. For example, when the early printed texts read *sith* or *apricokes* or *porpentine*, we have not modernized to *since, apricots, porcupine*. When the forms *an, and,* or *and if* appear instead of the modern form *if*, we have reduced *and* to *an* but have not changed any of these forms to their modern equivalent, *if*. We also modernize and, where necessary, correct passages in foreign languages, unless an error in the early printed text can be reasonably explained as a joke.

Whenever we change the wording of the quarto or add anything to its stage directions, we mark the change by enclosing it in superior half-brackets (⌜⌝). (Within the "Deposition Scene" in 4.1, which already appears in superior half-brackets because it is drawn from the Folio, we mark changes to the Folio lines by enclosing them in pointed brackets [⟨⟩].) We want our readers to be immediately aware when we have intervened. (Only when we correct an obvious typographical error in the quarto does the change not get marked.) Whenever we change the quarto's wording or its punctuation so that meaning changes, we list the change in the textual notes at the back of the book, even if all we have done is fix an obvious error.

We regularize a number of the proper names, as is the usual practice in editions of the play. For example, the name "Fitzwater" appears variously in *Richard II* as "Fitzwater," "Fitzwaters," and "Fitz." We reduce this diversity to "Fitzwater" in both the dialogue and speech prefixes. *Richard II*, which focuses specifically on the transfer of the title of king from one man to another, presents an interesting problem in the naming of the two kings. Our general policy is to leave a character's name unchanged throughout a given play; in *Richard II*, we alter this policy in order to follow the quarto designations of Richard and Bolingbroke. The quarto names Richard "King" until partway through Act 5. Then the speech prefix "King" is transferred to Bolingbroke, and Richard becomes "Richard" or "Ric." As in the quarto, Richard is "King Richard" in our edition until Bolingbroke becomes "King Henry," at which time the former king becomes simply "Richard" in stage directions and speech prefixes. As can be observed in these examples, we expand the often severely abbreviated forms of names used as speech headings in early printed texts into the full names of the characters. Variations in the speech headings of the early printed texts are recorded in the textual notes.

This edition differs from many earlier ones in its efforts to aid the reader in imagining the play as a performance. Nevertheless, when Q1's stage directions give prominence to the fictional, we adjust our additions to these stage directions accordingly. Thus when Richard is about to appear "on the walls," as Q1 puts it in 3.3, we have Northumberland approach "the battlements," rather than, say, "the rear of the stage." Whenever it is reasonably certain, in our view, that a speech is accompanied by a particular action, we provide a stage direction describing the action. (Occasional exceptions to this rule occur when the action is so obvious that to add a stage direction would insult the reader.) Stage directions for the entrance of characters in mid-scene are, with rare exceptions, placed so that they immediately precede the characters' participation in the scene, even though these entrances may appear somewhat earlier in the early printed texts. Whenever we move a stage direction, we record this change in the textual notes. Latin stage directions (e.g., *Exeunt*) are translated into English (e.g., *They exit*).

In the present edition, as well, we mark with a dash any change of address within a speech, unless a stage direction intervenes. When the *-ed* ending of a word is to be pronounced, we mark it with an accent. Like editors for the past two centuries we print metrically linked lines in the following way:

> BOLINGBROKE
>   Yea, my good lord.
>   KING RICHARD   Then I must not say no.

However, when there are a number of short verse lines that can be linked in more than one way, we do not, with rare exceptions, indent any of them.

The Explanatory Notes

The notes that appear on the pages facing the text are designed to provide readers with the help that they may need to enjoy the play. Whenever the meaning of a word in the text is not readily accessible in a good contemporary dictionary, we offer the meaning in a note. Sometimes we provide a note even when the relevant meaning is to be found in the dictionary but when the word has acquired since Shakespeare's time other potentially confusing meanings. In our notes, we try to offer modern synonyms for Shakespeare's words. We also try to indicate to the reader the connection between the word in the play and the modern synonym. For example, Shakespeare sometimes uses the word *head* to mean "source," but, for modern readers, there may be no connection evident between these two words. We provide the connection by explaining Shakespeare's usage as follows: "**head:** fountainhead, source." On some occasions, a whole phrase or clause needs explanation. Then, when space allows, we rephrase in our own words the difficult passage, and add at the end synonyms for individual words in the

passage. When scholars have been unable to determine
the meaning of a word or phrase, we acknowledge the
uncertainty.

In the explanatory notes and longer notes, quotations from the Bible are, unless otherwise noted, taken
from the Geneva Bible (1560), with spelling and punctuation modernized; quotations from Raphael Holinshed's *Chronicles* are taken from a Folger Shakespeare
Library copy of the 1587 edition (3:487–517), with
spelling and punctuation modernized.

The Tragedy of

RICHARD II

The Line of Edward III

[Characters in *Richard II* appear in bold]

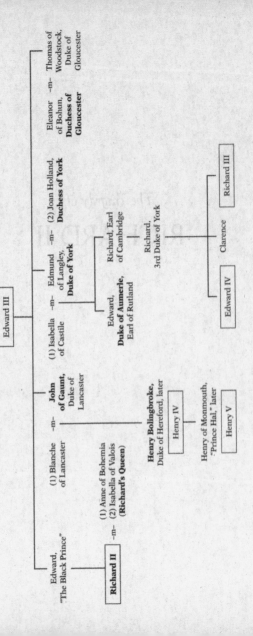

Characters in the Play

KING RICHARD II
Sir John BUSHY ⎫
Sir John BAGOT ⎬ *Richard's friends*
Sir Henry GREEN ⎭

Richard's QUEEN
Queen's LADIES-IN-WAITING

JOHN OF GAUNT, Duke of Lancaster
HENRY BOLINGBROKE, Duke of HEREFORD, son to John of
   Gaunt, and later King Henry IV

DUCHESS OF GLOUCESTER, widow to Thomas, Duke of
   Gloucester

Edmund, DUKE OF YORK
DUCHESS OF YORK
DUKE OF AUMERLE, Earl of Rutland, son to Duke and
   Duchess of York
York's SERVINGMAN

Thomas MOWBRAY, Duke of Norfolk
LORD MARSHAL ⎫
FIRST HERALD ⎬ *officials in trial by combat*
SECOND HERALD ⎭

EARL OF SALISBURY ⎫
BISHOP OF CARLISLE ⎪
SIR STEPHEN SCROOP ⎬ *supporters of King Richard*
LORD BERKELEY ⎪
ABBOT OF WESTMINSTER ⎪
WELSH CAPTAIN ⎭

3

Henry Percy, EARL OF NORTHUM-
  BERLAND
LORD ROSS
LORD WILLOUGHBY
HARRY PERCY, son of Northumber-
  land, later known as "Hotspur"

} *supporters of
  Bolingbroke*

LORD FITZWATER
DUKE OF SURREY
ANOTHER LORD

GARDENER
Gardener's Servingmen

GROOM of Richard's stable
KEEPER of prison at Pomfret Castle

SIR PIERCE OF EXTON
Servingman to Exton

Lords, Attendants, Officers, Soldiers, Servingmen,
  Exton's Men

The Tragedy of

RICHARD II

ACT 1

1.1 Henry Bolingbroke, King Richard's cousin, publicly accuses Thomas Mowbray, duke of Norfolk, of treason. Among Bolingbroke's charges is that Mowbray was responsible for the murder of Henry's and Richard's uncle the duke of Gloucester. When Richard and Gaunt, Bolingbroke's father, are unable to reconcile Bolingbroke and Mowbray, Richard orders them to trial by combat at Coventry.

---

1. **Lancaster:** i.e., duke of **Lancaster**
2. **band:** i.e., bond, duty, obligation
3. **Henry Hereford:** Henry Bolingbroke, son to the duke of Lancaster, was duke of Hereford.
4. **boist'rous:** violent, fierce; **late:** recent; **appeal:** charge, accusation
5. **our:** i.e., my (the royal "we," which Richard uses to refer to himself throughout most of this public scene in such words as *ourselves, we,* and *us*); **leisure:** i.e., convenience
8. **sounded:** i.e., questioned
9. **If:** i.e., whether; **appeal:** accuse; **ancient:** long-established, long-standing
12. **As near as I could sift him:** i.e., **as** far **as I could** determine by examining **him** closely; **argument:** subject
13. **apparent:** visible, obvious

⌜ACT 1⌝

⌜Scene 1⌝

*Enter King Richard, John of Gaunt, with other Nobles
and Attendants.*

KING RICHARD
Old John of Gaunt, time-honored Lancaster,
Hast thou, according to thy oath and band,
Brought hither Henry Hereford, thy bold son,
Here to make good the boist'rous late appeal,
Which then our leisure would not let us hear,   5
Against the Duke of Norfolk, Thomas Mowbray?
GAUNT   I have, my liege.
KING RICHARD
Tell me, moreover, hast thou sounded him
If he appeal the Duke on ancient malice
Or worthily, as a good subject should,   10
On some known ground of treachery in him?
GAUNT
As near as I could sift him on that argument,
On some apparent danger seen in him
Aimed at your Highness, no inveterate malice.
KING RICHARD
Then call them to our presence.   15
                          ⌜*An Attendant exits.*⌝
                          Face to face
And frowning brow to brow, ourselves will hear

7

19. **High stomached:** haughty

23. **still better:** i.e., continue to exceed; **other's:** i.e., the previous day's

24. **hap:** fortune

26. **but:** merely

27. **by the cause you come:** i.e., from the nature of the **cause** for which **you come**

28. **appeal:** accuse

29. **object:** bring as a charge

33. **Tend'ring:** holding dear; valuing, esteeming

34. **misbegotten:** illegally conceived, illegitimate (here used figuratively)

35. **appellant:** i.e., as the accuser

37. **mark . . . well:** i.e., pay close attention to what I say

38. **make good:** carry out, perform

39. **divine:** immortal

40. **miscreant:** villain (originally, a heretic)

41. **Too good:** perhaps, too highborn

44. **aggravate:** intensify, exacerbate; **note:** sign of disgrace (The word **note** comes from the Latin *nota*, one of whose meanings is "mark of ignominy, sign of official censure.")

46. **ere:** before

The accuser and the accusèd freely speak.
High stomached are they both and full of ire,
In rage deaf as the sea, hasty as fire.   20

Enter Bolingbroke and Mowbray.

BOLINGBROKE
Many years of happy days befall
My gracious sovereign, my most loving liege.
MOWBRAY
Each day still better other's happiness
Until the heavens, envying Earth's good hap,
Add an immortal title to your crown.   25
KING RICHARD
We thank you both. Yet one but flatters us,
As well appeareth by the cause you come:
Namely, to appeal each other of high treason.
Cousin of Hereford, what dost thou object
Against the Duke of Norfolk, Thomas Mowbray?   30
BOLINGBROKE
First—heaven be the record to my speech!—
In the devotion of a subject's love,
Tend'ring the precious safety of my prince
And free from other misbegotten hate,
Come I appellant to this princely presence.—   35
Now, Thomas Mowbray, do I turn to thee;
And mark my greeting well, for what I speak
My body shall make good upon this earth
Or my divine soul answer it in heaven.
Thou art a traitor and a miscreant,   40
Too good to be so and too bad to live,
Since the more fair and crystal is the sky,
The uglier seem the clouds that in it fly.
Once more, the more to aggravate the note,
With a foul traitor's name stuff I thy throat,   45
And wish, so please my sovereign, ere I move,

47. **right-drawn:** i.e., drawn in a just cause

51. **eager:** sharp; acid (from the French *aigre*)

52. **Can:** i.e., that **can; betwixt us twain:** between us two

58. **post:** ride quickly, as in riding post-horses (The words **curbs, reins,** and **spurs,** like the word **post,** compare **speech** to horseback riding [lines 56–57].)

59. **These terms of treason:** i.e., such **terms** as **traitor** and **miscreant** (line 40)

60. **high:** i.e., noble

61. **let him be:** i.e., acting as if he were (Bolingbroke and Richard were first cousins. See family tree, page 2.)

65. **tied:** obliged, bound

67. **inhabitable:** not habitable, unfit for human habitation

68. **durst:** i.e., dares

69. **this:** i.e., the oath that he swears; or, perhaps, his sword (the hilt of which he may clasp)

70. **hopes:** i.e., **hopes** of salvation

71. **gage:** pledge (By throwing down a glove or hood or some other object, the person pledges himself to meet his adversary in combat. See pictures, pages 26 and 154.)

72. **kindred:** kinship

74. **except:** exclude (See line 60.)

76. **pawn:** i.e., gage (See picture, page 26.)

77. **all . . . else:** i.e., **all** the other **rites of knighthood**

78. **make good:** See note to line 38.

79. **or thou . . . devise:** perhaps, **or** deeds even **worse** than **I have** named

What my tongue speaks my right-drawn sword may
    prove.
MOWBRAY
  Let not my cold words here accuse my zeal.
  'Tis not the trial of a woman's war, 50
  The bitter clamor of two eager tongues,
  Can arbitrate this cause betwixt us twain.
  The blood is hot that must be cooled for this.
  Yet can I not of such tame patience boast
  As to be hushed and naught at all to say. 55
  First, the fair reverence of your Highness curbs me
  From giving reins and spurs to my free speech,
  Which else would post until it had returned
  These terms of treason doubled down his throat.
  Setting aside his high blood's royalty, 60
  And let him be no kinsman to my liege,
  I do defy him, and I spit at him,
  Call him a slanderous coward and a villain,
  Which to maintain I would allow him odds
  And meet him, were I tied to run afoot 65
  Even to the frozen ridges of the Alps
  Or any other ground inhabitable
  Wherever Englishman durst set his foot.
  Meantime let this defend my loyalty:
  By all my hopes, most falsely doth he lie. 70
BOLINGBROKE, ⌈*throwing down a gage*⌉
  Pale trembling coward, there I throw my gage,
  Disclaiming here the kindred of the King,
  And lay aside my high blood's royalty,
  Which fear, not reverence, makes thee to except.
  If guilty dread have left thee so much strength 75
  As to take up mine honor's pawn, then stoop.
  By that and all the rites of knighthood else
  Will I make good against thee, arm to arm,
  What I have spoke or thou canst worse devise.

80–81. **by that sword . . . shoulder:** When a man was knighted, the king touched his **shoulder** with a **sword.**

82. **answer thee:** i.e., meet you in combat

84. **light:** alight (from my horse)

85. **unjustly:** i.e., in an unjust cause

87. **inherit us:** i.e., make me possess

88. **ill:** evil, badness

89. **Look what:** whatever

90. **nobles:** gold coins worth about seven shillings

91. **lendings:** money advanced to soldiers when the regular pay cannot be given

92. **lewd employments:** base uses

95. **Or:** i.e., either

98. **Complotted:** conspired, plotted secretly

99. **head:** i.e., fountainhead, source

101–2. **will maintain . . . good:** perhaps, will prove (**make . . . good**) by taking his life

103. **Duke of Gloucester:** brother to John of Gaunt and uncle to Richard and to Bolingbroke, killed in 1397, the year before the action reflected in this scene of the play (See longer note, page 223.)

104. **Suggest:** prompt

105. **consequently:** subsequently

108–10. **blood . . . cries . . . for justice:** In Genesis 4.10–11, "the voice of" the **blood** of Cain's brother, the murdered Abel, "cryeth unto [the Lord] from the ground," and the Earth is said to have "opened her mouth to receive [Cain's] brother's blood." **sacrificing Abel:** Cain kills his brother, Abel, because Abel's sacrificial offering of "the first fruits of his sheep" was pleasing to God while Cain's offering of "the fruit of the ground" was not.

(continued)

12

MOWBRAY, ⌜*picking up the gage*⌝
   I take it up, and by that sword I swear   80
   Which gently laid my knighthood on my shoulder,
   I'll answer thee in any fair degree
   Or chivalrous design of knightly trial;
   And when I mount, alive may I not light
   If I be traitor or unjustly fight.   85

KING RICHARD
   What doth our cousin lay to Mowbray's charge?
   It must be great that can inherit us
   So much as of a thought of ill in him.

BOLINGBROKE
   Look what I speak, my life shall prove it true:
   That Mowbray hath received eight thousand nobles   90
   In name of lendings for your Highness' soldiers,
   The which he hath detained for lewd employments,
   Like a false traitor and injurious villain.
   Besides I say, and will in battle prove,
   Or here or elsewhere to the furthest verge   95
   That ever was surveyed by English eye,
   That all the treasons for these eighteen years
   Complotted and contrivèd in this land
   Fetch from false Mowbray their first head and
      spring.   100
   Further I say, and further will maintain
   Upon his bad life to make all this good,
   That he did plot the Duke of Gloucester's death,
   Suggest his soon-believing adversaries,
   And consequently, like a traitor coward,   105
   Sluiced out his innocent soul through streams of
      blood,
   Which blood, like sacrificing Abel's, cries
   Even from the tongueless caverns of the Earth
   To me for justice and rough chastisement.   110
   And, by the glorious worth of my descent,
   This arm shall do it, or this life be spent.

110. **rough:** harsh

111. **descent:** i.e., hereditary lineage, ancestry

113. **pitch:** i.e., height (The image is from falconry, where the term **pitch** refers to the highest point of the falcon's flight.)

117. **slander of his blood:** i.e., disgrace to his family line (namely, Bolingbroke)

122. **my scepter's awe:** i.e., the power of my scepter to inspire dread or fear

124. **nothing privilege him:** i.e., give him no privilege at all; **partialize:** i.e., make partial, bias

128–29. **as low . . . thou liest:** The seriousness of a lie was measured by the point in the body from which the lie supposedly emanated. One could be accused of lying in one's teeth, in one's throat, or, as here, **as low as to** [one's] **heart.**

130. **Three parts of that receipt:** i.e., three-quarters of the money I received

132. **by consent:** i.e., according to a prior agreement with the king

133. **For that:** because

134. **Upon . . . account:** i.e., for the balance of a heavy debt

136. **For:** i.e., as **for**

144. **exactly:** expressly

KING RICHARD
　How high a pitch his resolution soars!—
　Thomas of Norfolk, what sayst thou to this?

MOWBRAY
　O, let my sovereign turn away his face　　　　　　115
　And bid his ears a little while be deaf,
　Till I have told this slander of his blood
　How God and good men hate so foul a liar.

KING RICHARD
　Mowbray, impartial are our eyes and ears.
　Were he my brother, nay, my kingdom's heir,　　120
　As he is but my father's brother's son,
　Now by ⌜my⌝ scepter's awe I make a vow:
　Such neighbor nearness to our sacred blood
　Should nothing privilege him nor partialize
　The unstooping firmness of my upright soul.　　125
　He is our subject, Mowbray; so art thou.
　Free speech and fearless I to thee allow.

MOWBRAY
　Then, Bolingbroke, as low as to thy heart,
　Through the false passage of thy throat, thou liest.
　Three parts of that receipt I had for Calais　　130
　Disbursed I duly to his Highness' soldiers;
　The other part reserved I by consent,
　For that my sovereign liege was in my debt
　Upon remainder of a dear account
　Since last I went to France to fetch his queen.　　135
　Now swallow down that lie. For Gloucester's death,
　I slew him not, but to my own disgrace
　Neglected my sworn duty in that case.—
　For you, my noble Lord of Lancaster,
　The honorable father to my foe,　　　　　　　　140
　Once did I lay an ambush for your life,
　A trespass that doth vex my grievèd soul.
　But ere I last received the sacrament,
　I did confess it and exactly begged

146. **my fault:** i.e., what I did wrong; **appealed:** charged against me

149. **Which in myself I:** i.e., the truth of **which** statement **I myself**

150. **interchangeably:** in turn, reciprocally

153. **chambered:** enclosed

154. **In haste whereof:** i.e., in order to hasten my self-justification

157–61. **Let's purge . . . bleed:** i.e., let's cure this anger **without** bloodshed (Richard's language plays with the idea of bloodletting as a medical cure, or purge, for **choler**—biliousness, anger, or other signs of an excess of bile. To **bleed** was to draw blood from the body to remove such excess fluid.)

168. **bids:** commands, enjoins; **bid:** request, beg

169. **we bid:** I command; **boot:** remedy

Your Grace's pardon, and I hope I had it.—   145
This is my fault. As for the rest appealed,
It issues from the rancor of a villain,
A recreant and most degenerate traitor,
Which in myself I boldly will defend,
And interchangeably hurl down my gage   150
Upon this overweening traitor's foot,

⌈*He throws down a gage.*⌉

To prove myself a loyal gentleman,
Even in the best blood chambered in his bosom;
In haste whereof most heartily I pray
Your Highness to assign our trial day.   155

⌈*Bolingbroke picks up the gage.*⌉

KING RICHARD
Wrath-kindled ⌈gentlemen,⌉ be ruled by me.
Let's purge this choler without letting blood.
This we prescribe, though no physician.
Deep malice makes too deep incision.
Forget, forgive; conclude and be agreed.   160
Our doctors say this is no month to bleed.—
Good uncle, let this end where it begun;
We'll calm the Duke of Norfolk, you your son.

GAUNT
To be a make-peace shall become my age.—
Throw down, my son, the Duke of Norfolk's gage.   165

KING RICHARD
And, Norfolk, throw down his.

GAUNT   When, Harry, when?
Obedience bids I should not bid again.

KING RICHARD
Norfolk, throw down, we bid; there is no boot.

MOWBRAY
Myself I throw, dread sovereign, at thy foot.   170

⌈*Mowbray kneels.*⌉

My life thou shalt command, but not my shame.
The one my duty owes, but my fair name,

173. **that lives:** i.e., **my fair name** will live

175. **impeached:** (1) disparaged; (2) accused of treason; **baffled:** subjected to public disgrace

177. **The which:** i.e., the wound caused by **slander's venomed spear** (line 176)

180. **Lions make leopards tame:** an allusion to the link between the king and the lion, "king of the beasts," as well as to Richard's and Mowbray's heraldic emblems

181. **not change his spots:** See Jeremiah 13.23: "Can the black Moor change his skin? or the leopard his spots?"

183. **mortal times:** i.e., our time on this Earth

185. **gilded loam or painted clay:** The reference here is to the idea that humans were made from the dust of the earth (Genesis 2.7, 3.19). Without **spotless reputation,** according to Mowbray, we are nothing but that dust (in the form of **loam** or **clay**) decorated with gold or with paint.

190. **try:** prove

192. **throw up your gage:** i.e., give me Mowbray's **gage,** which you picked up (The phrasing suggests that Bolingbroke is to **throw** the **gage up** to Richard, sitting above him.)

194. **crestfallen:** humbled, abashed

195. **impeach my height:** i.e., disgrace my noble standing

196. **out-dared:** cowed, overcome by daring

197. **such feeble wrong:** perhaps, a **wrong** that would brand me a weakling

198. **sound so base a parle:** i.e., ask for such an ignominious truce (The metaphor is from the trumpet sound for a parley between opposing armies.)

(continued)

Despite of death that lives upon my grave,
To dark dishonor's use thou shalt not have.
I am disgraced, impeached, and baffled here,   175
Pierced to the soul with slander's venomed spear,
The which no balm can cure but his heart-blood
Which breathed this poison.

KING RICHARD   Rage must be withstood.
Give me his gage. Lions make leopards tame.   180

MOWBRAY, ⌈*standing*⌉
Yea, but not change his spots. Take but my shame
And I resign my gage. My dear dear lord,
The purest treasure mortal times afford
Is spotless reputation; that away,
Men are but gilded loam or painted clay.   185
A jewel in a ten-times-barred-up chest
Is a bold spirit in a loyal breast.
Mine honor is my life; both grow in one.
Take honor from me and my life is done.
Then, dear my liege, mine honor let me try.   190
In that I live, and for that will I die.

KING RICHARD, ⌈*to Bolingbroke*⌉
Cousin, throw up your gage. Do you begin.

BOLINGBROKE
O, God defend my soul from such deep sin!
Shall I seem crestfallen in my father's sight?
Or with pale beggar-fear impeach my height   195
Before this out-dared dastard? Ere my tongue
Shall wound my honor with such feeble wrong
Or sound so base a ⌈*parle*,⌉ my teeth shall tear
The slavish motive of recanting fear
And spit it bleeding in his high disgrace,   200
Where shame doth harbor, even in Mowbray's face.

KING RICHARD
We were not born to sue, but to command,
Which, since we cannot do, to make you friends,
Be ready, as your lives shall answer it,

199. **motive:** instrument, organ (Bolingbroke says that he will bite out his own tongue rather than use it to take back his accusation.)

200. **in his high disgrace:** i.e., in the tongue's terrible **disgrace** (because it will be made to **harbor** in **Mowbray's face** [line 201])

201. **face:** See longer note, page 223.

202. **sue:** woo, beseech

205. **Coventry:** a town northwest of London; **Saint Lambert's day:** i.e., September 17

207. **settled:** fixed, unchanging

208. **atone:** reconcile

209. **Justice . . . chivalry:** It was believed that in trial by combat, God (or, here, **Justice**) rewards the innocent party with victory. **chivalry:** warlike distinction or glory

211. **home alarms:** i.e., domestic broils (in contrast to foreign wars)

1.2 The widow of the duke of Gloucester begs John of Gaunt to avenge the murder of her husband. Gaunt says that the king was responsible for Gloucester's murder and that, since the king is God's deputy, only God can take vengeance.

———

1. **the part . . . blood:** i.e., my kinship with Thomas of Woodstock, duke of Gloucester

2. **exclaims:** outcries

3. **stir:** i.e., take action

4. **correction:** punishment

4–5. **those hands . . . fault:** i.e., the **hands** of the person who committed the crime. (The implication
(continued)

20

At Coventry upon Saint Lambert's day.   205
There shall your swords and lances arbitrate
The swelling difference of your settled hate.
Since we cannot atone you, we shall see
Justice design the victor's chivalry.—
Lord Marshal, command our officers-at-arms   210
Be ready to direct these home alarms.

                       ⌜*They*⌝ *exit.*

⌜Scene 2⌝

Enter John of Gaunt with the Duchess of Gloucester.

GAUNT
Alas, the part I had in Woodstock's blood
Doth more solicit me than your exclaims
To stir against the butchers of his life.
But since correction lieth in those hands
Which made the fault that we cannot correct,   5
Put we our quarrel to the will of heaven,
Who, when they see the hours ripe on Earth,
Will rain hot vengeance on offenders' heads.

DUCHESS
Finds brotherhood in thee no sharper spur?
Hath love in thy old blood no living fire?   10
Edward's seven sons, whereof thyself art one,
Were as seven vials of his sacred blood
Or seven fair branches springing from one root.
Some of those seven are dried by nature's course,
Some of those branches by the Destinies cut.   15
But Thomas, my dear lord, my life, my Gloucester,
One vial full of Edward's sacred blood,
One flourishing branch of his most royal root,
Is cracked and all the precious liquor spilt,
Is hacked down, and his summer leaves all faded,   20
By envy's hand and murder's bloody ax.

here—made as an open accusation in lines 39–41—
is that the king was responsible for Gloucester's
murder. See longer note to 1.1.103, page 223.)

6. **quarrel:** cause

7. **they:** i.e., the heavens

11. **Edward's:** i.e., King Edward III's

14. **are . . . course:** i.e., died a natural death

15. **by . . . cut:** i.e., were cut off early in life **Destinies:** i.e., the Fates, the goddesses who, in Greek
mythology, wove one's life and brought about one's
death by cutting one's thread of life (See picture,
page 52.)

19. **liquor:** fluid (here, the **sacred blood** [line 12]
he had inherited from Edward III)

21. **envy's:** hatred's; malice's

24. **metal:** substance of which a person is made;
self: i.e., selfsame, same

27–28. **consent . . . to:** acquiesce . . . in

30. **model:** image, perfect representation

31. **patience:** i.e., the virtue of bearing suffering
quietly while waiting for something to happen (as
Gaunt described himself in lines 6–8)

32. **suff'ring:** allowing, permitting

33. **naked:** plain, obvious, clear

35. **mean men: men** of low social status

39. **quarrel:** cause; **for:** i.e., as **for; God's substitute:** i.e., the king (who was thought to rule on
Earth as **God's deputy**)

43. **minister:** agent

44. **complain myself:** utter my lamentations

48. **cousin:** kinsman; **fell:** cruel, fierce

51. **if misfortune miss the first career:** i.e., **if**
the **first** charge or encounter fails to kill Mowbray
misfortune: i.e., **misfortune** to Mowbray

22

Ah, Gaunt, his blood was thine! That bed, that
   womb,
That metal, that self mold that fashioned thee
Made him a man; and though thou livest and   25
   breathest,
Yet art thou slain in him. Thou dost consent
In some large measure to thy father's death
In that thou seest thy wretched brother die,
Who was the model of thy father's life.   30
Call it not patience, Gaunt. It is despair.
In suff'ring thus thy brother to be slaughtered,
Thou showest the naked pathway to thy life,
Teaching stern murder how to butcher thee.
That which in mean men we entitle patience   35
Is pale, cold cowardice in noble breasts.
What shall I say? To safeguard thine own life,
The best way is to venge my Gloucester's death.

GAUNT
God's is the quarrel; for God's substitute,
His deputy anointed in His sight,   40
Hath caused his death, the which if wrongfully
Let heaven revenge, for I may never lift
An angry arm against His minister.

DUCHESS
Where, then, alas, may I complain myself?

GAUNT
To God, the widow's champion and defense.   45

DUCHESS
Why then I will. Farewell, old Gaunt.
Thou goest to Coventry, there to behold
Our cousin Hereford and fell Mowbray fight.
O, ⌜sit⌝ my husband's wrongs on Hereford's spear,
That it may enter butcher Mowbray's breast!   50
Or if misfortune miss the first career,
Be Mowbray's sins so heavy in his bosom

54. **lists:** arena set up for tournaments (See picture, page 28.)

55. **caitiff recreant:** (1) wretched captive; (2) cowardly wretch; (3) captured apostate

56. **sometime:** former

60–61. **Grief . . . weight:** i.e., **grief** is like a ball that keeps rebounding not because it is hollow but because it is so heavy

64. **Commend me:** offer my greetings

68. **Plashy:** Gloucester's estate in Essex

70. **unfurnished walls:** bare **walls** from which the tapestries and hangings have been removed

71. **offices:** domestic areas where servants did their work

1.3 Bolingbroke and Mowbray prepare to fight to the death. King Richard suddenly calls off the fight and banishes Mowbray for life and Bolingbroke for many years.

———

1. **Lord Aumerle:** Holinshed records that **Aumerle** was "that day High Constable of England." He and the lord marshal were in charge of the trial by combat.

2. **at all points:** at every point, in every respect

That they may break his foaming courser's back
And throw the rider headlong in the lists,
A caitiff recreant to my cousin Hereford!   55
Farewell, old Gaunt. Thy sometime brother's wife
With her companion, grief, must end her life.
GAUNT
   Sister, farewell. I must to Coventry.
   As much good stay with thee as go with me.
DUCHESS
   Yet one word more. Grief boundeth where ⌜it⌝ falls,   60
   Not with the empty hollowness, but weight.
   I take my leave before I have begun,
   For sorrow ends not when it seemeth done.
   Commend me to thy brother, Edmund York.
   Lo, this is all. Nay, yet depart not so!   65
   Though this be all, do not so quickly go;
   I shall remember more. Bid him—ah, what?—
   With all good speed at Plashy visit me.
   Alack, and what shall good old York there see
   But empty lodgings and unfurnished walls,   70
   Unpeopled offices, untrodden stones?
   And what hear there for welcome but my groans?
   Therefore commend me; let him not come there
   To seek out sorrow that dwells everywhere.
   Desolate, desolate, will I hence and die.   75
   The last leave of thee takes my weeping eye.
                                          They exit.

                        ⌜Scene 3⌝
        Enter Lord Marshal and the Duke ⌜of⌝ Aumerle.

MARSHAL
   My Lord Aumerle, is Harry Hereford armed?
AUMERLE
   Yea, at all points, and longs to enter in.

3. **sprightfully:** full of spirit
4. **Stays but:** waits only for
5. **champions:** combatants
7. **demand of:** ask
9. **orderly:** duly, in accordance with the rules
10. **swear him in:** i.e., have **him swear** to
13. **quarrel:** cause
18. **God defend:** i.e., **God** forbid
20. **my succeeding issue:** i.e., my offspring
21. **appeals:** accuses

A knight taking up a gage. (1.1.76)
From Olaus Magnus, *Historia de gentibus
septentrionalibus . . .* (1555).

MARSHAL
  The Duke of Norfolk, sprightfully and bold,
  Stays but the summons of the appellant's trumpet.

AUMERLE
  Why then, the champions are prepared and stay   5
  For nothing but his Majesty's approach.

The trumpets sound and the King enters with his Nobles
⌜*and Officers;*⌝ *when they are set, enter* ⌜*Mowbray,*⌝ *the*
Duke of Norfolk in arms, defendant, ⌜*with a Herald.*⌝

KING RICHARD
  Marshal, demand of yonder champion
  The cause of his arrival here in arms,
  Ask him his name, and orderly proceed
  To swear him in the justice of his cause.   10

MARSHAL, ⌜*to Mowbray*⌝
  In God's name and the King's, say who thou art
  And why thou comest thus knightly clad in arms,
  Against what man thou com'st, and what thy quarrel.
  Speak truly on thy knighthood and thy oath,
  As so defend thee heaven and thy valor.   15

MOWBRAY
  My name is Thomas Mowbray, Duke of Norfolk,
  Who hither come engagèd by my oath—
  Which God defend a knight should violate!—
  Both to defend my loyalty and truth
  To God, my king, and my succeeding issue,   20
  Against the Duke of Hereford that appeals me,
  And by the grace of God and this mine arm
  To prove him, in defending of myself,
  A traitor to my God, my king, and me;
  And as I truly fight, defend me heaven.   25

  The trumpets sound. Enter ⌜*Bolingbroke,*⌝ *Duke of*
  Hereford, appellant, in armor, ⌜*with a Herald.*⌝

KING RICHARD   Marshal, ask yonder knight in arms

28. **plated . . . war:** i.e., dressed in armor

30. **Depose him in:** examine him on oath about

32. **lists:** arena set up for trials by combat (Holinshed reports that "the king caused a sumptuous scaffold or theater and **royal lists** . . . to be erected and prepared.") See picture, below.

38. **In lists:** i.e., in a formal trial by combat

43. **touch the lists:** Holinshed reports a proclamation forbidding any man to "attempt to approach or **touch** any part of **the lists** upon pain of death."

45. **these fair designs:** i.e., the orderly conduct of the tournament

Combat in lists. (1.2.54; 1.3.32)
From [Sir William Segar,] *The booke of honor and armes . . .* (1590).

Both who he is and why he cometh hither
Thus plated in habiliments of war,
And formally, according to our law,
Depose him in the justice of his cause.   30

MARSHAL, ⌜*to Bolingbroke*⌝
What is thy name? And wherefore com'st thou hither,
Before King Richard in his royal lists?
Against whom comest thou? And what's thy quarrel?
Speak like a true knight, so defend thee heaven.

BOLINGBROKE
Harry of Hereford, Lancaster, and Derby   35
Am I, who ready here do stand in arms
To prove, by God's grace and my body's valor,
In lists, on Thomas Mowbray, Duke of Norfolk,
That he is a traitor foul and dangerous
To God of heaven, King Richard, and to me.   40
And as I truly fight, defend me heaven.

MARSHAL
On pain of death, no person be so bold
Or daring-hardy as to touch the lists,
Except the Marshal and such officers
Appointed to direct these fair designs.   45

BOLINGBROKE
Lord Marshal, let me kiss my sovereign's hand
And bow my knee before his Majesty;
For Mowbray and myself are like two men
That vow a long and weary pilgrimage.
Then let us take a ceremonious leave   50
And loving farewell of our several friends.

MARSHAL, ⌜*to King Richard*⌝
The appellant in all duty greets your Highness
And craves to kiss your hand and take his leave.

KING RICHARD, ⌜*coming down*⌝
We will descend and fold him in our arms.
                              ⌜*He embraces Bolingbroke.*⌝
Cousin of Hereford, as thy cause is right,   55

57. **my blood ... shed:** Richard plays with the figurative sense of **my blood** as "my kinsman" and the literal **blood** that Bolingbroke might **shed.**

58. **not revenge thee:** Bolingbroke's death in this trial by combat would signal his guiltiness. (See note to 1.1.209.)

59. **profane a tear:** i.e., put even one **tear** to an unworthy use

65. **have to do with: have** dealings or business **with**

66. **lusty:** lively, healthy; **cheerly:** heartily

67–68. **at English feasts ... sweet:** The reference is to the custom, associated at the time with England, of ending a banquet with sweets and fruits. **regreet:** salute, greet **daintiest:** finest, most pleasing to the palate

69. **the earthly author of my blood:** i.e., my father

70. **in me regenerate:** i.e., reborn **in me**

73. **proof:** impenetrability, invulnerability

75. **waxen coat:** i.e., suit of armor as penetrable as wax

77. **lusty havior:** vigorous bearing or behavior

81. **amazing thunder:** i.e., terrifying, stupefying thunderbolts or thunderstones (thought to be emitted during thunder and lightning storms); **casque:** helmet (See picture, page 32.)

84. **Mine ... thrive:** i.e., may my **innocence and Saint George** bring me success (**Saint George** was the patron saint of England. See picture, page xvii.)

So be thy fortune in this royal fight.
Farewell, my blood—which, if today thou shed,
Lament we may but not revenge thee dead.
BOLINGBROKE
  O, let no noble eye profane a tear
  For me if I be gored with Mowbray's spear.   60
  As confident as is the falcon's flight
  Against a bird do I with Mowbray fight.
  My loving lord, I take my leave of you.—
  Of you, my noble cousin, Lord Aumerle;
  Not sick, although I have to do with death,   65
  But lusty, young, and cheerly drawing breath.—
  Lo, as at English feasts, so I regreet
  The daintiest last, to make the end most sweet.
  O, thou the earthly author of my blood,
  Whose youthful spirit in me regenerate   70
  Doth with a twofold vigor lift me up
  To reach at victory above my head,
  Add proof unto mine armor with thy prayers,
  And with thy blessings steel my lance's point
  That it may enter Mowbray's waxen coat   75
  And furbish new the name of John o' Gaunt,
  Even in the lusty havior of his son.
GAUNT
  God in thy good cause make thee prosperous.
  Be swift like lightning in the execution,
  And let thy blows, doubly redoubled,   80
  Fall like amazing thunder on the casque
  Of thy adverse pernicious enemy.
  Rouse up thy youthful blood, be valiant, and live.
BOLINGBROKE
  Mine innocence and Saint George to thrive!
MOWBRAY
  However God or fortune cast my lot,   85
  There lives or dies, true to King Richard's throne,
  A loyal, just, and upright gentleman.

90. **golden . . . enfranchisement:** i.e., freedom

92. **feast:** i.e., fete, festivity

94. **Take . . . years:** i.e., accept **my wish** that you may enjoy many **happy years**

95. **to jest:** i.e., **to** a **jest** (an entertainment)

96. **Truth hath a quiet breast:** Proverbial: "**Truth** fears no trial."

97. **Securely:** confidently

98. **couchèd:** lodged; or, expressed

106. **On . . . recreant:** i.e., the penalty to be suffered, should Bolingbroke fail **to prove the Duke of Norfolk . . . A traitor** (lines 107–8), is that he will himself **be found false and recreant**

112. **approve:** demonstrate, prove

A casque. (1.3.81)
From Louis de Gaya, *Traité des armes, des machines de guerre . . .* (1678).

Never did captive with a freer heart
Cast off his chains of bondage and embrace
His golden uncontrolled enfranchisement   90
More than my dancing soul doth celebrate
This feast of battle with mine adversary.
Most mighty liege and my companion peers,
Take from my mouth the wish of happy years.
As gentle and as jocund as to jest   95
Go I to fight. Truth hath a quiet breast.

KING RICHARD
Farewell, my lord. Securely I espy
Virtue with valor couchèd in thine eye.—
Order the trial, marshal, and begin.

MARSHAL
Harry of Hereford, Lancaster, and Derby,   100
Receive thy lance; and God defend the right.
          ⌜*He presents a lance to Bolingbroke.*⌝

BOLINGBROKE
Strong as a tower in hope, I cry "Amen!"

MARSHAL, ⌜*to an Officer*⌝
Go bear this lance to Thomas, Duke of Norfolk.
          ⌜*An Officer presents a lance to Mowbray.*⌝

⌜FIRST⌝ HERALD
Harry of Hereford, Lancaster, and Derby
Stands here for God, his sovereign, and himself,   105
On pain to be found false and recreant,
To prove the Duke of Norfolk, Thomas Mowbray,
A traitor to his God, his king, and him,
And dares him to set forward to the fight.

SECOND HERALD
Here standeth Thomas Mowbray, Duke of Norfolk,   110
On pain to be found false and recreant,
Both to defend himself and to approve
Henry of Hereford, Lancaster, and Derby
To God, his sovereign, and to him disloyal,

116. **Attending but:** awaiting only, listening only for

117 SD. **warder:** staff or truncheon carried as a symbol of office

118. **Stay:** stop, wait

119. **lay by:** put aside

123. **While:** until; **we return:** I tell

125. **list:** i.e., listen to, hear

126. **For that:** i.e., in order **that**

128. **for:** because; **aspect:** pronounced **aspèct**

132. **set on you:** i.e., **set you on,** incited **you**

135. **Which:** perhaps, **which** civil disturbance, or **which ambitious thoughts** and **envy** (Grammatically, **Which** refers to the word **peace** as its antecedent, but at the same time it serves as the subject of the clause **"Which . . . Might . . . fright fair peace."**)

142. **upon pain of life:** i.e., your **life** will be the penalty if you disobey

144. **regreet:** salute or greet again

145. **stranger:** foreign

Courageously and with a free desire   115
Attending but the signal to begin.

MARSHAL

Sound, trumpets, and set forward, combatants.
⌜*Trumpets sound. Richard throws down his warder.*⌝
Stay! The King hath thrown his warder down.

KING RICHARD

Let them lay by their helmets and their spears,
And both return back to their chairs again.   120
⌜*To his council.*⌝ Withdraw with us, and let the
   trumpets sound
While we return these dukes what we decree.
   ⌜*Trumpets sound while Richard consults with Gaunt
                              and other Nobles.*⌝
⌜*To Bolingbroke and Mowbray.*⌝ Draw near,
And list what with our council we have done.   125
For that our kingdom's earth should not be soiled
With that dear blood which it hath fosterèd;
And for our eyes do hate the dire aspect
Of civil wounds plowed up with neighbor's sword;
And for we think the eagle-wingèd pride   130
Of sky-aspiring and ambitious thoughts,
With rival-hating envy, set on you
To wake our peace, which in our country's cradle
Draws the sweet infant breath of gentle sleep,
Which, so roused up with boist'rous untuned   135
   drums,
With harsh resounding trumpets' dreadful bray,
And grating shock of wrathful iron arms,
Might from our quiet confines fright fair peace
And make us wade even in our kindred's blood: 140
Therefore we banish you our territories.
You, cousin Hereford, upon pain of life,
Till twice five summers have enriched our fields
Shall not regreet our fair dominions,
But tread the stranger paths of banishment.   145

150. **heavier doom:** graver sentence

152. **determinate:** put an end to

153. **dateless limit:** prescribed period without end; **dear:** dire

158. **dearer:** more precious; **merit:** reward; **maim:** wound, injury (For the context of Mowbray's claim that he deserves from Richard a reward instead of severe punishment, see longer note to 1.1.103, page 223.)

165. **cunning:** ingenious, skillfully contrived

166. **open:** i.e., out of its case

166–67. **into his hands / That:** i.e., **into** the **hands** of someone who

169. **Doubly portcullised:** i.e., as if put behind a double portcullis or grate (See picture, page 44.)

171. **attend on:** wait upon, serve as attendant to

172. **nurse:** i.e., nursemaid, one of whose tasks would have been to help a young child to speak

177. **boots:** benefits, profits; **compassionate:** self-pitying; or, appealing for pity

178. **plaining:** complaining, lamenting

BOLINGBROKE
    Your will be done. This must my comfort be:
    That sun that warms you here shall shine on me,
    And those his golden beams to you here lent
    Shall point on me and gild my banishment.

KING RICHARD
    Norfolk, for thee remains a heavier doom,	150
    Which I with some unwillingness pronounce:
    The sly, slow hours shall not determinate
    The dateless limit of thy dear exile.
    The hopeless word of "never to return"
    Breathe I against thee, upon pain of life.	155

MOWBRAY
    A heavy sentence, my most sovereign liege,
    And all unlooked-for from your Highness' mouth.
    A dearer merit, not so deep a maim
    As to be cast forth in the common air,
    Have I deservèd at your Highness' hands.	160
    The language I have learnt these forty years,
    My native English, now I must forgo;
    And now my tongue's use is to me no more
    Than an unstringèd viol or a harp,
    Or like a cunning instrument cased up,	165
    Or, being open, put into his hands
    That knows no touch to tune the harmony.
    Within my mouth you have enjailed my tongue,
    Doubly portcullised with my teeth and lips,
    And dull unfeeling barren ignorance	170
    Is made my jailor to attend on me.
    I am too old to fawn upon a nurse,
    Too far in years to be a pupil now.
    What is thy sentence ⌜then⌝ but speechless death,
    Which robs my tongue from breathing native	175
      breath?

KING RICHARD
    It boots thee not to be compassionate.
    After our sentence plaining comes too late.

179. **me:** i.e., myself
180. **shades:** darkness
185. **therein:** i.e., in **the duty that you owe**
190. **regreet:** greet, salute
192. **by advisèd purpose:** i.e., deliberately
193. **complot:** plot together, conspire; **ill:** evil
197. **so far as to mine enemy:** perhaps an indication that the words to follow, though addressed directly to Mowbray, are not to be mistaken for a friendly overture (See longer note, page 224.)
198. **permitted us:** i.e., allowed us to fight to the death
200. **Banished:** i.e., **banished** from
204. **clogging:** Clogs were blocks of wood or other weights attached to animals or humans to impede movement or prevent escape. (See picture, page 218.)
206. **My name be:** i.e., may **my name be**

MOWBRAY
　　Then thus I turn me from my country's light,
　　To dwell in solemn shades of endless night.   180
　　　　　　　　　　　　　⌜*He begins to exit.*⌝
KING RICHARD
　　Return again, and take an oath with thee.
　　⌜*To Mowbray and Bolingbroke.*⌝ Lay on our royal
　　　sword your banished hands.
　　　　　　　⌜*They place their right hands on the hilts of*
　　　　　　　　　　　　　　Richard's sword.⌝
　　Swear by the duty that you owe to God—
　　Our part therein we banish with yourselves—   185
　　To keep the oath that we administer:
　　You never shall, so help you truth and God,
　　Embrace each other's love in banishment,
　　Nor never look upon each other's face,
　　Nor never write, regreet, nor reconcile   190
　　This louring tempest of your homebred hate,
　　Nor never by advisèd purpose meet
　　To plot, contrive, or complot any ill
　　'Gainst us, our state, our subjects, or our land.
BOLINGBROKE　I swear.   195
MOWBRAY　And I, to keep all this.
　　　　　　　　　　　　　　⌜*They step back.*⌝
BOLINGBROKE
　　Norfolk, so far as to mine enemy:
　　By this time, had the King permitted us,
　　One of our souls had wandered in the air,
　　Banished this frail sepulcher of our flesh,   200
　　As now our flesh is banished from this land.
　　Confess thy treasons ere thou fly the realm.
　　Since thou hast far to go, bear not along
　　The clogging burden of a guilty soul.
MOWBRAY
　　No, Bolingbroke; if ever I were traitor,   205
　　My name be blotted from the book of life,

210. **stray:** i.e., go the wrong way

212. **glasses:** looking **glasses,** mirrors

213. **aspect:** In the sixteenth century, this word could be pronounced **aspèct.**

214. **banished years:** i.e., **years** of banishment

219. **wanton:** luxuriant

221. **in regard of:** i.e., because of your **regard** for

227–29. **lamp, light, taper:** Human life is often (as in the Bible) compared to candles and lamps. Gaunt imagines his own death as the extinguishing of these sources of light and heat. **extinct:** extinguished

235. **furrow:** Here, old **age** is imaged in the wrinkled brow, pictured as a field that time has plowed into furrows.

236. **his pilgrimage:** i.e., its progress (A **pilgrimage** was a journey to a sacred place, but the term was often used to describe the course of a human life from youth to old age and death.)

And I from heaven banished as from hence.
But what thou art, God, thou, and I do know,
And all too soon, I fear, the King shall rue.—
Farewell, my liege. Now no way can I stray;   210
Save back to England, all the world's my way.

He exits.

KING RICHARD, ⌜*to Gaunt*⌝
Uncle, even in the glasses of thine eyes
I see thy grievèd heart. Thy sad aspect
Hath from the number of his banished years
Plucked four away. ⌜*To Bolingbroke.*⌝ Six frozen   215
    winters spent,
Return with welcome home from banishment.

BOLINGBROKE
How long a time lies in one little word!
Four lagging winters and four wanton springs
End in a word; such is the breath of kings.   220

GAUNT
I thank my liege that in regard of me
He shortens four years of my son's exile.
But little vantage shall I reap thereby;
For, ere the six years that he hath to spend
Can change their moons and bring their times   225
    about,
My oil-dried lamp and time-bewasted light
Shall be extinct with age and endless ⌜night;⌝
My inch of taper will be burnt and done,
And blindfold death not let me see my son.   230

KING RICHARD
Why, uncle, thou hast many years to live.

GAUNT
But not a minute, king, that thou canst give.
Shorten my days thou canst with sullen sorrow,
And pluck nights from me, but not lend a morrow.
Thou canst help time to furrow me with age,   235
But stop no wrinkle in his pilgrimage.

237. **current:** genuine, authentic (a term applied to money that is valid—as opposed to counterfeit—currency); **him:** i.e., time

238. **But dead:** i.e., **but** once I am **dead**

240. **a party verdict:** a vote that shared in the joint **verdict**

242. **Things . . . sour:** proverbial

246. **To smooth his fault:** i.e., in order to make **his fault** less offensive

247. **A partial slander:** i.e., the accusation of partiality

249. **looked when:** expected that

250. **to make mine own away:** i.e., in making away with, destroying, my **own** child

251. **gave leave to:** i.e., allowed

255–56. **Cousin . . . show:** It is possible that Aumerle should exit following this couplet; see longer note, page 224.   **What . . . know:** i.e., that which I cannot learn from personal contact **remain:** reside, dwell

260. **greeting:** courteous words

262. **office:** function

262–63. **prodigal / To breathe:** i.e., lavish in breathing

Thy word is current with him for my death,
But dead, thy kingdom cannot buy my breath.
KING RICHARD
Thy son is banished upon good advice,
Whereto thy tongue a party verdict gave.   240
Why at our justice seem'st thou then to lour?
GAUNT
Things sweet to taste prove in digestion sour.
You urged me as a judge, but I had rather
You would have bid me argue like a father.
O, had it been a stranger, not my child,   245
To smooth his fault I should have been more mild.
A partial slander sought I to avoid,
And in the sentence my own life destroyed.
Alas, I looked when some of you should say
I was too strict, to make mine own away.   250
But you gave leave to my unwilling tongue
Against my will to do myself this wrong.
KING RICHARD, ⌐*to Bolingbroke*¬
Cousin, farewell.—And, uncle, bid him so.
Six years we banish him, and he shall go.
  ⌐*Flourish. King Richard*¬ exits ⌐*with his Attendants.*¬
AUMERLE, ⌐*to Bolingbroke*¬
Cousin, farewell. What presence must not know,   255
From where you do remain let paper show.
MARSHAL, ⌐*to Bolingbroke*¬
My lord, no leave take I, for I will ride,
As far as land will let me, by your side.
GAUNT, ⌐*to Bolingbroke*¬
O, to what purpose dost thou hoard thy words,
That thou returnest no greeting to thy friends?   260
BOLINGBROKE
I have too few to take my leave of you,
When the tongue's office should be prodigal
To breathe the abundant dolor of the heart.

264. **thy absence:** i.e., your being absent

271. **sullen:** gloomy, dark

272. **foil:** setting for a **jewel** (line 273)

275. **remember me:** i.e., remind me

277. **apprenticehood:** i.e., apprenticeship

278. **passages:** (1) experiences; (2) journeys

279. **freedom:** (1) from his contract as an apprentice; (2) from his sentence of exile

280. **journeyman:** one who has finished his apprenticeship and works for daily hire (with a pun on **journeyman** as "a man who journeys")

281–82. **All . . . havens:** Proverbial: "**A wise man** makes every country his own."   **the eye of heaven:** i.e., the sun

284. **There is no virtue like necessity:** proverbial

287. **faintly:** feebly

Door with a portcullis. (1.3.169)
Print tipped into John Foxe, *Actes and monuments . . .* (1563).

GAUNT
  Thy grief is but thy absence for a time.
BOLINGBROKE
  Joy absent, grief is present for that time.   265
GAUNT
  What is six winters? They are quickly gone.
BOLINGBROKE
  To men in joy; but grief makes one hour ten.
GAUNT
  Call it a travel that thou tak'st for pleasure.
BOLINGBROKE
  My heart will sigh when I miscall it so,
  Which finds it an enforcèd pilgrimage.   270
GAUNT
  The sullen passage of thy weary steps
  Esteem as foil wherein thou art to set
  The precious jewel of thy home return.
BOLINGBROKE
  Nay, rather every tedious stride I make
  Will but remember me what a deal of world   275
  I wander from the jewels that I love.
  Must I not serve a long apprenticehood
  To foreign passages, and in the end,
  Having my freedom, boast of nothing else
  But that I was a journeyman to grief?   280
GAUNT
  All places that the eye of heaven visits
  Are to a wise man ports and happy havens.
  Teach thy necessity to reason thus:
  There is no virtue like necessity.
  Think not the King did banish thee,   285
  But thou the King. Woe doth the heavier sit
  Where it perceives it is but faintly borne.
  Go, say I sent thee forth to purchase honor,
  And not the King exiled thee; or suppose
  Devouring pestilence hangs in our air   290
  And thou art flying to a fresher clime.

292. **Look what:** whatever

295. **the presence:** i.e., **the** king's **presence** chamber

296. **strewed:** i.e., strewn or spread with rushes or carpet

298. **measure:** a kind of stately dancing

299. **gnarling:** snarling

300. **sets it light:** i.e., makes **light** of **it**

306. **fantastic:** imagined

307. **apprehension:** imagination, conception

308. **the worse:** i.e., the bad, that which is **worse**

309. **Fell:** cruel, destructive

310. **when he bites:** The reference here is to Gaunt's statement at lines 299–300 about **gnarling sorrow.**

314. **nurse:** i.e., one who cares for a young child (a nursemaid or a wet nurse)

1.4 Richard makes plans to fight in person in Ireland. To obtain money for the war against the Irish, he leases out crown lands and revenues in exchange for cash, and he gives his deputies in England power to demand large sums of money from the wealthy. News comes that John of Gaunt is gravely ill. Richard looks forward to using Gaunt's property to help fund the war.

---

1. **We did observe:** Richard enters in mid-conversation with Green and Bagot.

2. **high:** (1) noble; (2) haughty, arrogant

Look what thy soul holds dear, imagine it
To lie that way thou goest, not whence thou com'st.
Suppose the singing birds musicians,
The grass whereon thou tread'st the presence 295
 strewed,
The flowers fair ladies, and thy steps no more
Than a delightful measure or a dance;
For gnarling sorrow hath less power to bite
The man that mocks at it and sets it light. 300

BOLINGBROKE
O, who can hold a fire in his hand
By thinking on the frosty Caucasus?
Or cloy the hungry edge of appetite
By bare imagination of a feast?
Or wallow naked in December snow 305
By thinking on fantastic summer's heat?
O no, the apprehension of the good
Gives but the greater feeling to the worse.
Fell sorrow's tooth doth never rankle more
Than when he bites but lanceth not the sore. 310

GAUNT
Come, come, my son, I'll bring thee on thy way.
Had I thy youth and cause, I would not stay.

BOLINGBROKE
Then, England's ground, farewell; sweet soil, adieu,
My mother and my nurse that bears me yet.
Where'er I wander, boast of this I can, 315
Though banished, yet a trueborn Englishman.
         They exit.

⌜Scene 4⌝
Enter the King with ⌜*Green and Bagot,*⌝ *at one door, and
the Lord Aumerle at another.*

KING RICHARD We did observe.—Cousin Aumerle,
How far brought you high Hereford on his way?

4. **next highway:** nearest public road

5. **store:** abundance

6. **Faith:** a mild oath; **for me:** i.e., from me; **except:** i.e., **except** that

8. **rheum:** tears

12. **for:** i.e., because

14. **To counterfeit . . . grief:** i.e., to pretend to be so oppressed by sorrow

16. **Marry:** a mild oath (originally an oath "by the Virgin Mary")

20. **none of:** i.e., **none** from

21. **our cousin, cousin:** Richard, Aumerle, and Bolingbroke were first cousins; **'tis doubt:** it is doubtful; or, it is to be doubted

23. **friends:** i.e., cousins (literally, kinsmen, relatives)

30. **underbearing:** endurance

31. **As 'twere to banish their affects with him:** i.e., as if to carry their kind feelings with him into banishment

32. **bonnet:** hat; **oysterwench:** a girl or woman who sells oysters

33. **brace:** pair

AUMERLE
  I brought high Hereford, if you call him so,
  But to the next highway, and there I left him.
KING RICHARD
  And say, what store of parting tears were shed?   5
AUMERLE
  Faith, none for me, except the northeast wind,
  Which then blew bitterly against our faces,
  Awaked the sleeping rheum and so by chance
  Did grace our hollow parting with a tear.
KING RICHARD
  What said our cousin when you parted with him?   10
AUMERLE   "Farewell."
  And, for my heart disdainèd that my tongue
  Should so profane the word, that taught me craft
  To counterfeit oppression of such grief
  That words seemed buried in my sorrow's grave.   15
  Marry, would the word "farewell" have lengthened
    hours
  And added years to his short banishment,
  He should have had a volume of farewells.
  But since it would not, he had none of me.   20
KING RICHARD
  He is our ⌈cousin,⌉ cousin, but 'tis doubt,
  When time shall call him home from banishment,
  Whether our kinsman come to see his friends.
  Ourself and Bushy, ⌈Bagot here and Green,⌉
  Observed his courtship to the common people,   25
  How he did seem to dive into their hearts
  With humble and familiar courtesy,
  What reverence he did throw away on slaves,
  Wooing poor craftsmen with the craft of smiles
  And patient underbearing of his fortune,   30
  As 'twere to banish their affects with him.
  Off goes his bonnet to an oysterwench;
  A brace of draymen bid God speed him well

36. **As were our England:** i.e., as if my **England were; in reversion his:** i.e., destined to become his

37. **next degree in hope:** nearest step (perhaps, heir to the throne) in their expectations

38. **with . . . thoughts:** i.e., let **these thoughts go with him**

39. **stand out:** hold out, resist

40. **Expedient:** expeditious; **manage:** management, direction, control

41. **leisure:** opportunity afforded by unoccupied time

43. **We will ourself in person:** i.e., I will go myself

44. **for:** i.e., because; **too great a court:** i.e., too large a retinue of courtiers (At 4.1.293–94, Richard describes himself as one who "every day under his household roof / Did keep ten thousand men.")

46. **farm our royal realm:** i.e., lease out all crown lands and expected tax revenues in exchange for large cash payments (See longer note, page 224.)

48. **our affairs in hand:** i.e., my present business **in hand:** in process

49–51. **substitutes . . . sums of gold:** See longer note, page 224. **Whereto:** i.e., in which **them:** perhaps, the names of the rich men; perhaps, the charters

52. **them:** probably, the **large sums of gold** (line 51); perhaps, the **charters** (line 49) as filled out

53. **make for:** proceed toward; **presently:** immediately

56. **taken:** i.e., **taken** ill

59. **Ely House:** palace of the bishop of **Ely** (often rented out to noblemen visiting London)

62. **lining:** i.e., contents; **coats: coats** of mail

And had the tribute of his supple knee,
With "Thanks, my countrymen, my loving friends,"   35
As were our England in reversion his
And he our subjects' next degree in hope.

GREEN
Well, he is gone, and with him go these thoughts.
Now for the rebels which stand out in Ireland,
Expedient manage must be made, my liege,   40
Ere further leisure yield them further means
For their advantage and your Highness' loss.

KING RICHARD
We will ourself in person to this war.
And, for our coffers, with too great a court
And liberal largess, are grown somewhat light,   45
We are enforced to farm our royal realm,
The revenue whereof shall furnish us
For our affairs in hand. If that come short,
Our substitutes at home shall have blank charters,
Whereto, when they shall know what men are rich,   50
They shall subscribe them for large sums of gold
And send them after to supply our wants,
For we will make for Ireland presently.

⌜*Enter Bushy.*⌝

Bushy, what news?⌝

BUSHY
Old John of Gaunt is grievous sick, my lord,   55
Suddenly taken, and hath sent posthaste
To entreat your Majesty to visit him.

KING RICHARD   Where lies he?

BUSHY   At Ely House.

KING RICHARD
Now put it, God, in the physician's mind   60
To help him to his grave immediately!
The lining of his coffers shall make coats

The Destinies or Fates. (1.2.15)
From Vincenzo Cartari, *Imagines deorum . . .* (1581).

To deck our soldiers for these Irish wars.
Come, gentlemen, let's all go visit him.
Pray God we may make haste and come too late.   65
⌜ALL⌝ Amen!

They exit.

The Tragedy of

RICHARD II

ACT 2

2.1 John of Gaunt, knowing that he is dying, speaks plainly to Richard about his deficiencies as king. Richard expresses his fury. Gaunt is taken offstage and word comes that he has died. Richard declares that all of Gaunt's possessions now belong to the crown and will be used to help fund his war in Ireland. After Richard exits, Northumberland and two other nobles lament the injustice done to Bolingbroke, and Northumberland reveals that Bolingbroke is on his way back to England. The three nobles set out to join him.

---

 0 **SD. sick:** Gaunt would probably have been carried onstage in a chair to indicate his illness.

 1. **last:** i.e., **last** breath, or **last** words

 2. **unstaid:** unrestrained, unregulated

 11. **is listened more:** i.e., **is more** heeded

 13. **gloze:** talk smoothly and speciously

 14. **marked:** paid attention to

 18. **my life's counsel:** i.e., my advice while I lived

 19. **My death's sad tale:** i.e., what I tell him as I am dying

⌜ACT 2⌝

⌜Scene 1⌝

Enter John of Gaunt sick, with the Duke of York, ⌜and Attendants.⌝

GAUNT
Will the King come, that I may breathe my last
In wholesome counsel to his unstaid youth?
YORK
Vex not yourself nor strive not with your breath,
For all in vain comes counsel to his ear.
GAUNT
O, but they say the tongues of dying men   5
Enforce attention like deep harmony.
Where words are scarce, they are seldom spent in
    vain,
For they breathe truth that breathe their words in
    pain.   10
He that no more must say is listened more
    Than they whom youth and ease have taught to
        gloze.
More are men's ends marked than their lives before.
    The setting sun and music at the close,   15
As the last taste of sweets, is sweetest last,
Writ in remembrance more than things long past.
Though Richard my life's counsel would not hear,
My death's sad tale may yet undeaf his ear.

57

21. **As ... fond:** i.e., such **as** praise, which even **the wise** enjoy (**Fond** also meant "foolishly credulous.")

22. **venom:** venomous, malignant

25. **still:** continually, always

27. **vanity:** idle tale; worthless idea or statement

28. **So:** i.e., as long as; **there's no respect:** i.e., it doesn't matter   **respect:** regard, consideration

31. **will:** desire; determination; **wit's regard:** reason's design or purpose

35. **Methinks:** it seems to me

37. **riot:** wasteful living, dissipation, extravagance

39. **Small:** i.e., light (literally, composed of tiny particles)

41. **betimes:** quickly (used later in this line to mean "at an early time"); **spurs:** rides quickly by urging the horse with spurs

43. **Light:** frivolous, unthinking; **vanity:** pride, conceit; idle or unprofitable conduct; **cormorant:** voracious seabird (See picture, page 200.)

44. **means:** resources at its disposal

45. **sceptered isle:** This phrase, like **royal throne of kings** and **earth of majesty** (line 46), emphasizes England's status as an island kingdom.

46. **seat:** residence, abode; **Mars:** i.e., military prowess (literally, the Roman god of war)

47. **demi-paradise:** i.e., an earthly replica of **paradise** (as a demi-god is half divine, half mortal)

50. **happy:** fortunate

52. **office:** function

53. **defensive to:** defending against attack, protective of

YORK
No, it is stopped with other flattering sounds,   20
As praises, of whose taste the wise are ⌈fond;⌉
Lascivious meters, to whose venom sound
The open ear of youth doth always listen;
Report of fashions in proud Italy,
Whose manners still our tardy-apish nation   25
Limps after in base imitation.
Where doth the world thrust forth a vanity—
So it be new, there's no respect how vile—
That is not quickly buzzed into his ears?
Then all too late comes counsel to be heard   30
Where will doth mutiny with wit's regard.
Direct not him whose way himself will choose.
'Tis breath thou lack'st, and that breath wilt thou
    lose.

GAUNT
Methinks I am a prophet new inspired   35
And thus expiring do foretell of him:
His rash fierce blaze of riot cannot last,
For violent fires soon burn out themselves;
Small showers last long, but sudden storms are
    short;   40
He tires betimes that spurs too fast betimes;
With eager feeding food doth choke the feeder;
Light vanity, insatiate cormorant,
Consuming means, soon preys upon itself.
This royal throne of kings, this sceptered isle,   45
This earth of majesty, this seat of Mars,
This other Eden, demi-paradise,
This fortress built by Nature for herself
Against infection and the hand of war,
This happy breed of men, this little world,   50
This precious stone set in the silver sea,
Which serves it in the office of a wall
Or as ⌈a⌉ moat defensive to a house,

54. **envy:** malice; **less happier:** i.e., **less** happy

57. **teeming:** fertile

58. **Feared by:** i.e., causing fear by; **breed:** lineage

59–62. **Renownèd . . . Mary's son:** The reference here is to the prowess of England's **kings** (line 57) in the Crusades, the series of wars (from 1095 to c. 1450) fought by Christians to recover Christ's **sepulcher** in Jerusalem from the Muslims. **chivalry:** bravery or prowess in war **stubborn Jewry:** i.e., the land of the Jews, here called **stubborn** because it refused Christianity **the world's ransom:** See 1 Timothy 2.5–6: "the man Christ Jesus, who gave himself a **ransom** for all men."

66. **tenement:** property leased to a tenant; **pelting:** paltry, worthless

67. **with:** i.e., by

68. **envious:** malicious, spiteful

69. **wat'ry Neptune:** i.e., the sea (literally, the Roman god of the sea)

70. **inky blots and rotten parchment bonds:** i.e., the "blank charters" referred to at 1.4.49

73. **would the scandal vanish:** i.e., if **the scandal would vanish**

79. **composition:** condition, state

82. **meat:** food

Against the envy of less happier lands,
This blessèd plot, this earth, this realm, this
   England,   55
This nurse, this teeming womb of royal kings,
Feared by their breed and famous by their birth,
Renownèd for their deeds as far from home
For Christian service and true chivalry   60
As is the sepulcher in stubborn Jewry
Of the world's ransom, blessèd Mary's son,
This land of such dear souls, this dear dear land,
Dear for her reputation through the world,
Is now leased out—I die pronouncing it—   65
Like to a tenement or pelting farm.
England, bound in with the triumphant sea,
Whose rocky shore beats back the envious siege
Of wat'ry Neptune, is now bound in with shame,
With inky blots and rotten parchment bonds.   70
That England that was wont to conquer others
Hath made a shameful conquest of itself.
Ah, would the scandal vanish with my life,
How happy then were my ensuing death!

Enter King and Queen, ⌜*Aumerle, Bushy, Green, Bagot,*
           Ross, Willoughby,⌝ *etc.*

YORK
  The King is come. Deal mildly with his youth,   75
  For young hot colts being ⌜reined⌝ do rage the more.
QUEEN, ⌜*to Gaunt*⌝
  How fares our noble uncle Lancaster?
KING RICHARD, ⌜*to Gaunt*⌝
  What comfort, man? How is 't with agèd Gaunt?
GAUNT
  O, how that name befits my composition!
  Old Gaunt indeed and gaunt in being old.   80
  Within me grief hath kept a tedious fast,
  And who abstains from meat that is not gaunt?

83. **watched:** i.e., acted as a nightwatchman, stayed awake

89. **inherits:** possesses, owns

90. **nicely:** precisely, subtly

91. **makes sport to mock itself:** entertains **itself** by mocking **itself**

94. **flatter with:** try to please, fawn upon

100. **Ill . . . ill:** Gaunt here plays with the meanings of **ill** as "sick" and as "evil." Both meanings are implied in the following lines (lines 101–5) about Richard's "sickness."

101. **no lesser than:** i.e., as large as

108. **yet:** i.e., even though they are; **verge:** Gaunt may be playing with two meanings of this word: (1) circumference and (2) "an area . . . defined as extending to a distance of twelve miles around the king's court" (*Oxford English Dictionary*).

109. **waste:** destruction; devastation; squandering, prodigality; any unauthorized act of a tenant that is destructive of the tenement

For sleeping England long time have I watched;
Watching breeds leanness, leanness is all gaunt.
The pleasure that some fathers feed upon   85
Is my strict fast—I mean my children's looks—
And, therein fasting, hast thou made me gaunt.
Gaunt am I for the grave, gaunt as a grave,
Whose hollow womb inherits naught but bones.

KING RICHARD
Can sick men play so nicely with their names?   90

GAUNT
No, misery makes sport to mock itself.
Since thou dost seek to kill my name in me,
I mock my name, great king, to flatter thee.

KING RICHARD
Should dying men flatter with those that live?

GAUNT
No, no, men living flatter those that die.   95

KING RICHARD
Thou, now a-dying, sayest thou flatterest me.

GAUNT
O, no, thou diest, though I the sicker be.

KING RICHARD
I am in health, I breathe, and see thee ill.

GAUNT
Now He that made me knows I see thee ill,
Ill in myself to see, and in thee, seeing ill.   100
Thy deathbed is no lesser than thy land,
Wherein thou liest in reputation sick;
And thou, too careless-patient as thou art,
Commit'st thy anointed body to the cure
Of those physicians that first wounded thee.   105
A thousand flatterers sit within thy crown,
Whose compass is no bigger than thy head,
And yet ⌈encagèd⌉ in so small a verge,
The waste is no whit lesser than thy land.

110. **thy grandsire:** i.e., Edward III (See picture, page 92.)

112. **From forth:** outside, beyond

113. **possessed:** i.e., in possession of the crown (In the following line, the word carries the sense of demonic possession or of obsession.)

115. **regent:** ruler

116. **shame:** matter for severe reproach or reprobation; **let . . . by lease:** rent out . . . on a contract

117. **for thy world enjoying:** i.e., since the **world** you have the use of; **but:** is only

120. **state of law:** status under the **law; bondslave:** slave

123. **ague's privilege:** immunity granted to the ill (An *ague* was chills and fever.)

126. **his:** its

127. **seat's . . . majesty:** i.e., kingship (Literally, the seat is his throne.)

128. **great Edward's son:** i.e., Richard's father, Edward the Black Prince

129. **runs:** wags freely; **roundly:** bluntly

130. **run thy head:** cause your head to roll quickly; **unreverent:** irreverent

132. **For that:** i.e., because

133. **like the pelican:** Pelicans were believed to "tap out" their own blood to feed their young. (See picture, page 72.) Gaunt accuses Richard of having **tapped out** (line 134) the **blood** of Edward III by killing Edward's son **Gloucester** (line 135).

134. **caroused:** drained, swilled, quaffed

136. **Whom fair befall:** i.e., to whom may good things happen

(continued)

O, had thy grandsire with a prophet's eye   110
Seen how his son's son should destroy his sons,
From forth thy reach he would have laid thy shame,
Deposing thee before thou wert possessed,
Which art possessed now to depose thyself.
Why, cousin, wert thou regent of the world,   115
It were a shame to let this land by lease;
But, for thy world enjoying but this land,
Is it not more than shame to shame it so?
Landlord of England art thou now, not king.
Thy state of law is bondslave to the law,   120
And thou—
KING RICHARD   A lunatic lean-witted fool,
  Presuming on an ague's privilege,
  Darest with thy frozen admonition
  Make pale our cheek, chasing the royal blood   125
  With fury from his native residence.
  Now, by my seat's right royal majesty,
  Wert thou not brother to great Edward's son,
  This tongue that runs so roundly in thy head
  Should run thy head from thy unreverent shoulders.   130
GAUNT
  O, spare me not, my ⌜brother⌝ Edward's son,
  For that I was his father Edward's son!
  That blood already, like the pelican,
  Hast thou tapped out and drunkenly caroused.
  My brother Gloucester—plain, well-meaning soul,   135
  Whom fair befall in heaven 'mongst happy souls—
  May be a precedent and witness good
  That thou respect'st not spilling Edward's blood.
  Join with the present sickness that I have,
  And thy unkindness be like crooked age   140
  To crop at once a too-long withered flower.
  Live in thy shame, but die not shame with thee!
  These words hereafter thy tormentors be!—

137. **a precedent:** an instance, an example

138. **respect'st not:** i.e., are not concerned about

140. **And thy:** and let your

146. **sullens:** ill humor, sulkiness

147. **become:** are suited for

150–51. **He . . . Hereford:** i.e., **he loves you** as dearly as he loves his son **Hereford** (Richard responds as if York's words meant "he loves you as much as Hereford loves you.")

154. **commends him:** asks to be kindly remembered

160. **poor:** This description of death as poverty-stricken picks up from the earlier words **spent** and **bankrupt.**

162. **pilgrimage:** i.e., life's journey; **must be:** i.e., remains to be finished

164. **supplant:** get rid of, oust; **rugheaded:** shaggy-headed (also, a likely allusion to the Irish mantle, called by the English a "rug," and to the Irish glib, or shaggy forelock) See picture, page xix. **kern:** foot soldiers (Most editors follow the Folio and print *kerns.* This reading is also found in one extant copy of the First Quarto, but the other three extant copies of the First Quarto print *kern,* which was often used at the time as a collective plural.) See picture, page 86.

165–66. **where no . . . to live:** an allusion to the fact that there are no snakes in Ireland (The word **venom** is a synecdoche for "poisonous snakes.")

167. **for:** because; **charge:** expense

Convey me to my bed, then to my grave.
Love they to live that love and honor have.   145
                    He exits, ⌜carried off by Attendants.⌝

KING RICHARD
And let them die that age and sullens have,
For both hast thou, and both become the grave.

YORK
I do beseech your Majesty, impute his words
To wayward sickliness and age in him.
He loves you, on my life, and holds you dear   150
As Harry, Duke of Hereford, were he here.

KING RICHARD
Right, you say true: as Hereford's love, so his;
As theirs, so mine; and all be as it is.

                    ⌜*Enter Northumberland.*⌝

NORTHUMBERLAND
My liege, old Gaunt commends him to your Majesty.

KING RICHARD
What says he?   155

NORTHUMBERLAND
                    Nay, nothing; all is said.
His tongue is now a stringless instrument;
Words, life, and all, old Lancaster hath spent.

YORK
Be York the next that must be bankrupt so!
Though death be poor, it ends a mortal woe.   160

KING RICHARD
The ripest fruit first falls, and so doth he;
His time is spent, our pilgrimage must be.
So much for that. Now for our Irish wars:
We must supplant those rough rugheaded kern,
Which live like venom where no venom else   165
But only they have privilege to live.
And, for these great affairs do ask some charge,
Towards our assistance we do seize to us

169. **plate:** gold and silver utensils and ornaments; **movables:** furniture, clothing, jewels

170. **did stand possessed:** i.e., owned

172. **tender:** affectionate; **suffer:** allow, endure

174. **Gaunt's rebukes:** i.e., **rebukes** to Gaunt

175–76. **prevention . . . marriage:** According to Holinshed's *Chronicles*, Bolingbroke would have married the king of France's cousin had not Richard prevented the marriage.

185. **Accomplished with:** literally, furnished with (The line means "when he was as old as you.")

193. **compare between:** Richard's question in the following line may suggest that York breaks down at this point and leaves the phrase unfinished.

197. **withal:** i.e., with whatever punishment my boldness brings down on me

198. **gripe:** take, grasp

199. **royalties:** royal privileges, **rights** granted a subject by a king

201. **Harry:** i.e., Henry Bolingbroke; **true:** loyal

The plate, coin, revenues, and movables
Whereof our uncle Gaunt did stand possessed.   170
YORK
How long shall I be patient? Ah, how long
Shall tender duty make me suffer wrong?
Not Gloucester's death, nor Hereford's banishment,
Nor Gaunt's rebukes, nor England's private wrongs,
Nor the prevention of poor Bolingbroke   175
About his marriage, nor my own disgrace,
Have ever made me sour my patient cheek
Or bend one wrinkle on my sovereign's face.
I am the last of noble Edward's sons,
Of whom thy father, Prince of Wales, was first.   180
In war was never lion raged more fierce,
In peace was never gentle lamb more mild,
Than was that young and princely gentleman.
His face thou hast, for even so looked he,
Accomplished with ⌜the⌝ number of thy hours;   185
But when he frowned, it was against the French
And not against his friends. His noble hand
Did win what he did spend, and spent not that
Which his triumphant father's hand had won.
His hands were guilty of no kindred blood,   190
But bloody with the enemies of his kin.
O, Richard! York is too far gone with grief,
Or else he never would compare between.
KING RICHARD
Why, uncle, what's the matter?
YORK   O, my liege,   195
Pardon me if you please. If not, I, pleased
Not to be pardoned, am content withal.
Seek you to seize and gripe into your hands
The royalties and rights of banished Hereford?
Is not Gaunt dead? And doth not Hereford live?   200
Was not Gaunt just? And is not Harry true?
Did not the one deserve to have an heir?

204. **Take ... and take:** i.e., if you **take** ... you thereby **take**

205. **His ... his:** i.e., its ... its (Such conventions as **customary rights** belong to **time** in that **rights** of inheritance are passed down through the course of **time.**)

209. **I say true:** i.e., that what **I** am about to **say** should come **true**

211–13. **Call in ... livery:** i.e., revoke his right to make a claim (through his representatives) for the delivery of his father's lands **letters patents:** royal grants **attorneys general:** those to whom he has given power of attorney to represent him **livery:** delivery (of his property) (See longer note, page 225.)

213. **deny:** refuse; **homage:** Part of the ceremony of receiving inherited lands was to pay homage to the king.

214. **pluck:** pull down

216. **prick:** incite

220. **by:** nearby

222–23. **by bad courses ... good:** i.e., the results of **bad courses** of action are **never good** **events:** results

224. **straight:** straightway, immediately

225. **repair:** come; **Ely House:** See note to 1.4.59.

226. **see:** i.e., **see** to

227. **We will:** i.e., **I will** depart; **trow:** believe

Is not his heir a well-deserving son?
Take Hereford's rights away, and take from time
His charters and his customary rights;   205
Let not tomorrow then ensue today;
Be not thyself; for how art thou a king
But by fair sequence and succession?
Now afore God—God forbid I say true!—
If you do wrongfully seize Hereford's rights,   210
Call in the letters patents that he hath
By his attorneys general to sue
His livery, and deny his offered homage,
You pluck a thousand dangers on your head,
You lose a thousand well-disposèd hearts,   215
And prick my tender patience to those thoughts
Which honor and allegiance cannot think.

KING RICHARD
  Think what you will, we seize into our hands
  His plate, his goods, his money, and his lands.

YORK
  I'll not be by the while. My liege, farewell.   220
  What will ensue hereof there's none can tell;
  But by bad courses may be understood
  That their events can never fall out good.   *He exits.*

KING RICHARD
  Go, Bushy, to the Earl of Wiltshire straight.
  Bid him repair to us to Ely House   225
  To see this business. Tomorrow next
  We will for Ireland, and 'tis time, I trow.
  And we create, in absence of ourself,
  Our uncle York Lord Governor of England,
  For he is just and always loved us well.—   230
  Come on, our queen. Tomorrow must we part.
  Be merry, for our time of stay is short.
              King and Queen exit ⌈with others;⌉
    Northumberland, ⌈Willoughby, and Ross⌉ remain.

237. **great:** i.e., big (pregnant) with sorrow

238. **liberal:** free, unrestrained

240. **speaks thy words again:** i.e., repeats your words

241. **Tends . . . to:** i.e., does what you have to say concern

247. **gelded:** deprived

249. **In him:** i.e., in his case

251. **basely:** treacherously, ignobly

252. **what:** i.e., whatever

256. **The commons:** the third estate in the English Parliament (The first two estates were the Lords Temporal and the Lords Spiritual.) **pilled:** i.e., stripped bare (literally, peeled)

A pelican tapping out its blood. (2.1.133–34)
From Conrad Lycosthenes, *Prodigiorum . . .* (1557).

NORTHUMBERLAND
  Well, lords, the Duke of Lancaster is dead.
ROSS
  And living too, for now his son is duke.
WILLOUGHBY
  Barely in title, not in revenues.   235
NORTHUMBERLAND
  Richly in both, if justice had her right.
ROSS
  My heart is great, but it must break with silence
  Ere 't be disburdened with a liberal tongue.
NORTHUMBERLAND
  Nay, speak thy mind, and let him ne'er speak more
  That speaks thy words again to do thee harm!   240
WILLOUGHBY, ⌈to Ross⌉
  Tends that thou wouldst speak to the Duke of
      Hereford?
  If it be so, out with it boldly, man.
  Quick is mine ear to hear of good towards him.
ROSS
  No good at all that I can do for him,   245
  Unless you call it good to pity him,
  Bereft and gelded of his patrimony.
NORTHUMBERLAND
  Now, afore God, 'tis shame such wrongs are borne
  In him, a royal prince, and many more
  Of noble blood in this declining land.   250
  The King is not himself, but basely led
  By flatterers; and what they will inform
  Merely in hate 'gainst any of us all,
  That will the King severely prosecute
  'Gainst us, our lives, our children, and our heirs.   255
ROSS
  The commons hath he pilled with grievous taxes,
  And quite lost their hearts. The nobles hath he fined
  For ancient quarrels, and quite lost their hearts.

260. **blanks:** blank charters; **benevolences:** forced loans; **wot:** know

261. **this:** i.e., this money he has collected

262. **Wars hath:** i.e., **wars** have

263. **basely:** contemptibly, in a cowardly manner

266. **in farm:** on lease (The **Earl of Wiltshire** was one of Richard's great favorites and lord treasurer of England. He is referred to often in the play, but never actually appears.)

267. **King:** Most editions follow the later quartos and the Folio and print "King's"; the First Quarto reading, followed here, allows the "hath" of the preceding line to govern **grown bankrupt.**

268. **hangeth:** i.e., hang

271. **But by:** i.e., except through

275. **sore:** oppressively

276. **strike not:** (1) do **not strike** our sails; (2) do not fight back; **securely:** self-confidently, carelessly

277. **wrack:** ruin, destruction

278. **unavoided:** unavoidable

279. **For suffering so:** i.e., because we have thus permitted

282. **is:** i.e., are

WILLOUGHBY
  And daily new exactions are devised,
  As blanks, benevolences, and I wot not what.   260
  But what i' God's name doth become of this?

NORTHUMBERLAND
  Wars hath not wasted it, for warred he hath not,
  But basely yielded upon compromise
  That which his noble ancestors achieved with blows.
  More hath he spent in peace than they in wars.   265

ROSS
  The Earl of Wiltshire hath the realm in farm.

WILLOUGHBY
  The King grown bankrupt like a broken man.

NORTHUMBERLAND
  Reproach and dissolution hangeth over him.

ROSS
  He hath not money for these Irish wars,
  His burdenous taxations notwithstanding,   270
  But by the robbing of the banished duke.

NORTHUMBERLAND
  His noble kinsman. Most degenerate king!
  But, lords, we hear this fearful tempest sing,
  Yet seek no shelter to avoid the storm;
  We see the wind sit sore upon our sails,   275
  And yet we strike not, but securely perish.

ROSS
  We see the very wrack that we must suffer,
  And unavoided is the danger now
  For suffering so the causes of our wrack.

NORTHUMBERLAND
  Not so. Even through the hollow eyes of death   280
  I spy life peering; but I dare not say
  How near the tidings of our comfort is.

WILLOUGHBY
  Nay, let us share thy thoughts, as thou dost ours.

285. **speaking so:** i.e., **speaking** to others who **are but thyself**

288. **Brittany:** a province on the northwest coast of France; **intelligence:** news

291. **That late broke:** i.e., who recently escaped (In Holinshed's *Chronicles* it was the son of the earl of Arundel, not Rainold Lord Cobham, who had recently escaped from the duke of Exeter. Many editions thus insert a line preceding our line 291 that reads "The son of Richard Earl of Arundel." See longer note, page 226.)

292. **archbishop late:** formerly archbishop (See longer note to 2.1.291.)

298. **expedience:** speed

300. **stay:** await

303. **Imp out:** mend by grafting new feathers on a **broken wing** (a term from falconry)

304. **Redeem from broking pawn:** i.e., save from the pawnbrokers

305. **gilt:** gilding, i.e., a thin layer of gold (with a pun on *guilt*)

307. **Away with me:** i.e., come **away with me; in post:** i.e., quickly (perhaps riding in relay on posthorses); **Ravenspurgh:** a port city on the Humber River

308. **faint:** lose courage

311. **Hold . . . and:** i.e., if **my horse** holds out

ROSS
 Be confident to speak, Northumberland.
 We three are but thyself, and speaking so   285
 Thy words are but as thoughts. Therefore be bold.
NORTHUMBERLAND
 Then thus: I have from Le Port ⌈Blanc,⌉
 A bay in Brittany, received intelligence
 That Harry Duke of Hereford, Rainold Lord
    Cobham,   290
 That late broke from the Duke of Exeter,
 His brother, archbishop late of Canterbury,
 Sir Thomas Erpingham, Sir John Ramston,
 Sir John Norbery, Sir Robert Waterton, and Francis
    Coint—   295
 All these well furnished by the Duke of Brittany
 With eight tall ships, three thousand men of war,
 Are making hither with all due expedience
 And shortly mean to touch our northern shore.
 Perhaps they had ere this, but that they stay   300
 The first departing of the King for Ireland.
 If then we shall shake off our slavish yoke,
 Imp out our drooping country's broken wing,
 Redeem from broking pawn the blemished crown,
 Wipe off the dust that hides our scepter's gilt,   305
 And make high majesty look like itself,
 Away with me in post to Ravenspurgh.
 But if you faint, as fearing to do so,
 Stay and be secret, and myself will go.
ROSS
 To horse, to horse! Urge doubts to them that fear.   310
WILLOUGHBY
 Hold out my horse, and I will first be there.
                                                  They exit.

2.2   As the Queen grieves for Richard's departure, news comes that Bolingbroke has landed in England with an army. As York attempts to find means to oppose him, Bushy, Bagot, and Green, in fear for their lives, prepare to flee.

———————

3. **heaviness:** sorrow
4. **entertain:** receive (as a guest)
8. **Save bidding:** i.e., except having had to bid
9. **methinks:** it seems to me
10. **ripe:** ready for birth; **in Fortune's womb:** Here, a future **sorrow** is imaged as an **unborn** baby in the **womb** of the goddess Fortuna. (See picture, page 174.)
14. **Each . . . shadows:** i.e., for every real **grief** there are **twenty** imaginary ones
15. **shows . . . is:** i.e., show . . . are
17. **Divides . . . to:** i.e., divide **one** single **thing** into
18. **perspectives:** i.e., perspective glasses, optical devices, imagined here as distorting the appearance of whatever one viewed through them
19. **awry:** askance, at an angle
21. **awry:** amiss, wrongly
22. **shapes:** i.e., images; **himself:** i.e., grief itself
23. **shadows:** illusions

⌜Scene 2⌝
Enter the Queen, Bushy, ⌜*and*⌝ *Bagot.*

BUSHY
  Madam, your Majesty is too much sad.
  You promised, when you parted with the King,
  To lay aside life-harming heaviness
  And entertain a cheerful disposition.
QUEEN
  To please the King I did; to please myself   5
  I cannot do it. Yet I know no cause
  Why I should welcome such a guest as grief,
  Save bidding farewell to so sweet a guest
  As my sweet Richard. Yet again methinks
  Some unborn sorrow ripe in Fortune's womb   10
  Is coming towards me, and my inward soul
  With nothing trembles. At some thing it grieves
  More than with parting from my lord the King.
BUSHY
  Each substance of a grief hath twenty shadows
  Which shows like grief itself but is not so;   15
  For sorrow's eyes, glazed with blinding tears,
  Divides one thing entire to many objects,
  Like perspectives, which rightly gazed upon
  Show nothing but confusion, eyed awry
  Distinguish form. So your sweet Majesty,   20
  Looking awry upon your lord's departure,
  Find shapes of grief more than himself to wail,
  Which, looked on as it is, is naught but shadows
  Of what it is not. Then, thrice-gracious queen,
  More than your lord's departure weep not. More is   25
      not seen,
  Or if it be, 'tis with false sorrow's eye,
  Which for things true weeps things imaginary.
QUEEN
  It may be so, but yet my inward soul
  Persuades me it is otherwise. Howe'er it be,   30

32. **As thought:** Many editions here print the words *As though,* which is what is found in the later quartos and the Folio. We follow the First Quarto reading, since the substitution of *though* does not appreciably improve the sense of this difficult passage.

33. **faint:** lose heart or spirit

34. **conceit:** imagination, thought

35. **still:** always

38. **something hath:** i.e., **something hath** begot

39. **'Tis in reversion that I do possess:** i.e., what I own is (merely) destined to come into my possession in the future

41. **wot:** know

45. **designs crave:** plans require; **his haste:** i.e., **his haste** requires

46. **wherefore:** why

47. **retired his power:** withdrawn or led back his army

49. **set footing:** entered

50. **repeals himself:** calls himself back (from exile)

51. **uplifted arms:** raised weapons

54. **that is:** i.e., what **is, that** which **is**

I cannot but be sad—so heavy sad
As thought, on thinking on no thought I think,
Makes me with heavy nothing faint and shrink.

BUSHY
'Tis nothing but conceit, my gracious lady.

QUEEN
'Tis nothing less. Conceit is still derived   35
From some forefather grief. Mine is not so,
For nothing hath begot my something grief—
Or something hath the nothing that I grieve.
'Tis in reversion that I do possess,
But what it is that is not yet known what,   40
I cannot name. 'Tis nameless woe, I wot.

⌈*Enter Green.*⌉

GREEN
God save your Majesty!—And well met, gentlemen.
I hope the King is not yet shipped for Ireland.

QUEEN
Why hopest thou so? 'Tis better hope he is,
For his designs crave haste, his haste good hope.   45
Then wherefore dost thou hope he is not shipped?

GREEN
That he, our hope, might have retired his power
And driven into despair an enemy's hope,
Who strongly hath set footing in this land.
The banished Bolingbroke repeals himself   50
And with uplifted arms is safe arrived
At Ravenspurgh.

QUEEN   Now God in heaven forbid!

GREEN
Ah, madam, 'tis too true. And that is worse,
The Lord Northumberland, his son young Harry   55
  Percy,
The Lords of Ross, Beaumont, and Willoughby,
With all their powerful friends, are fled to him.

60. **all the rest revolted faction:** i.e., **all the** remaining mutinous **faction** or rebels

61. **Worcester:** Thomas Percy, lord high steward in the royal household and brother of Northumberland

62. **staff:** i.e., **staff** of office (According to Holinshed, "Sir Thomas Percy, Earl of Worcester, lord steward of the king's house, . . . brake his white staff, which is the representing figure and token of his office.")

63. **household servants:** i.e., those, some of them noblemen, who attend the king in the royal **household**

67. **prodigy:** monstrous birth (the **unborn sorrow** of line 10)

73. **cozening:** deceiving; **He:** i.e., hope

75. **bands of life:** connections by which **life** is held together

76. **lingers in extremity:** i.e., causes to linger *in extremis* (at the point of death)

78. **With signs of war . . . neck:** He is presumably wearing an iron collar called a "gorget," which protected the throat. (See picture, page 84.)

79. **careful:** anxious; **business:** distress

80. **comfortable:** comforting

83. **crosses:** obstacles, obstructions

84. **save:** safeguard (his possessions)

86. **underprop:** support

BUSHY

Why have you not proclaimed Northumberland
And all the rest revolted faction traitors? 60

GREEN

We have; whereupon the Earl of Worcester
Hath broken his staff, resigned his stewardship,
And all the household servants fled with him
To Bolingbroke.

QUEEN

So, Green, thou art the midwife to my woe, 65
And Bolingbroke my sorrow's dismal heir.
Now hath my soul brought forth her prodigy,
And I, a gasping new-delivered mother,
Have woe to woe, sorrow to sorrow joined.

BUSHY

Despair not, madam. 70

QUEEN   Who shall hinder me?
I will despair and be at enmity
With cozening hope. He is a flatterer,
A parasite, a keeper-back of death,
Who gently would dissolve the bands of life 75
Which false hope lingers in extremity.

⌜*Enter York.*⌝

GREEN   Here comes the Duke of York.

QUEEN

With signs of war about his agèd neck.
O, full of careful business are his looks!—
Uncle, for God's sake speak comfortable words. 80

YORK

Should I do so, I should belie my thoughts.
Comfort's in heaven, and we are on the Earth,
Where nothing lives but crosses, cares, and grief.
Your husband, he is gone to save far off
Whilst others come to make him lose at home. 85
Here am I left to underprop his land,

88. **surfeit:** excesses (literally, overindulgence)
89. **try:** put to the test
90. **your son:** i.e., Aumerle
92. **commons:** See note to 2.1.256.
93. **cold:** indifferent, apathetic
95. **Sirrah:** a term of address to an inferior (a servant or a boy); **sister Gloucester:** i.e., sister-in-law, duchess of **Gloucester**
96. **Bid her:** i.e., tell her (or ask her) to; **presently:** at once
97. **Hold:** i.e., wait a minute; **ring:** proof that the request comes from York
103. **God for His mercy:** i.e., **God** be merciful
106. **So my untruth . . . it:** i.e., so long as my disloyalty was not the cause
107. **my brother's:** i.e., the duke of Gloucester's
108. **posts:** messengers
109. **How:** i.e., what
112. **home:** to York's estate

Neck armor, a hausse-col or gorget. (2.2.78)
From Louis de Gaya, *Traité des armes, des machines de guerre . . .* (1678).

Who, weak with age, cannot support myself.
Now comes the sick hour that his surfeit made;
Now shall he try his friends that flattered him.

⌜*Enter a Servingman.*⌝

SERVINGMAN
My lord, your son was gone before I came.   90
YORK
He was? Why, so go all which way it will.
The nobles they are fled; the commons they are
    cold
And will, I fear, revolt on Hereford's side.
Sirrah, get thee to Plashy, to my sister Gloucester;   95
Bid her send me presently a thousand pound.
Hold, take my ring.
SERVINGMAN
My lord, I had forgot to tell your Lordship:
Today as I came by I callèd there—
But I shall grieve you to report the rest.   100
YORK   What is 't, knave?
SERVINGMAN
An hour before I came, the Duchess died.
YORK
God for His mercy, what a tide of woes
Comes rushing on this woeful land at once!
I know not what to do. I would to God,   105
So my untruth had not provoked him to it,
The King had cut off my head with my brother's!
What, are there no posts dispatched for Ireland?
How shall we do for money for these wars?—
Come, sister—cousin I would say, pray pardon   110
    me.—
Go, fellow, get thee home. Provide some carts
And bring away the armor that is there.
                              ⌜*Servingman exits.*⌝
Gentlemen, will you go muster men?

116. **Thus disorderly:** in this state of disorder
121. **kindred:** kinship; **to right:** i.e., **to set right**
122. **somewhat:** something
124. **dispose of:** make proper arrangements for
126. **Berkeley:** a castle northeast of Bristol
129. **at six and seven:** i.e., in a state of confusion
130–31. **The wind ... returns:** i.e., the direction of the wind is favorable for sending **news to Ireland but none** can come back to us from there
135. **those love not:** i.e., **those** who do **not love**
137. **them:** i.e., **their purses**
140. **If judgment lie in them:** i.e., if the power to condemn lies with the commons; **then so do we:** i.e., **we,** too, stand **condemned** (line 139)

An Irish kern. (2.1.164)
From John Derricke, *The image of Irelande, with a discouerie of woodkarne . . .* (1883 facsimile).

If I know how or which way to order these affairs 115
Thus disorderly thrust into my hands,
Never believe me. Both are my kinsmen.
T' one is my sovereign, whom both my oath
And duty bids defend; t' other again
Is my kinsman, whom the King hath wronged, 120
Whom conscience and my kindred bids to right.
Well, somewhat we must do. ⌜*To Queen.*⌝ Come, cousin,
I'll dispose of you.—Gentlemen, go muster up your men 125
And meet me presently at Berkeley.
I should to Plashy too,
But time will not permit. All is uneven,
And everything is left at six and seven.

> *Duke ⌜of York and⌝ Queen exit.*
> *Bushy, Green, ⌜and Bagot⌝ remain.*

BUSHY
The wind sits fair for news to go for Ireland, 130
But none returns. For us to levy power
Proportionable to the enemy
Is all unpossible.

GREEN
Besides, our nearness to the King in love
Is near the hate of those love not the King. 135

BAGOT
And that is the wavering commons, for their love
Lies in their purses, and whoso empties them
By so much fills their hearts with deadly hate.

BUSHY
Wherein the King stands generally condemned.

BAGOT
If judgment lie in them, then so do we, 140
Because we ever have been near the King.

GREEN
Well, I will for refuge straight to Bristow Castle.
The Earl of Wiltshire is already there.

144. **office:** service

149. **vain:** worthless, idle

153. **numb'ring sands and drinking oceans dry:** i.e., counting the grains of sand on a beach or drinking all the water in the ocean (proverbial expressions for trying to do the impossible)

155. **for once, for all: once** as a final act (usually phrased "**once** and **for all**")

2.3 Bolingbroke and Northumberland, just outside Berkeley Castle, meet young Henry Percy, Northumberland's son. When the duke of York enters, he chastises Bolingbroke for coming back to England, but admits to being powerless to stop him, and finally offers him hospitality at Berkeley Castle.

-----

5. **Draws . . . makes:** i.e., draw . . . make

6. **fair discourse:** pleasant conversation

7. **delectable:** delightful (In the sixteenth century, this word could be pronounced **dèlectàble.**)

9. **Cotshall:** i.e., the Cotswold Hills in Gloucestershire

BUSHY
  Thither will I with you, for little office
  Will the hateful commons perform for us,   145
  Except like curs to tear us all to pieces.—
  Will you go along with us?
BAGOT
  No, I will to Ireland to his Majesty.
  Farewell. If heart's presages be not vain,
  We three here part that ne'er shall meet again.   150
BUSHY
  That's as York thrives to beat back Bolingbroke.
GREEN
  Alas, poor duke, the task he undertakes
  Is numb'ring sands and drinking oceans dry.
  Where one on his side fights, thousands will fly.
  Farewell at once, for once, for all, and ever.   155
BUSHY
  Well, we may meet again.
BAGOT   I fear me, never.
                         ⌜*They exit.*⌝

⌜Scene 3⌝
Enter ⌜*Bolingbroke, Duke of*⌝ *Hereford,* ⌜*and*⌝
Northumberland.

BOLINGBROKE
  How far is it, my lord, to Berkeley now?
NORTHUMBERLAND   Believe me, noble lord,
  I am a stranger here in Gloucestershire.
  These high wild hills and rough uneven ways
  Draws out our miles and makes them wearisome.   5
  And yet your fair discourse hath been as sugar,
  Making the hard way sweet and delectable.
  But I bethink me what a weary way
  From Ravenspurgh to Cotshall will be found

10. **In:** i.e., by; **wanting:** lacking
11. **beguiled:** diverted attention from
12. **tediousness and process:** i.e., tedious **process**
15. **to:** i.e., of
16. **By this:** i.e., through this expectation
22. **whencesoever:** i.e., from wherever he is
23. **your uncle:** i.e., the earl of Worcester
24–25. **of you:** i.e., from you
36. **power:** troops
37. **repair:** go, travel

Crows, symbolizing flattery, feed on
a dead body. (2.2.73–74)
From Guillaume de La Perrière, *Le théâtre des bons
engins* . . . (1539?).

In Ross and Willoughby, wanting your company, 10
Which, I protest, hath very much beguiled
The tediousness and process of my travel.
But theirs is sweetened with the hope to have
The present benefit which I possess,
And hope to joy is little less in joy 15
Than hope enjoyed. By this the weary lords
Shall make their way seem short as mine hath done
By sight of what I have, your noble company.

BOLINGBROKE
Of much less value is my company
Than your good words. But who comes here? 20

Enter Harry Percy.

NORTHUMBERLAND It is my son, young Harry Percy,
Sent from my brother Worcester whencesoever.—
Harry, how fares your uncle?

PERCY
I had thought, my lord, to have learned his health of
 you. 25

NORTHUMBERLAND Why, is he not with the Queen?

PERCY
No, my good lord, he hath forsook the court,
Broken his staff of office, and dispersed
The household of the King.

NORTHUMBERLAND
What was his reason? He was not so resolved 30
When last we spake together.

PERCY
Because your Lordship was proclaimèd traitor.
But he, my lord, is gone to Ravenspurgh
To offer service to the Duke of Hereford,
And sent me over by Berkeley to discover 35
What power the Duke of York had levied there,
Then with directions to repair to Ravenspurgh.

43. **tender:** offer (Percy probably kneels at this point.)

46. **approvèd:** tried, tested

51. **It:** i.e., **my fortune** (line 50); **still:** always

53. **stir:** activity

54. **men of war:** soldiers

59. **name:** title, fame; **estimate:** repute, reputation

61. **Bloody with spurring:** i.e., stained with blood from their spurred horses

King Edward III. (2.1.110)
From John Taylor, *All the workes of . . .* (1630).

NORTHUMBERLAND
  Have you forgot the Duke of ⌈Hereford,⌉ boy?
PERCY
  No, my good lord, for that is not forgot
  Which ne'er I did remember. To my knowledge   40
  I never in my life did look on him.
NORTHUMBERLAND
  Then learn to know him now. This is the Duke.
PERCY, ⌈*to Bolingbroke*⌉
  My gracious lord, I tender you my service,
  Such as it is, being tender, raw, and young,
  Which elder days shall ripen and confirm   45
  To more approvèd service and desert.
BOLINGBROKE
  I thank thee, gentle Percy, and be sure
  I count myself in nothing else so happy
  As in a soul rememb'ring my good friends;
  And as my fortune ripens with thy love,   50
  It shall be still thy true love's recompense.
  My heart this covenant makes, my hand thus seals it.
                       ⌈*Gives Percy his hand.*⌉
NORTHUMBERLAND, ⌈*to Percy*⌉
  How far is it to Berkeley, and what stir
  Keeps good old York there with his men of war?
PERCY
  There stands the castle by yon tuft of trees,   55
  Manned with three hundred men, as I have heard,
  And in it are the Lords of York, Berkeley, and
    Seymour,
  None else of name and noble estimate.

           ⌈*Enter Ross and Willoughby.*⌉

NORTHUMBERLAND
  Here come the Lords of Ross and Willoughby,   60
  Bloody with spurring, fiery red with haste.

64. **unfelt:** intangible

67. **attain it:** i.e., reach **your presence** (line 66)

68. **thank's:** i.e., thank (gratitude) is; **exchequer:** treasure, store of funds

69. **comes to years:** i.e., matures

70. **Stands for:** i.e., serves as

73. **to "Lancaster":** Bolingbroke here insists on being addressed by the title he should have inherited from his father.

78. **rase:** erase, slash

79. **what lord you will:** i.e., whatever title you wish to use

81. **pricks you on:** incites you

82. **the absent time:** i.e., **the time** of the king's absence

83. **self-borne arms:** i.e., weapons carried on one's own behalf rather than for the protection of the kingdom (Some editors prefer "self-born"— i.e., arising among ourselves—which emphasizes Bolingbroke's stirring up of civil war.)

84. **need transport:** i.e., **need** to send

BOLINGBROKE
Welcome, my lords. I wot your love pursues
A banished traitor. All my treasury
Is yet but unfelt thanks, which, more enriched,
Shall be your love and labor's recompense.   65
ROSS
Your presence makes us rich, most noble lord.
WILLOUGHBY
And far surmounts our labor to attain it.
BOLINGBROKE
Evermore thank's the exchequer of the poor,
Which, till my infant fortune comes to years,
Stands for my bounty. But who comes here?   70

⌜*Enter Berkeley.*⌝

NORTHUMBERLAND
It is my Lord of Berkeley, as I guess.
BERKELEY, ⌜*to Bolingbroke*⌝
My Lord of Hereford, my message is to you.
BOLINGBROKE
My lord, my answer is—to "Lancaster";
And I am come to seek that name in England.
And I must find that title in your tongue   75
Before I make reply to aught you say.
BERKELEY
Mistake me not, my lord, 'tis not my meaning
To rase one title of your honor out.
To you, my lord, I come, what lord you will,
From the most gracious regent of this land,   80
The Duke of York, to know what pricks you on
To take advantage of the absent time,
And fright our native peace with self-borne arms.

⌜*Enter York.*⌝

BOLINGBROKE
I shall not need transport my words by you.

88. **Whose duty:** i.e., whose gesture in thus kneeling; **deceivable:** deceptive

93. **an ungracious:** a wicked

95. **a dust:** a grain of **dust**

99. **ostentation . . . arms:** display of vile weapons

103. **but:** even

105. **the Black Prince:** i.e., Edward, prince of Wales, father of Richard II; **Mars of men:** i.e., exemplary warrior (**Mars** was the Roman god of war.)

109. **correction:** punishment; **fault:** misdeed

111. **On . . . wherein:** i.e., according to what provision in law is it a misdeed and how is it a misdeed according to that provision   **condition:** provision in law

113. **detested:** vile

116. **braving:** defiant

"Like a shooting star." (2.4.19)
From Hartmann Schedel, *Liber chronicorum* (1493).

Here comes his Grace in person.   ⌜*He kneels.*⌝   85
                              My noble uncle.
YORK
  Show me thy humble heart and not thy knee,
  Whose duty is deceivable and false.
BOLINGBROKE, ⌜*standing*⌝ My gracious uncle—
YORK Tut, tut!   90
  Grace me no grace, nor uncle me no uncle.
  I am no traitor's uncle, and that word "grace"
  In an ungracious mouth is but profane.
  Why have those banished and forbidden legs
  Dared once to touch a dust of England's ground?   95
  But then, more why: why have they dared to march
  So many miles upon her peaceful bosom,
  Frighting her pale-faced villages with war
  And ostentation of despisèd arms?
  Com'st thou because the anointed king is hence?   100
  Why, foolish boy, the King is left behind
  And in my loyal bosom lies his power.
  Were I but now lord of such hot youth
  As when brave Gaunt thy father and myself
  Rescued the Black Prince, that young Mars of men, 105
  From forth the ranks of many thousand French,
  O, then, how quickly should this arm of mine,
  Now prisoner to the palsy, chastise thee
  And minister correction to thy fault!
BOLINGBROKE
  My gracious uncle, let me know my fault.   110
  On what condition stands it and wherein?
YORK
  Even in condition of the worst degree,
  In gross rebellion and detested treason.
  Thou art a banished man and here art come,
  Before the expiration of thy time,   115
  In braving arms against thy sovereign.

120. **indifferent:** impartial

123–24. **condemned / A:** i.e., **condemned** to be a

125. **arms:** coat of **arms; perforce:** by force

126. **unthrifts:** spendthrifts; **Wherefore:** why

132. **rouse:** drive from hiding (as if they were hunted animals); **the bay:** the quarry's last stand

133–36. **I am denied . . . employed:** See note to 2.1.211–13 and longer note, page 225. **leave:** permission **distrained:** seized **and all:** i.e., and everything else

138. **challenge law:** demand my legal rights; **Attorneys are denied me:** See the reference at 2.1.211–13 to the attorneys general who had been given power of attorney to "sue his livery" for him.

140. **of free descent:** perhaps, which comes to me by direct, legal inheritance

141. **abused:** wronged, injured

142. **stands . . . upon:** is your Grace's duty

143. **Base:** lowborn; inferior; **by his endowments:** through enrichment **by his** properties

147. **kind:** manner, fashion

BOLINGBROKE
　As I was banished, I was banished Hereford,
　But as I come, I come for Lancaster.
　And, noble uncle, I beseech your Grace
　Look on my wrongs with an indifferent eye.　　　　120
　You are my father, for methinks in you
　I see old Gaunt alive. O, then, my father,
　Will you permit that I shall stand condemned
　A wandering vagabond, my rights and royalties
　Plucked from my arms perforce and given away　　125
　To upstart unthrifts? Wherefore was I born?
　If that my cousin king be king in England,
　It must be granted I am Duke of Lancaster.
　You have a son, Aumerle, my noble cousin.
　Had you first died and he been thus trod down,　　130
　He should have found his uncle Gaunt a father
　To rouse his wrongs and chase them to the bay.
　I am denied to sue my livery here,
　And yet my letters patents give me leave.
　My father's goods are all distrained and sold,　　135
　And these, and all, are all amiss employed.
　What would you have me do? I am a subject,
　And I challenge law. Attorneys are denied me,
　And therefore personally I lay my claim
　To my inheritance of free descent.　　　　　　140
NORTHUMBERLAND, ⌈to York⌉
　The noble duke hath been too much abused.
ROSS, ⌈to York⌉
　It stands your Grace upon to do him right.
WILLOUGHBY, ⌈to York⌉
　Base men by his endowments are made great.
YORK
　My lords of England, let me tell you this:
　I have had feeling of my cousin's wrongs　　　　145
　And labored all I could to do him right.
　But in this kind to come, in braving arms,

148. **Be his own carver:** i.e., help himself (as at a dinner table)

149. **find out right with wrong:** i.e., seek rights by doing **wrong**

156. **issue:** outcome

158. **power:** army; **ill-left:** left in a bad state (without adequate means, or in disarray)

160. **attach:** arrest

163. **as neuter:** neutral

169. **Bagot:** We learn soon that **Bagot** is not at Bristow Castle. (And see note to 4.1.1.) **complices:** accomplices

170. **caterpillars:** a conventional term of abuse for those seen as feeding off **the commonwealth**

171. **Weed:** remove

174. **Nor:** neither as

175. **Things past ... care:** Proverbial. See *Macbeth* 3.2.13–14: "Things without all remedy / Should be without regard." **care:** heed, attention

Be his own carver and cut out his way
To find out right with wrong, it may not be.
And you that do abet him in this kind   150
Cherish rebellion and are rebels all.

NORTHUMBERLAND
The noble duke hath sworn his coming is
But for his own, and for the right of that
We all have strongly sworn to give him aid.
And let him never see joy that breaks that oath.   155

YORK
Well, well. I see the issue of these arms.
I cannot mend it, I must needs confess,
Because my power is weak and all ill-left.
But if I could, by Him that gave me life,
I would attach you all and make you stoop   160
Unto the sovereign mercy of the King.
But since I cannot, be it known unto you
I do remain as neuter. So fare you well—
Unless you please to enter in the castle
And there repose you for this night.   165

BOLINGBROKE
An offer, uncle, that we will accept.
But we must win your Grace to go with us
To Bristow Castle, which they say is held
By Bushy, Bagot, and their complices,
The caterpillars of the commonwealth,   170
Which I have sworn to weed and pluck away.

YORK
It may be I will go with you; but yet I'll pause,
For I am loath to break our country's laws.
Nor friends nor foes, to me welcome you are.
Things past redress are now with me past care.   175
                                        They exit.

2.4 The Welsh troops, having waited ten days for Richard's return, disperse. The earl of Salisbury predicts that Richard stands at the edge of defeat.

---

1. **stayed:** waited
2. **hardly:** i.e., with great difficulty
3. **yet:** still
9. **fixèd stars:** In Ptolemaic astronomy, **the stars** (in distinction from, e.g., **meteors**) were **fixed** within a crystalline sphere that circled **the Earth**. (See picture, page xxxv.)
11. **lean-looked prophets:** lean-looking soothsayers; **fearful:** frightening, terrible
13, 14. **enjoy:** possess, delight in
15. **forerun:** are the precursors of
18. **heavy:** sorrowful
21. **Thy sun:** Since the king and the **sun** were often linked, each being put forward as the topmost link in its part of a "great chain of being," this reference to Richard's setting **sun** carries special resonance.
22. **Witnessing:** being proof of
23. **wait upon:** serve, follow
24. **crossly:** adversely

⌜Scene 4⌝
Enter Earl of Salisbury and a Welsh Captain.

WELSH CAPTAIN
My Lord of Salisbury, we have stayed ten days
And hardly kept our countrymen together,
And yet we hear no tidings from the King.
Therefore we will disperse ourselves. Farewell.

SALISBURY
Stay yet another day, thou trusty Welshman.   5
The King reposeth all his confidence in thee.

WELSH CAPTAIN
'Tis thought the King is dead. We will not stay.
The bay trees in our country are all withered,
And meteors fright the fixèd stars of heaven;
The pale-faced moon looks bloody on the Earth,   10
And lean-looked prophets whisper fearful change;
Rich men look sad, and ruffians dance and leap,
The one in fear to lose what they enjoy,
The other to enjoy by rage and war.
These signs forerun the death or fall of kings.   15
Farewell. Our countrymen are gone and fled,
As well assured Richard their king is dead.
⌜*He exits.*⌝

SALISBURY
Ah, Richard! With the eyes of heavy mind
I see thy glory like a shooting star
Fall to the base earth from the firmament.   20
Thy sun sets weeping in the lowly west,
Witnessing storms to come, woe, and unrest.
Thy friends are fled to wait upon thy foes,
And crossly to thy good all fortune goes.
⌜*He exits.*⌝

The Tragedy of

RICHARD II

ACT 3

3.1 Bolingbroke sentences Bushy and Green to death.

———

3. **part:** separate from
4. **urging:** emphasizing, calling attention to
7. **unfold:** disclose, reveal; **of:** for
9. **A happy gentleman in:** i.e., a man fortunate in; **blood:** inheritance, birth
10. **clean:** entirely
11. **in manner:** as it were
13. **Broke . . . bed:** The play gives no evidence of unhappiness between Richard and his queen, but Holinshed says that in Richard's court "there reigned abundantly the filthy sin of lechery and fornication, with abominable adultery, specially in the king."
20. **in foreign clouds:** perhaps, adding my breath to **clouds** over **foreign** lands; or, perhaps, **in foreign** air

The "double-fatal yew." (3.2.120)
From John Gerard, *The herball or generall historie of plantes . . .* (1597).

⌐Scene 1⌐

Enter ⌐*Bolingbroke,*⌐ *Duke of Hereford, York,*
Northumberland, ⌐*with other Lords, and*⌐ *Bushy and*
Green prisoners.

BOLINGBROKE   Bring forth these men.—
Bushy and Green, I will not vex your souls,
Since presently your souls must part your bodies,
With too much urging your pernicious lives,
For 'twere no charity; yet to wash your blood   5
From off my hands, here in the view of men
I will unfold some causes of your deaths:
You have misled a prince, a royal king,
A happy gentleman in blood and lineaments
By you unhappied and disfigured clean.   10
You have in manner with your sinful hours
Made a divorce betwixt his queen and him,
Broke the possession of a royal bed,
And stained the beauty of a fair queen's cheeks
With tears drawn from her eyes by your foul wrongs.   15
Myself, a prince by fortune of my birth,
Near to the King in blood, and near in love
Till you did make him misinterpret me,
Have stooped my neck under your injuries
And sighed my English breath in foreign clouds,   20
Eating the bitter bread of banishment,

22. **seigniories:** estates, territories
23. **Disparked:** thrown open
24. **From . . . coat:** i.e., broken the stained-glass or painted **windows** in which **my coat** of arms was displayed
25. **Rased out:** erased; **imprese:** heraldic device
37. **dispatched:** put to death
40. **entreated:** treated
41. **commends:** greetings
44. **at large:** in full, at length
46. **Glendower:** Owen **Glendower** plays a large role in Shakespeare's *Henry IV, Part 1.* (See longer note, page 226.) **complices:** accomplices
47. **after:** afterward

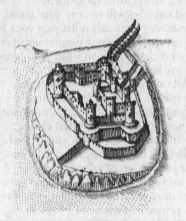

"Barkloughly" (Harlech) Castle. (3.2.1)
From John Speed, *The theatre of the empire of Great Britaine . . .* (1627 [i.e., 1631]).

Whilst you have fed upon my seigniories,
Disparked my parks and felled my forest woods,
From my own windows torn my household coat,
Rased out my imprese, leaving me no sign,   25
Save men's opinions and my living blood,
To show the world I am a gentleman.
This and much more, much more than twice all
    this,
Condemns you to the death.—See them delivered   30
    over
To execution and the hand of death.

BUSHY
More welcome is the stroke of death to me
Than Bolingbroke to England. Lords, farewell.

GREEN
My comfort is that heaven will take our souls   35
And plague injustice with the pains of hell.

BOLINGBROKE
My Lord Northumberland, see them dispatched.
        ⌐*Northumberland exits with Bushy and Green.*⌐
⌐*To York.*⌐ Uncle, you say the Queen is at your
    house.
For God's sake, fairly let her be entreated.   40
Tell her I send to her my kind commends.
Take special care my greetings be delivered.

YORK
A gentleman of mine I have dispatched
With letters of your love to her at large.

BOLINGBROKE
Thanks, gentle uncle.—Come, lords, away,   45
To fight with Glendower and his complices.
A while to work, and after holiday.
                                    They exit.

3.2 Richard, landing in England, greets his kingdom and expresses certainty that God will protect him against Bolingbroke's threat. He learns that the Welsh troops have dispersed, that his close friends have been executed, and that York and Richard's other supporters have joined with Bolingbroke. Richard orders his army discharged and retreats to Flint Castle.

———————

0 SD. **Flourish and colors:** i.e., a trumpet fanfare and a display of banners; **Carlisle:** i.e., the bishop of **Carlisle**

1. **Barkloughly:** Holinshed's incorrect name for Harlech, which is on the west coast of Wales (See picture, page 108.) **at hand:** nearby

2. **brooks:** enjoys

3. **late:** recent

4. **Needs must I:** i.e., **I must** necessarily

6. **salute:** greet

8. **long-parted mother with:** i.e., **mother long-parted** from

9. **fondly:** (1) with love; (2) foolishly

13. **sense:** appetite

15. **in their way:** i.e., in the path of the king's enemies

16. **annoyance:** injury

20. **lurking adder:** See picture, page 130.

21. **mortal:** fatal

23. **senseless conjuration:** i.e., imploring of inanimate things

25. **Prove:** i.e., show themselves to be; **native:** natural, legitimate

⌈Scene 2⌉

⌈*Drums. Flourish and colors.*⌉ *Enter the King, Aumerle,*
Carlisle, ⌈*and Soldiers.*⌉

KING RICHARD
  Barkloughly Castle call they this at hand?
AUMERLE
  Yea, my lord. How brooks your Grace the air
  After your late tossing on the breaking seas?
KING RICHARD
  Needs must I like it well. I weep for joy
  To stand upon my kingdom once again. ⌈*He kneels.*⌉   5
  Dear earth, I do salute thee with my hand,
  Though rebels wound thee with their horses' hoofs.
  As a long-parted mother with her child
  Plays fondly with her tears and smiles in meeting,
  So, weeping, smiling, greet I thee, my earth,   10
  And do thee favors with my royal hands.
  Feed not thy sovereign's foe, my gentle earth,
  Nor with thy sweets comfort his ravenous sense,
  But let thy spiders, that suck up thy venom,
  And heavy-gaited toads lie in their way,   15
  Doing annoyance to the treacherous feet
  Which with usurping steps do trample thee.
  Yield stinging nettles to mine enemies,
  And when they from thy bosom pluck a flower,
  Guard it, I pray thee, with a lurking adder,   20
  Whose double tongue may with a mortal touch
  Throw death upon thy sovereign's enemies.
  Mock not my senseless conjuration, lords.
  This earth shall have a feeling, and these stones
  Prove armèd soldiers, ere her native king   25
  Shall falter under foul rebellion's arms.
CARLISLE
  Fear not, my lord. That power that made you king
  Hath power to keep you king in spite of all.

29–32. The means . . . redress: In these difficult lines, the bishop of Carlisle advises Richard to act now and not refuse the help the bishop believes that heaven offers. **heavens yield:** i.e., the **heavens yield,** or heaven yields

34. security: foolish absence of anxiety, overconfidence

35. in substance and in power: i.e., in resources and in troops

36. Discomfortable: discouraging, disheartening

37. searching eye of heaven: i.e., sun (Richard here begins a comparison of the sun's absence at nighttime to his own absence in Ireland. In Ptolemaic astronomy, the sun travels around **the globe**—the Earth; it departs at night in order to light **the lower world**—i.e., the other side of the world.)

38. that lights: i.e., while it is lighting

41. this terrestrial ball: i.e., the Earth

42. He: i.e., it (the sun); **fires:** i.e., shines its light on (literally, sets on fire)

43. guilty hole: i.e., place where the guilty are hiding

50. Antipodes: i.e., those who live on the opposite side of the globe (See picture, page 114.)

56. balm: fragrant oil used for anointing a monarch in the coronation ceremony

57. breath: speech, words; **worldly:** earthly, mortal

59. pressed: impressed, conscripted

60. shrewd: keen, harsh

The means that heavens yield must be embraced
And not neglected. Else heaven would,   30
And we will not—heaven's offer we refuse,
The proffered means of succor and redress.

AUMERLE
He means, my lord, that we are too remiss,
Whilst Bolingbroke, through our security,
Grows strong and great in substance and in power.   35

KING RICHARD
Discomfortable cousin, know'st thou not
That when the searching eye of heaven is hid
Behind the globe that lights the lower world,
Then thieves and robbers range abroad unseen
In murders and in outrage boldly here?   40
But when from under this terrestrial ball
He fires the proud tops of the eastern pines
And darts his light through every guilty hole,
Then murders, treasons, and detested sins,
The cloak of night being plucked from off their   45
  backs,
Stand bare and naked, trembling at themselves.
So when this thief, this traitor Bolingbroke,
Who all this while hath reveled in the night
Whilst we were wand'ring with the Antipodes,   50
Shall see us rising in our throne, the east,
His treasons will sit blushing in his face,
Not able to endure the sight of day,
But self-affrighted, tremble at his sin.
Not all the water in the rough rude sea   55
Can wash the balm off from an anointed king.
The breath of worldly men cannot depose
The deputy elected by the Lord.
For every man that Bolingbroke hath pressed
To lift shrewd steel against our golden crown,   60
God for His Richard hath in heavenly pay

63. **still:** always
64. **power:** army
65. **Nor near:** neither closer
66. **Discomfort:** disheartenment, discouragement
73. **state:** royal authority
76, 83. **Comfort:** take **comfort**
77. **But now:** even **now**
78. **triumph:** look triumphant, exult
82. **pride:** glory, honor

World map with the Antipodes. (3.2.50)
From Ambrosius Aurelius Theodosius Macrobius, *In Somnium Scipionis . . .* (1492).

A glorious angel. Then, if angels fight,
Weak men must fall, for heaven still guards the right.

Enter Salisbury.

Welcome, my lord. How far off lies your power?
SALISBURY
Nor near nor farther off, my gracious lord,   65
Than this weak arm. Discomfort guides my tongue
And bids me speak of nothing but despair.
One day too late, I fear me, noble lord,
Hath clouded all thy happy days on Earth.
O, call back yesterday, bid time return,   70
And thou shalt have twelve thousand fighting men.
Today, today, unhappy day too late,
Overthrows thy joys, friends, fortune, and thy state;
For all the Welshmen, hearing thou wert dead,
Are gone to Bolingbroke, dispersed, and fled.   75
AUMERLE
Comfort, my liege. Why looks your Grace so pale?
KING RICHARD
But now the blood of twenty thousand men
    Did triumph in my face, and they are fled;
And till so much blood thither come again
    Have I not reason to look pale and dead?   80
All souls that will be safe, fly from my side,
For time hath set a blot upon my pride.
AUMERLE
Comfort, my liege. Remember who you are.
KING RICHARD
I had forgot myself. Am I not king?
Awake, thou coward majesty, thou sleepest!   85
Is not the King's name twenty thousand names?
Arm, arm, my name! A puny subject strikes
At thy great glory. Look not to the ground,
You favorites of a king. Are we not high?
High be our thoughts. I know my Uncle York   90

96. **unfold:** disclose

97. **care:** i.e., object of **care** or concern

101. **his fellow:** i.e., Bolingbroke's equal

103. **as us: as** to me

105. **his day:** i.e., its **day** (See picture, page 122.)

111. **his limits:** i.e., its banks

117. **clap:** i.e., thrust; **female:** i.e., unmanly

118. **In:** into; **arms:** armor

119. **beadsmen:** almsmen who offer prayers on behalf of a benefactor

120. **double-fatal yew:** The **yew** tree is deadly in two ways: its leaves and berries are poisonous, and its wood is used to make **bows.** (See picture, page 106.)

121. **distaff women:** spinning **women** (The **distaff** is a staff used for spinning thread from wool or flax. See picture, below.) **manage rusty bills:** wield pikes or halberds **rusty** from disuse

Woman with a distaff. (3.2.121)
From Johann Engel, *Astrolabium . . .* (1488).

116

Hath power enough to serve our turn.—But who
  comes here?

Enter Scroop.

SCROOP
More health and happiness betide my liege
Than can my care-tuned tongue deliver him.
KING RICHARD
Mine ear is open and my heart prepared.   95
The worst is worldly loss thou canst unfold.
Say, is my kingdom lost? Why, 'twas my care,
And what loss is it to be rid of care?
Strives Bolingbroke to be as great as we?
Greater he shall not be. If he serve God,   100
We'll serve Him too and be his fellow so.
Revolt our subjects? That we cannot mend.
They break their faith to God as well as us.
Cry woe, destruction, ruin, and decay.
The worst is death, and death will have his day.   105
SCROOP
Glad am I that your Highness is so armed
To bear the tidings of calamity.
Like an unseasonable stormy day
Which makes the silver rivers drown their shores
As if the world were all dissolved to tears,   110
So high above his limits swells the rage
Of Bolingbroke, covering your fearful land
With hard bright steel and hearts harder than steel.
Whitebeards have armed their thin and hairless
  scalps   115
Against thy Majesty; boys with women's voices
Strive to speak big and clap their female joints
In stiff unwieldy arms against thy crown;
Thy very beadsmen learn to bend their bows
Of double-fatal yew against thy state.   120
Yea, distaff women manage rusty bills

122. **seat:** throne

124. **ill:** bad, distressing

128. **Measure our confines:** travel across my land; **with such peaceful steps:** i.e., without opposition

134. **heart blood:** i.e., heart's blood

136. **Judas:** betrayer of Jesus (See note to 4.1.178–79.)

138. **spotted:** corrupt, morally stained

139. **his property:** i.e., its character or nature

145. **graved:** buried

"Through the hollow eyes of death/I
spy life peering." (2.1.280–81)
From Francis Quarles, *Emblemes . . .* (1635).

Against thy seat. Both young and old rebel,
And all goes worse than I have power to tell.

KING RICHARD
Too well, too well thou tell'st a tale so ill.
Where is the Earl of Wiltshire? Where is Bagot?   125
What is become of Bushy? Where is Green,
That they have let the dangerous enemy
Measure our confines with such peaceful steps?
If we prevail, their heads shall pay for it!
I warrant they have made peace with Bolingbroke.   130

SCROOP
Peace have they made with him indeed, my lord.

KING RICHARD
O villains, vipers, damned without redemption!
Dogs easily won to fawn on any man!
Snakes in my heart blood warmed, that sting my
   heart!   135
Three Judases, each one thrice worse than Judas!
Would they make peace? Terrible hell
Make war upon their spotted souls for this!

SCROOP
Sweet love, I see, changing his property,
Turns to the sourest and most deadly hate.   140
Again uncurse their souls. Their peace is made
With heads and not with hands. Those whom you
   curse
Have felt the worst of death's destroying wound
And lie full low, graved in the hollow ground.   145

AUMERLE
Is Bushy, Green, and the Earl of Wiltshire dead?

SCROOP
Ay, all of them at Bristow lost their heads.

AUMERLE
Where is the Duke my father with his power?

KING RICHARD
No matter where. Of comfort no man speak.

155. **deposèd:** i.e., discarded

158. **that small . . . earth:** i.e., our body (The comparison of human flesh to dust was common—see Genesis 3.19—as was the image of the human body as a small model, or microcosm, of the Earth or the cosmos.)

159. **paste and cover:** i.e., a covering (as in the pastry covering of a pie)

163. **ghosts:** i.e., **ghosts** of kings

166. **rounds:** encircles

167. **antic:** jester, grotesque (The image of Death here is of the mocking skeleton familiar in pictures of "the dance of Death." See picture, page 122.)

168. **Scoffing his state:** i.e., **scoffing** at the king's majestic rule

170. **monarchize:** i.e., play at being a monarch

171. **self and vain conceit:** i.e., foolish and empty notions of himself

173–74. **humored thus/Comes:** i.e., when the king has been thus indulged, **Death comes**

175. **his castle wall:** i.e., **this flesh which walls about our life** (line 172)

176. **Cover your heads:** i.e., put on your hats (which would not be worn in the presence of the king, in order to show proper respect)

180. **feel want:** experience needs and deficiencies

181. **Subjected thus:** (1) made to undergo such human experiences; (2) thus turned into (or revealed to be) a subject

184. **presently:** quickly, immediately; **prevent:** block off or counter in advance; **the ways to wail:** perhaps, those things that would cause grief

Let's talk of graves, of worms, and epitaphs,   150
Make dust our paper, and with rainy eyes
Write sorrow on the bosom of the earth.
Let's choose executors and talk of wills.
And yet not so, for what can we bequeath
Save our deposèd bodies to the ground?   155
Our lands, our lives, and all are Bolingbroke's,
And nothing can we call our own but death
And that small model of the barren earth
Which serves as paste and cover to our bones.
For God's sake, let us sit upon the ground   160
And tell sad stories of the death of kings—
How some have been deposed, some slain in war,
Some haunted by the ghosts they have deposed,
Some poisoned by their wives, some sleeping killed,
All murdered. For within the hollow crown   165
That rounds the mortal temples of a king
Keeps Death his court, and there the antic sits,
Scoffing his state and grinning at his pomp,
Allowing him a breath, a little scene,
To monarchize, be feared, and kill with looks,   170
Infusing him with self and vain conceit,
As if this flesh which walls about our life
Were brass impregnable; and humored thus,
Comes at the last and with a little pin
Bores through his castle wall, and farewell, king!   175
Cover your heads, and mock not flesh and blood
With solemn reverence. Throw away respect,
Tradition, form, and ceremonious duty,
For you have but mistook me all this while.
I live with bread like you, feel want,   180
Taste grief, need friends. Subjected thus,
How can you say to me I am a king?
CARLISLE
  My lord, wise men ne'er sit and wail their woes,
  But presently prevent the ways to wail.

188. **Fear . . . fight:** i.e., both cowardice and valor can lead to death

191. **a power:** an army

194. **change:** exchange; **doom:** judgment

195. **ague fit:** i.e., period of trembling or shivering; **is overblown:** i.e., has blown over

201. **heavy:** gloomy, sorrowful

203. **by small and small:** i.e., little by little

208. **Upon his party:** on his side

210. **Beshrew thee:** a mild oath; **which:** who

"Death will have his day." (3.2.105)
From *Todten-Tantz . . .* (1696).

To fear the foe, since fear oppresseth strength,   185
Gives in your weakness strength unto your foe,
And so your follies fight against yourself.
Fear, and be slain—no worse can come to fight;
And fight and die is death destroying death,
Where fearing dying pays death servile breath.   190

AUMERLE
My father hath a power. Inquire of him,
And learn to make a body of a limb.

KING RICHARD
Thou chid'st me well.—Proud Bolingbroke, I come
To change blows with thee for our day of doom.—
This ague fit of fear is overblown.   195
An easy task it is to win our own.—
Say, Scroop, where lies our uncle with his power?
Speak sweetly, man, although thy looks be sour.

SCROOP
Men judge by the complexion of the sky
　　The state and inclination of the day;   200
So may you by my dull and heavy eye.
　　My tongue hath but a heavier tale to say.
I play the torturer by small and small
To lengthen out the worst that must be spoken.
Your uncle York is joined with Bolingbroke,   205
And all your northern castles yielded up,
And all your southern gentlemen in arms
Upon his party.

KING RICHARD   Thou hast said enough.
⌜*To Aumerle.*⌝ Beshrew thee, cousin, which didst   210
　　lead me forth
Of that sweet way I was in to despair.
What say you now? What comfort have we now?
By heaven, I'll hate him everlastingly
That bids me be of comfort anymore.   215
Go to Flint Castle. There I'll pine away;
A king, woe's slave, shall kingly woe obey.

218. **power:** army
219. **ear:** plow, cultivate
223. **wrong:** injury

3.3 Bolingbroke, approaching Flint Castle, learns that Richard is within. In answer to Bolingbroke's trumpets, Richard and Aumerle appear on the battlements. Northumberland presents Bolingbroke's demand that Richard yield Bolingbroke's "lineal royalties" and lift the sentence of banishment. Richard agrees. Northumberland returns and asks that Richard descend to Bolingbroke, who awaits him in the outer court. The cousins meet and Richard expresses willingness to yield to Bolingbroke and accompany him to London.

---

1. **intelligence:** information (Bolingbroke may be reading a dispatch or may simply be in midconversation as the scene opens.)
7. **beseem:** become

That power I have, discharge, and let them go
To ear the land that hath some hope to grow,
For I have none. Let no man speak again   220
To alter this, for counsel is but vain.

AUMERLE
My liege, one word.

KING RICHARD   He does me double wrong
That wounds me with the flatteries of his tongue.
Discharge my followers. Let them hence away,   225
From Richard's night to Bolingbroke's fair day.
                                      ⌜*They exit.*⌝

⌜Scene 3⌝
Enter ⌜*with Drum and Colors*⌝ *Bolingbroke, York,*
Northumberland, ⌜*with Soldiers and Attendants.*⌝

BOLINGBROKE
So that by this intelligence we learn
The Welshmen are dispersed, and Salisbury
Is gone to meet the King, who lately landed
With some few private friends upon this coast.

NORTHUMBERLAND
The news is very fair and good, my lord: 5
Richard not far from hence hath hid his head.

YORK
It would beseem the Lord Northumberland
To say "King Richard." Alack the heavy day
When such a sacred king should hide his head!

NORTHUMBERLAND
Your Grace mistakes; only to be brief   10
Left I his title out.

YORK
The time hath been, would you have been so brief
    with him,
He would have been so brief to shorten you,

15. **taking so the head:** perhaps, thus omitting his title

16. **Mistake not:** do not misapprehend the meaning

17. **cousin:** kinsman, nephew

18. **mistake:** transgress, offend (See longer note, page 226.)

27. **the limits of yon lime and stone:** i.e., those castle walls   **limits of:** region enclosed by

31. **belike:** probably

33. **rude:** rough; **ribs:** i.e., walls

34. **breath of parley:** i.e., signal for a conference

35. **his ruined ears:** i.e., the castle ruins (The words may also allude to the king.) **deliver:** say

41. **my banishment repealed:** i.e., the repeal of **my banishment**

42. **lands restored:** i.e., the restoration of my **lands**

Flint Castle. (3.2.216; 3.3)
From John Speed, *The theatre of the empire of Great Britaine . . .* (1627 [i.e., 1631]).

126

For taking so the head, your whole head's length. 15

BOLINGBROKE
Mistake not, uncle, further than you should.

YORK
Take not, good cousin, further than you should,
Lest you mistake. The heavens are over our heads.

BOLINGBROKE
I know it, uncle, and oppose not myself
Against their will. But who comes here? 20

Enter Percy.

Welcome, Harry. What, will not this castle yield?

PERCY
The castle royally is manned, my lord,
Against thy entrance.

BOLINGBROKE
Royally? Why, it contains no king.

PERCY　Yes, my good lord, 25
It doth contain a king. King Richard lies
Within the limits of yon lime and stone,
And with him are the Lord Aumerle, Lord Salisbury,
Sir Stephen Scroop, besides a clergyman
Of holy reverence—who, I cannot learn. 30

NORTHUMBERLAND
O, belike it is the Bishop of Carlisle.

BOLINGBROKE, ⌜*to Northumberland*⌝　Noble ⌜lord,⌝
Go to the rude ribs of that ancient castle,
Through brazen trumpet send the breath of parley
Into his ruined ears, and thus deliver: 35
Henry Bolingbroke
On both his knees doth kiss King Richard's hand
And sends allegiance and true faith of heart
To his most royal person, hither come
Even at his feet to lay my arms and power, 40
Provided that my banishment repealed
And lands restored again be freely granted.

43. **advantage of my power:** superiority of my forces

48. **It is such:** i.e., **it is** that **such** a

50. **My stooping duty:** i.e., my obedient humbling of myself; **tenderly:** gently, affectionately

52 SD. **Trumpets:** trumpeters

54. **tottered:** i.e., tattered (having pointed projections; or, dilapidated)

55. **appointments:** equipment, outfits (Holinshed reports that Bolingbroke "mustered his army before the king's presence, which undoubtedly made a passing fair show.")

56. **Methinks:** it seems to me

58. **Of fire and water:** in the form of lightning and rain

61. **rain:** He promises to **rain** his **waters** (but there is a probable pun on *rain/reign*).

63. **mark:** observe

63 SD. **Richard appeareth:** Many editions follow the Folio here and have Scroop, Salisbury, and the bishop of Carlisle also appear **on the walls.**

65. **blushing discontented sun:** Proverbial: "A red morning foretells a stormy day."

67. **he:** i.e., it; **envious:** spiteful; **bent:** determined

71. **lightens forth:** i.e., sends **forth** like lightning

73. **so fair a show:** so beautiful a spectacle or sight

If not, I'll use the advantage of my power
And lay the summer's dust with showers of blood
Rained from the wounds of slaughtered   45
    Englishmen—
The which how far off from the mind of Bolingbroke
It is such crimson tempest should bedrench
The fresh green lap of fair King Richard's land,
My stooping duty tenderly shall show.   50
Go signify as much while here we march
Upon the grassy carpet of this plain.
                    ⌜*Northumberland and Trumpets*
                        approach the battlements.⌝
Let's march without the noise of threat'ning drum,
That from this castle's tottered battlements
Our fair appointments may be well perused.   55
Methinks King Richard and myself should meet
With no less terror than the elements
Of fire and water when their thund'ring shock
At meeting tears the cloudy cheeks of heaven.
Be he the fire, I'll be the yielding water;   60
The rage be his, whilst on the Earth I rain
My waters—on the Earth, and not on him.
March on, and mark King Richard how he looks.
    ⌜*Bolingbroke's Soldiers march,*⌝ *the trumpets sound.*
        Richard appeareth on the walls ⌜*with Aumerle.*⌝
See, see, King Richard doth himself appear
As doth the blushing discontented sun   65
From out the fiery portal of the east
When he perceives the envious clouds are bent
To dim his glory and to stain the track
Of his bright passage to the occident.
YORK
Yet looks he like a king. Behold, his eye,   70
As bright as is the eagle's, lightens forth
Controlling majesty. Alack, alack for woe
That any harm should stain so fair a show!

74. **We are amazed:** I am astounded

74–75. **stood / To watch:** i.e., **stood** silent waiting to see

77. **An if:** i.e., **if**

78. **awful:** reverential, profoundly respectful

79. **hand of God:** God's signature

82. **gripe:** seize

83. **Unless . . . usurp:** i.e., without committing sacrilege, theft, or usurpation

85. **Have torn . . . us:** i.e., **have** turned away **from** me, thus tearing **their souls** asunder

91. **That lift:** i.e., (the **children** of you) who **lift**

96. **purple testament:** i.e., bloody legacy

98. **crowns:** heads

104. **civil:** i.e., used in civil combat; **uncivil:** barbarous

"A lurking adder." (3.2.20)
From Claude Paradin, *The heroicall deuises of . . .* (1591).

KING RICHARD, ⌜*to Northumberland, below*⌝
  We are amazed, and thus long have we stood
  To watch the fearful bending of thy knee,   75
  Because we thought ourself thy lawful king.
  An if we be, how dare thy joints forget
  To pay their awful duty to our presence?
  If we be not, show us the hand of God
  That hath dismissed us from our stewardship,   80
  For well we know no hand of blood and bone
  Can gripe the sacred handle of our scepter,
  Unless he do profane, steal, or usurp.
  And though you think that all, as you have done,
  Have torn their souls by turning them from us,   85
  And we are barren and bereft of friends,
  Yet know, my master, God omnipotent,
  Is mustering in his clouds on our behalf
  Armies of pestilence, and they shall strike
  Your children yet unborn and unbegot,   90
  That lift your vassal hands against my head
  And threat the glory of my precious crown.
  Tell Bolingbroke—for yon methinks he stands—
  That every stride he makes upon my land
  Is dangerous treason. He is come to open   95
  The purple testament of bleeding war;
  But ere the crown he looks for live in peace,
  Ten thousand bloody crowns of mothers' sons
  Shall ill become the flower of England's face,
  Change the complexion of her maid-pale peace   100
  To scarlet indignation, and bedew
  Her pastures' grass with faithful English blood.
NORTHUMBERLAND
  The King of heaven forbid our lord the King
  Should so with civil and uncivil arms
  Be rushed upon! Thy thrice-noble cousin,   105
  Harry Bolingbroke, doth humbly kiss thy hand,
  And by the honorable tomb he swears

109. **royalties:** royal status; **bloods:** families, lineages

110. **head:** fountainhead, spring

114. **scope:** aim, goal

115. **lineal royalties:** hereditary rights due to one of royal blood

116. **Enfranchisement:** i.e., freedom from the sentence of banishment

117. **on thy royal party granted once:** i.e., **once** you have **granted** this

118. **commend:** commit

119. **barbèd steeds:** armored horses (A *barb* was a shield covering the horse's breast and flanks.)

123. **returns:** replies

126. **accomplished:** carried out

128. **commends:** regards

131. **look so poorly:** appear so abject; **fair:** courteously, flatteringly

Scales, or balances. (3.4.91–94)
From Silvestro Pietrasanta, . . . *Symbola heroica* (1682).

That stands upon your royal grandsire's bones,
And by the royalties of both your bloods,
Currents that spring from one most gracious head,   110
And by the buried hand of warlike Gaunt,
And by the worth and honor of himself,
Comprising all that may be sworn or said,
His coming hither hath no further scope
Than for his lineal royalties, and to beg   115
Enfranchisement immediate on his knees;
Which on thy royal party granted once,
His glittering arms he will commend to rust,
His barbèd steeds to stables, and his heart
To faithful service of your Majesty.   120
This swears he, as he is ⌐a prince and¬ just,
And as I am a gentleman I credit him.

KING RICHARD
Northumberland, say thus the King returns:
His noble cousin is right welcome hither,
And all the number of his fair demands   125
Shall be accomplished without contradiction.
With all the gracious utterance thou hast,
Speak to his gentle hearing kind commends.
         ⌐*Northumberland returns to Bolingbroke.*¬
⌐*To Aumerle.*¬ We do debase ourselves, cousin, do
    we not,   130
To look so poorly and to speak so fair?
Shall we call back Northumberland and send
Defiance to the traitor and so die?

AUMERLE
No, good my lord, let's fight with gentle words,
Till time lend friends, and friends their helpful   135
    swords.

KING RICHARD
O God, O God, that e'er this tongue of mine
That laid the sentence of dread banishment
On yon proud man should take it off again

140. **words of sooth:** flattering **words**

144. **scope:** space

146. **scope:** permission; opportunity

152. **set of beads:** i.e., rosary

154. **gay:** brilliant, fine; **almsman's gown: gown** of one supported by charitable gifts

156. **palmer's:** pilgrim's (See picture, below.)

160. **King's highway:** i.e., rather than in consecrated ground

161. **trade:** traffic

164. **buried once:** i.e., **once** I am **buried**

167. **lodge:** beat down; **corn:** wheat

168. **revolting:** rebelling

169. **play the wantons:** dally, trifle

170. **make . . . match:** i.e., devise a clever game

172. **fretted:** i.e., dug (literally, worn away)

173–74. **there lies . . . eyes:** These words are perhaps their imagined epitaph.

A palmer. (3.3.156)
From Henry Peacham, *Minerua Britanna* . . . (1612).

With words of sooth! O, that I were as great   140
As is my grief, or lesser than my name!
Or that I could forget what I have been,
Or not remember what I must be now.
Swell'st thou, proud heart? I'll give thee scope to
     beat,   145
Since foes have scope to beat both thee and me.

AUMERLE
Northumberland comes back from Bolingbroke.

KING RICHARD
What must the King do now? Must he submit?
The King shall do it. Must he be deposed?
The King shall be contented. Must he lose   150
The name of king? I' God's name, let it go.
I'll give my jewels for a set of beads,
My gorgeous palace for a hermitage,
My gay apparel for an almsman's gown,
My figured goblets for a dish of wood,   155
My scepter for a palmer's walking-staff,
My subjects for a pair of carvèd saints,
And my large kingdom for a little grave,
A little, little grave, an obscure grave;
Or I'll be buried in the King's highway,   160
Some way of common trade, where subjects' feet
May hourly trample on their sovereign's head;
For on my heart they tread now whilst I live
And, buried once, why not upon my head?
Aumerle, thou weep'st, my tender-hearted cousin.   165
We'll make foul weather with despisèd tears;
Our sighs and they shall lodge the summer corn
And make a dearth in this revolting land.
Or shall we play the wantons with our woes
And make some pretty match with shedding tears?   170
As thus, to drop them still upon one place
Till they have fretted us a pair of graves
Within the earth; and therein laid—there lies

175. **ill:** misfortune
176. **idly:** foolishly
180. **make a leg:** i.e., bow
181. **base court:** outermost courtyard (Holinshed says that Bolingbroke waited for Richard "within the first gate" of the castle.) **attend:** wait
183. **glist'ring:** glittering; **Phaëton:** son of Apollo, the sun god, killed while attempting to drive the chariot of the sun (See picture, below.)
184. **Wanting the manage of:** i.e., unable to control; **jades:** a contemptuous name for horses
187. **do them grace:** i.e., show them favor
194. **fondly:** foolishly; **frantic man:** madman
196. **Stand all apart:** i.e., everyone **stand** aside
201. **Me rather had:** i.e., **I had rather**

"Down I come, like glist'ring Phaëton." (3.3.183)
From Ovid, . . . *Metamorphoseos Libri XV* . . . (1527).

Two kinsmen digged their graves with weeping eyes.
Would not this ill do well? Well, well, I see   175
I talk but idly, and you laugh at me.
⌜*Northumberland approaches the battlements.*⌝
Most mighty prince, my Lord Northumberland,
What says King Bolingbroke? Will his Majesty
Give Richard leave to live till Richard die?
You make a leg, and Bolingbroke says ay.   180

NORTHUMBERLAND
My lord, in the base court he doth attend
To speak with you, may it please you to come down.

KING RICHARD
Down, down I come, like glist'ring Phaëton,
Wanting the manage of unruly jades.
In the base court—base court, where kings grow   185
   base,
To come at traitors' calls and do them grace.
In the base court come down—down court, down
   king,
For nightowls shriek where mounting larks should   190
   sing.
                    ⌜*Richard exits above*
        and Northumberland returns to Bolingbroke.⌝

BOLINGBROKE   What says his Majesty?
NORTHUMBERLAND   Sorrow and grief of heart
Makes him speak fondly like a frantic man,
Yet he is come.   195

              ⌜*Richard enters below.*⌝

BOLINGBROKE   Stand all apart,
And show fair duty to his Majesty.   *He kneels down.*
My gracious lord.

KING RICHARD
Fair cousin, you debase your princely knee
To make the base earth proud with kissing it.   200
Me rather had my heart might feel your love

208. **redoubted:** feared, reverenced
213. **want:** lack
216. **willing:** willingly

3.4 Richard's queen overhears a gardener describing Richard's downfall and probable deposition.

---

2. **heavy:** sad, sorrowful
3–5. **bowls, rubs, bias:** In the game of **bowls**, **rubs** are obstructions that hinder or deflect the course of the bowl; the **bias** is the curve that brings the ball to the desired point. (See picture, below.)

"We'll play at bowls." (3.4.3)
From *Le centre de l'amour* . . . (1650?).

Than my unpleased eye see your courtesy.
Up, cousin, up. Your heart is up, I know,
Thus high at least ⌜*indicating his crown,*⌝ although
    your knee be low.   205

BOLINGBROKE, ⌜*standing*⌝
My gracious lord, I come but for mine own.

KING RICHARD
Your own is yours, and I am yours, and all.

BOLINGBROKE
So far be mine, my most redoubted lord,
As my true service shall deserve your love.

KING RICHARD
Well you deserve. They well deserve to have   210
That know the strong'st and surest way to get.—
Uncle, give me your hands. Nay, dry your eyes.
Tears show their love but want their remedies.—
Cousin, I am too young to be your father,
Though you are old enough to be my heir.   215
What you will have I'll give, and willing too,
For do we must what force will have us do.
Set on towards London, cousin, is it so?

BOLINGBROKE
Yea, my good lord.

KING RICHARD   Then I must not say no.   220
                                    ⌜*They exit.*⌝

⌜Scene 4⌝
Enter the Queen with her ⌜*Ladies-in-waiting.*⌝

QUEEN
What sport shall we devise here in this garden
To drive away the heavy thought of care?

LADY   Madam, we'll play at bowls.

QUEEN
'Twill make me think the world is full of rubs
And that my fortune runs against the bias.   5

7. **can . . . measure:** cannot move rhythmically

8. **no measure keeps:** knows no limit or bounds

14. **wanting:** lacking

15. **remember:** remind

16. **had:** in my possession, as opposed to lacking (line 14)

17, 19. **want:** lack

19. **boots not:** does no good, does not help

25. **sing:** perhaps, **sing** for joy

29. **My wretchedness unto:** i.e., I would bet **my wretchedness** against

30. **state:** i.e., matters of **state**

31. **Against:** just before; **forerun with:** foreshadowed by

32. **young:** Some editions print "yon," from the Folio's "yond." **apricokes:** apricots (See picture, below.)

An apricot tree. (3.4.32)
From John Gerard, *The herball or generall historie of plantes . . .* (1633).

LADY   Madam, we'll dance.

QUEEN
  My legs can keep no measure in delight
  When my poor heart no measure keeps in grief.
  Therefore no dancing, girl. Some other sport.

LADY   Madam, we'll tell tales.   10

QUEEN
  Of sorrow or of ⌜joy?⌝

LADY   Of either, madam.

QUEEN   Of neither, girl,
  For if of joy, being altogether wanting,
  It doth remember me the more of sorrow;   15
  Or if of grief, being altogether had,
  It adds more sorrow to my want of joy.
  For what I have I need not to repeat,
  And what I want it boots not to complain.

LADY   20
  Madam, I'll sing.

QUEEN   'Tis well that thou hast cause,
  But thou shouldst please me better wouldst thou
      weep.

LADY
  I could weep, madam, would it do you good.

QUEEN
  And I could sing, would weeping do me good,   25
  And never borrow any tear of thee.

        Enter ⌜a Gardener and two Servingmen.⌝

  But stay, here come the gardeners.
  Let's step into the shadow of these trees.
  My wretchedness unto a row of ⌜pins,⌝
  They will talk of state, for everyone doth so   30
  Against a change. Woe is forerun with woe.
                      ⌜*Queen and Ladies step aside.*⌝

GARDENER, ⌜*to one Servingman*⌝
  Go, bind thou up young dangling apricokes

34. **of their prodigal weight:** i.e., from **their** excessive **weight** (The word **prodigal,** with its associations with wasteful children—as in the "**prodigal son**" story in Luke 15.11–32—continues the parallel between the fruit of the apricot and **unruly children** [line 33].)

37. **sprays:** twigs of trees or shrubs

41. **noisome:** harmful, injurious

43. **pale:** area enclosed by a fence (See picture, below.)

45. **firm estate:** sound or healthy condition

49. **knots:** intricately designed flower beds (See picture, page 202.)

52. **suffered:** allowed

63. **at time of year:** i.e., at the proper season

66. **it confound:** i.e., the tree destroy

A garden encompassed with pales. (3.4.43)
From Thomas Hill, *The gardeners labyrinth . . .* (1577).

Which, like unruly children, make their sire
Stoop with oppression of their prodigal weight.
Give some supportance to the bending twigs.—   35
Go thou, and like an executioner
Cut off the heads of ⌜too⌝-fast-growing sprays
That look too lofty in our commonwealth.
All must be even in our government.
You thus employed, I will go root away   40
The noisome weeds which without profit suck
The soil's fertility from wholesome flowers.

MAN
Why should we, in the compass of a pale,
Keep law and form and due proportion,
Showing as in a model our firm estate,   45
When our sea-wallèd garden, the whole land,
Is full of weeds, her fairest flowers choked up,
Her fruit trees all unpruned, her hedges ruined,
Her knots disordered, and her wholesome herbs
Swarming with caterpillars?   50

GARDENER   Hold thy peace.
He that hath suffered this disordered spring
Hath now himself met with the fall of leaf.
The weeds which his broad-spreading leaves did
      shelter,   55
That seemed in eating him to hold him up,
Are plucked up, root and all, by Bolingbroke—
I mean the Earl of Wiltshire, Bushy, Green.

MAN
What, are they dead?

GARDENER   They are. And Bolingbroke   60
Hath seized the wasteful king. O, what pity is it
That he had not so trimmed and dressed his land
As we this garden! ⌜We⌝ at time of year
Do wound the bark, the skin of our fruit trees,
Lest, being overproud in sap and blood,   65
With too much riches it confound itself.
Had he done so to great and growing men,

70. **bearing boughs:** i.e., **boughs** that bear fruit

74. **Depressed:** subjugated, overcome

75. **'Tis doubt:** there is fear

78. **pressed to death:** a reference to a method of torture in which the body of an accused person who refused to speak was crushed under a mass of stones (See picture, page 206.) **want:** lack

79. **old Adam's . . . garden:** a reference to Genesis 2.15: "Then the Lord God took the man [Adam] and put him into the **garden** of Eden, that he might **dress** it and keep it."

82–83. **Eve . . . man:** See Genesis 3 for the story of the **serpent,** the temptation of Adam and **Eve,** and the **fall of cursèd man. suggested:** tempted

87. **ill:** evil

91. **are weighed:** The gardener goes on to describe the **fortunes** of Richard and Bolingbroke as if they were being **weighed** in a balance—a weighing device with pans or scales. (See picture, page 132.) In line 94, the word **balance** is used to refer to one of these pans.

93. **vanities:** worthless things

96. **odds:** advantage

97. **Post you:** go quickly, as if by post-horses

They might have lived to bear and he to taste
Their fruits of duty. Superfluous branches
We lop away, that bearing boughs may live.   70
Had he done so, himself had borne the crown,
Which waste of idle hours hath quite thrown down.

MAN
What, think you the King shall be deposed?

GARDENER
Depressed he is already, and deposed
'Tis doubt he will be. Letters came last night   75
To a dear friend of the good Duke of York's
That tell black tidings.

QUEEN
O, I am pressed to death through want of speaking!
                                   ⌈*Stepping forward.*⌉
Thou old Adam's likeness, set to dress this garden,
How dares thy harsh rude tongue sound this   80
   unpleasing news?
What Eve, what serpent, hath suggested thee
To make a second fall of cursèd man?
Why dost thou say King Richard is deposed?
Dar'st thou, thou little better thing than earth,   85
Divine his downfall? Say where, when, and how
⌈Cam'st⌉ thou by this ill tidings? Speak, thou wretch!

GARDENER
Pardon me, madam. Little joy have I
To breathe this news, yet what I say is true.
King Richard, he is in the mighty hold   90
Of Bolingbroke. Their fortunes both are weighed.
In your lord's scale is nothing but himself
And some few vanities that make him light,
But in the balance of great Bolingbroke,
Besides himself, are all the English peers,   95
And with that odds he weighs King Richard down.
Post you to London and you will find it so.
I speak no more than everyone doth know.

99. **mischance:** disaster, calamity; evil fate

100. **embassage:** message

103. **Thy sorrow:** i.e., the **sorrow** carried by **mischance**

106. **triumph:** triumphal procession

110. **would:** i.e., wish

111. **fall:** shed

112. **rue, sour herb of grace:** Garden **rue** was called "**herb of grace**" because of its association with repentance. (See picture, page 204.)

113. **ruth:** pity

Gardeners pruning an arbor. (3.4.32–72)
From Thomas Hill, *The gardeners labyrinth . . .* (1577).

QUEEN
    Nimble mischance, that art so light of foot,
    Doth not thy embassage belong to me,   100
    And am I last that knows it? O, thou thinkest
    To serve me last that I may longest keep
    Thy sorrow in my breast. Come, ladies, go
    To meet at London London's king in woe.
    What, was I born to this, that my sad look   105
    Should grace the triumph of great Bolingbroke?—
    Gard'ner, for telling me these news of woe,
    Pray God the plants thou graft'st may never grow.
                                    She exits ⌈*with Ladies.*⌉
GARDENER
    Poor queen, so that thy state might be no worse,
    I would my skill were subject to thy curse.   110
    Here did she fall a tear. Here in this place
    I'll set a bank of rue, sour herb of grace.
    Rue even for ruth here shortly shall be seen
    In the remembrance of a weeping queen.
                                                They exit.

The Tragedy of

RICHARD II

ACT 4

4.1 Bolingbroke seeks information about the duke of Gloucester's death. Bagot implicates Aumerle, and several nobles challenge Aumerle and each other. York brings word that Richard resigns the crown. When Bolingbroke begins to ascend the throne, the bishop of Carlisle accuses him of treachery and predicts bloody civil war. Carlisle is arrested, and Bolingbroke orders Richard brought before him. Richard formally deposes himself and is taken off to the Tower. Aumerle learns from the abbot of Westminster that there is a plot against Bolingbroke.

---

1. **Bagot:** The play does not make clear Bagot's location following his farewell at 2.2.148–50, when he says he will join Richard in Ireland. Richard's question about Bagot at 3.2.125 makes it obvious that the two did not meet in Ireland. Now, as 4.1 opens, Bagot enters, presumably having been captured by Bolingbroke.

3. **Gloucester's death:** See note to 1.1.103 and longer note, page 223.

5. **timeless:** untimely

9. **delivered:** said

10. **dead:** past, long ago; also, perhaps, fatal, deadly

12. **of length:** long

13. **restful:** quiet

⌜ACT 4⌝

⌜Scene 1⌝

Enter Bolingbroke with the Lords ⌜Aumerle,
Northumberland, Harry Percy, Fitzwater, Surrey, the
Bishop of Carlisle, the Abbot of Westminster, and
another Lord, Herald, Officers⌝ to parliament.

BOLINGBROKE Call forth Bagot.

Enter ⌜Officers with⌝ Bagot.

Now, Bagot, freely speak thy mind
What thou dost know of noble Gloucester's death,
Who wrought it with the King, and who performed
The bloody office of his timeless end.   5

BAGOT
Then set before my face the Lord Aumerle.

BOLINGBROKE
Cousin, stand forth, and look upon that man.
                                            ⌜Aumerle steps forward.⌝

BAGOT
My Lord Aumerle, I know your daring tongue
Scorns to unsay what once it hath delivered.
In that dead time when Gloucester's death was   10
    plotted,
I heard you say "Is not my arm of length,
That reacheth from the restful English court
As far as Calais, to mine uncle's head?"
Amongst much other talk that very time   15

151

18. **Than Bolingbroke's return:** i.e., **than** have Bolingbroke **return** (The time scheme is in error here, since Gloucester was killed before Bolingbroke was exiled.)

19. **withal:** in addition

20. **this your cousin's:** i.e., Bolingbroke's

22. **base:** lowborn

23. **my fair stars:** i.e., my noble birth (Aumerle here credits the influence of the **stars** for his fortunate lineage.)

24. **On equal terms:** i.e., as if we were equals

26. **attainder:** accusation

26 SD. **gage:** See note to 1.1.71 and pictures, pages 26 and 154.

27. **the manual seal of death:** (1) the signature (*seal manual* or *sign manual*) of **Death;** (2) a glove from my hand that seals your fate

29–30. **maintain . . . In thy heart-blood:** i.e., uphold even **in** your heart's blood that **what** you have **said is false**

30–31. **though being . . . sword:** i.e., even **though** your blood is **too base** (lowborn) **to** be worthy of staining **my sword,** made of well-tempered steel

33. **one:** i.e., Bolingbroke

33–34. **I would . . . so:** i.e., I wish I had been provoked by the highest born in this company

35. **stand on sympathy:** i.e., insists on fighting someone of equal rank

39. **vauntingly:** boastfully

43. **forgèd:** made, fashioned

I heard you say that you had rather refuse
The offer of an hundred thousand crowns
Than Bolingbroke's return to England,
Adding withal how blest this land would be
In this your cousin's death.   20
AUMERLE   Princes and noble lords,
   What answer shall I make to this base man?
   Shall I so much dishonor my fair stars
   On equal terms to give ⌜him⌝ chastisement?
   Either I must or have mine honor soiled   25
   With the attainder of his slanderous lips.
                                   ⌜*He throws down a gage.*⌝
   There is my gage, the manual seal of death
   That marks thee out for hell. I say thou liest,
   And will maintain what thou hast said is false
   In thy heart-blood, though being all too base   30
   To stain the temper of my knightly sword.
BOLINGBROKE
   Bagot, forbear. Thou shalt not take it up.
AUMERLE
   Excepting one, I would he were the best
   In all this presence that hath moved me so.
FITZWATER, ⌜*throwing down a gage*⌝
   If that thy valor stand on sympathy,   35
   There is my gage, Aumerle, in gage to thine.
   By that fair sun which shows me where thou
      stand'st,
   I heard thee say, and vauntingly thou spak'st it,
   That thou wert cause of noble Gloucester's death.   40
   If thou deniest it twenty times, thou liest,
   And I will turn thy falsehood to thy heart,
   Where it was forgèd, with my rapier's point.
AUMERLE, ⌜*taking up the gage*⌝
   Thou dar'st not, coward, live to see that day.
FITZWATER
   Now, by my soul, I would it were this hour.   45

48. **appeal:** charge, accusation; **all:** completely

50–51. **to ... breathing:** i.e., with my dying breath; or, at the cost of my life, if necessary

52. **An if:** i.e., **if**

55. **I task ... like:** i.e., **I** give **the earth** a similar burden; **forsworn:** perjured, falsely sworn

56. **with full as many:** i.e., by accusing you of just **as many**

59. **Engage it:** perhaps, take it up as a gage

60. **sets me:** wagers against me; **throw:** cast (**Sets** and **throw** are terms from dicing.)

65. **in presence:** present; or, perhaps, in the king's presence chamber

Gantelet.

A gauntlet (often used as a gage).
(1.1.71; 4.1.27)
From Louis de Gaya, *Traité des armes, des machines de guerre* ... (1678).

AUMERLE
  Fitzwater, thou art damned to hell for this.
PERCY
  Aumerle, thou liest! His honor is as true
  In this appeal as thou art all unjust;
  And that thou art so, there I throw my gage,
                              ⌜*He throws down a gage.*⌝
  To prove it on thee to the extremest point   50
  Of mortal breathing. Seize it if thou dar'st.
AUMERLE, ⌜*taking up the gage*⌝
  An if I do not, may my hands rot off
  And never brandish more revengeful steel
  Over the glittering helmet of my foe!
ANOTHER LORD, ⌜*throwing down a gage*⌝
  I task the earth to the like, forsworn Aumerle,   55
  And spur thee on with full as many lies
  As may be holloed in thy treacherous ear
  From ⌜sun⌝ to ⌜sun.⌝ There is my honor's pawn.
  Engage it to the trial if thou darest.
AUMERLE, ⌜*taking up the gage*⌝
  Who sets me else? By heaven, I'll throw at all!   60
  I have a thousand spirits in one breast
  To answer twenty thousand such as you.
SURREY
  My Lord Fitzwater, I do remember well
  The very time Aumerle and you did talk.
FITZWATER
  'Tis very true. You were in presence then,   65
  And you can witness with me this is true.
SURREY
  As false, by heaven, as heaven itself is true.
FITZWATER
  Surrey, thou liest.
SURREY   Dishonorable boy,
  That lie shall lie so heavy on my sword   70
  That it shall render vengeance and revenge

76. **fondly:** foolishly; **a forward:** an eager
81. **correction:** punishment
83. **appeal:** accusation
84. **Norfolk:** Thomas Mowbray, duke of **Norfolk**
89. **repealed to try his honor:** i.e., called back from exile to put **his honor** on trial
90. **differences:** quarrels, disagreements; **under gage:** as challenges
93. **seigniories:** estates, territories
95. **his trial:** i.e., **trial** by combat
99. **Streaming the ensign:** flying the banner

"Yield stinging nettles to mine enemies." (3.2.18)
From John Gerard, *The herball or generall historie of plantes . . .* (1597).

Till thou the lie-giver and that lie do lie
In earth as quiet as thy father's skull.
⌈*He throws down a gage.*⌉
In proof whereof, there is my honor's pawn.
Engage it to the trial if thou dar'st.   75

FITZWATER, ⌈*taking up the gage*⌉
How fondly dost thou spur a forward horse!
If I dare eat or drink or breathe or live,
I dare meet Surrey in a wilderness
And spit upon him whilst I say he lies,
And lies, and lies. There is ⌈my⌉ bond of faith   80
To tie thee to my strong correction.
⌈*He throws down a gage.*⌉
As I intend to thrive in this new world,
Aumerle is guilty of my true appeal.—
Besides, I heard the banished Norfolk say
That thou, Aumerle, didst send two of thy men   85
To execute the noble duke at Calais.

AUMERLE
Some honest Christian trust me with a gage.
⌈*A lord hands him a gage.*
Aumerle throws it down.⌉
That Norfolk lies, here do I throw down this,
If he may be repealed to try his honor.

BOLINGBROKE
These differences shall all rest under gage   90
Till Norfolk be repealed. Repealed he shall be,
And though mine enemy, restored again
To all his lands and seigniories. When he is
    returned,
Against Aumerle we will enforce his trial.   95

CARLISLE
That honorable day shall never be seen.
Many a time hath banished Norfolk fought
For Jesu Christ in glorious Christian field,
Streaming the ensign of the Christian cross

101. **toiled:** fatigued, worn out

105. **colors:** flag, insignia

108–9. **bosom . . . Abraham:** See Luke 16.22: "And it was so that [the man] died and was carried by the angels into Abraham's **bosom**."

109. **Lords appellants:** i.e., you **lords** who have made accusations against each other

117. **descending:** i.e., passing to you

120. **Marry:** an oath (originally, "by the Virgin Mary")

121. **Worst:** i.e., least worthy, lowest in rank

122. **best beseeming me:** i.e., it **best** fits **me** (as bishop)

125. **noblesse:** nobility

126. **Learn:** teach

129. **but:** unless; **by:** i.e., present

130. **apparent:** obvious

Golgotha. (4.1.150)
From Martin Luther, *Ein sermon . . .* (1523).

Against black pagans, Turks, and Saracens;   100
And, toiled with works of war, retired himself
To Italy, and there at Venice gave
His body to that pleasant country's earth
And his pure soul unto his captain, Christ,
Under whose colors he had fought so long.   105

BOLINGBROKE   Why, bishop, is Norfolk dead?

CARLISLE   As surely as I live, my lord.

BOLINGBROKE
Sweet peace conduct his sweet soul to the bosom
Of good old Abraham! Lords appellants,
Your differences shall all rest under gage   110
Till we assign you to your days of trial.

Enter York.

YORK
Great Duke of Lancaster, I come to thee
From plume-plucked Richard, who with willing
    soul
Adopts thee heir, and his high scepter yields   115
To the possession of thy royal hand.
Ascend his throne, descending now from him,
And long live Henry, fourth of that name!

BOLINGBROKE
In God's name, I'll ascend the regal throne.

CARLISLE   Marry, God forbid!   120
Worst in this royal presence may I speak,
Yet best beseeming me to speak the truth.
Would God that any in this noble presence
Were enough noble to be upright judge
Of noble Richard! Then true noblesse would   125
Learn him forbearance from so foul a wrong.
What subject can give sentence on his king?
And who sits here that is not Richard's subject?
Thieves are not judged but they are by to hear,
Although apparent guilt be seen in them;   130
And shall the figure of God's majesty,

132. **elect:** chosen

133. **planted:** established

135. **forfend it God:** i.e., **God** forbid

136. **climate:** i.e., region

144. **future ages groan:** Carlisle's prophecy describes what happens to England in the Wars of the Roses, dramatized by Shakespeare in his plays about Henry VI and Richard III.

147. **kin . . . confound:** i.e., destroy (**confound**) kinsman by kinsman

149. **inhabit:** dwell

150. **Golgotha and dead men's skulls: Golgatha** (the hill of Calvary), where Jesus was crucified, was known as "the place of **dead men's skulls**" (Mark 15.22). See picture, page 158.

151–52. **If you raise . . . prove:** See Matthew 12.25: "And Jesus . . . said unto them, Every kingdom divided against itself shall be brought to naught, and every city or house divided against itself shall not stand." See also Mark 3.25.

157. **Of:** i.e., on a charge of

160–331. **May it please you . . . true king's fall:** These lines (often called "the Deposition Scene") were not in the first three quartos; they appeared first in the Fourth Quarto printing of 1608, again in Quarto 5 in 1615, and, in a different and far superior text, in the 1623 Folio. (See longer note, page 226.)

160–61. **the commons' suit:** i.e., the petition submitted on behalf of the commons (This is presumably the paper Northumberland will badger Richard to read aloud [lines 232–35, 254, 280].)

163. **surrender:** i.e., **surrender** the crown

165. **conduct:** guide, escort

His captain, steward, deputy elect,
Anointed, crowned, planted many years,
Be judged by subject and inferior breath,
And he himself not present? O, forfend it God   135
That in a Christian climate souls refined
Should show so heinous, black, obscene a deed!
I speak to subjects and a subject speaks,
Stirred up by God thus boldly for his king.
My Lord of Hereford here, whom you call king,   140
Is a foul traitor to proud Hereford's king,
And if you crown him, let me prophesy
The blood of English shall manure the ground
And future ages groan for this foul act,
Peace shall go sleep with Turks and infidels,   145
And in this seat of peace tumultuous wars
Shall kin with kin and kind with kind confound.
Disorder, horror, fear, and mutiny
Shall here inhabit, and this land be called
The field of Golgotha and dead men's skulls.   150
O, if you raise this house against this house,
It will the woefullest division prove
That ever fell upon this cursèd earth!
Prevent it, resist it, let it not be so,
Lest child, child's children, cry against you woe!   155

NORTHUMBERLAND
Well have you argued, sir, and, for your pains,
Of capital treason we arrest you here.—
My Lord of Westminster, be it your charge
To keep him safely till his day of trial.
⌜May it please you, lords, to grant the commons'   160
    suit?⌝

BOLINGBROKE
Fetch hither Richard, that in common view
He may surrender. So we shall proceed
Without suspicion.

YORK   I will be his conduct.   *He exits.*   165

167. **sureties . . . answer:** persons who will guarantee your appearance at your trials by combat

168. **beholding:** beholden, indebted

169. **looked for at:** i.e., expected from

173. **insinuate:** ingratiate myself

176. **favors:** (1) faces; (2) support, kindnesses

177. **sometime:** in the past, once

178–79. **So Judas . . . all but one:** See Matthew 26.20–21, 47–49: "So when the even was come, [Jesus] sat down with the twelve. And as they did eat, he said, Verily I say unto you, that one of you shall betray me. . . . Judas, one of the twelve [said to the high priests], whomsoever I shall kiss, that is he. . . . And forthwith [Judas] came to Jesus and said, God save thee, master, and kissed him."

182. **clerk:** i.e., responder (The **clerk** serving at the altar answered the priest's prayers, usually with "**amen.**")

186. **do that office:** perform that service

194. **owes:** possesses

BOLINGBROKE
Lords, you that here are under our arrest,
Procure your sureties for your days of answer.
Little are we beholding to your love
And little looked for at your helping hands.

Enter Richard and York.

KING RICHARD
Alack, why am I sent for to a king   170
Before I have shook off the regal thoughts
Wherewith I reigned? I hardly yet have learned
To insinuate, flatter, bow, and bend my knee.
Give sorrow leave awhile to tutor me
To this submission. Yet I well remember   175
The favors of these men. Were they not mine?
Did they not sometime cry "All hail" to me?
So Judas did to Christ, but He in twelve
Found truth in all but one; I, in twelve thousand,
     none.   180
God save the King! Will no man say "amen"?
Am I both priest and clerk? Well, then, amen.
God save the King, although I be not he,
And yet amen, if heaven do think him me.
To do what service am I sent for hither?   185
YORK
To do that office of thine own goodwill
Which tired majesty did make thee offer:
The resignation of thy state and crown
To Henry Bolingbroke.
KING RICHARD
Give me the crown.—Here, cousin, seize the crown.   190
Here, cousin,
On this side my hand, on that side thine.
Now is this golden crown like a deep well
That owes two buckets, filling one another,
The emptier ever dancing in the air,   195

204. **Your cares, my cares:** Here and in the next few lines Richard plays with the various meanings of the word **cares:** personal griefs, objects of responsibility, concerns of office, etc. His general point is that Bolingbroke's assuming the **cares** (responsibilities) of the crown does not lessen Richard's **cares** (griefs).

205. **by old care done:** perhaps, destroyed by my old (failure of) responsibility

208. **'tend:** i.e., attend, accompany

210–11. **Ay, no . . . to thee:** These lines pun on the words *I* and *ay,* and play with the equivalency of *no* and *nothing:* if "I am nothing," then "Ay is no." It has also been suggested that the first four words of line 210 can be heard as "I know no I."

212. **mark me:** notice, pay attention to; **undo:** (1) release; (2) undress; (3) cancel, annul; (4) destroy

216. **balm:** See note to 3.2.56.

218. **state:** position, status

221. **revenues:** pronounced **revènues**

222. **deny:** disavow, repudiate

223. **broke:** broken

224. **unbroke:** unbroken; **are made:** i.e., which **are made**

The other down, unseen, and full of water.
That bucket down and full of tears am I,
Drinking my griefs, whilst you mount up on high.

BOLINGBROKE
I thought you had been willing to resign.

KING RICHARD
My crown I am, but still my griefs are mine.　　200
You may my glories and my state depose
But not my griefs; still am I king of those.

BOLINGBROKE
Part of your cares you give me with your crown.

KING RICHARD
Your cares set up do not pluck my cares down.
My care is loss of care, by old care done;　　205
Your care is gain of care, by new care won.
The cares I give I have, though given away.
They 'tend the crown, yet still with me they stay.

BOLINGBROKE
Are you contented to resign the crown?

KING RICHARD
Ay, no; no, ay; for I must nothing be.　　210
Therefore no "no," for I resign to thee.
Now, mark me how I will undo myself.
I give this heavy weight from off my head
And this unwieldy scepter from my hand,
The pride of kingly sway from out my heart.　　215
With mine own tears I wash away my balm,
With mine own hands I give away my crown,
With mine own tongue deny my sacred state,
With mine own breath release all duteous oaths.
All pomp and majesty I do forswear.　　220
My manors, rents, revenues I forgo;
My acts, decrees, and statutes I deny.
God pardon all oaths that are broke to me.
God keep all vows unbroke are made to thee.
Make me, that nothing have, with nothing grieved,　　225

226. **with all pleased:** i.e., **pleased with** everything

227. **in Richard's seat:** i.e., on **Richard's** throne

235. **state:** government

240. **record:** pronounced **recòrd**

242. **a lecture:** a "lesson" read out for moral instruction; **wouldst:** i.e., would read them

249. **bait:** i.e., torment (The image is from bearbaiting, where the bear is tied to a stake and set upon by dogs. [See picture, below.] Here the spectators watch Richard being attacked by his own **wretchedness.**)

250. **with . . . hands:** See Matthew 27.24: "When Pilate saw that he availed nothing . . . he took water and washed his hands before the multitude, saying, I am innocent of the blood of this just man."

254. **dispatch:** make haste

257. **sort:** group, set, band

A bearbaiting. (4.1.249)
From [William Lily,] *Antibossicon* (1521).

And thou with all pleased that hast all achieved.
Long mayst thou live in Richard's seat to sit,
And soon lie Richard in an earthy pit.
God save King Henry, unkinged Richard says,
And send him many years of sunshine days.   230
What more remains?
NORTHUMBERLAND, (*offering Richard a paper*)
                    No more, but that you read
These accusations and these grievous crimes
Committed by your person and your followers
Against the state and profit of this land;   235
That, by confessing them, the souls of men
May deem that you are worthily deposed.
KING RICHARD
Must I do so? And must I ravel out
My weaved-up follies? Gentle Northumberland,
If thy offenses were upon record,   240
Would it not shame thee in so fair a troop
To read a lecture of them? If thou wouldst,
There shouldst thou find one heinous article
Containing the deposing of a king
And cracking the strong warrant of an oath,   245
Marked with a blot, damned in the book of
    heaven.—
Nay, all of you that stand and look upon me
Whilst that my wretchedness doth bait myself,
Though some of you, with Pilate, wash your hands,   250
Showing an outward pity, yet you Pilates
Have here delivered me to my sour cross,
And water cannot wash away your sin.
NORTHUMBERLAND
My lord, dispatch. Read o'er these articles.
KING RICHARD
Mine eyes are full of tears; I cannot see.   255
And yet salt water blinds them not so much
But they can see a sort of traitors here.

261. **T' undeck:** to strip, unclothe; **pompous:** magnificent, glorious

263. **state:** magnificence

265. **haught:** haughty, arrogant

267. **font:** i.e., baptismal **font** (See picture, below.)

271. **mockery:** imitation, counterfeit

275. **An if:** i.e., if; **be sterling yet:** i.e., is still worth anything, still passes as valid currency

276. **hither straight:** i.e., brought here immediately

278. **his:** i.e., its

"That name . . . given me at the font." (4.1.267)
From [Richard Day,] *A booke of christian prayers . . .* (1578).

Nay, if I turn mine eyes upon myself,
I find myself a traitor with the rest,
For I have given here my soul's consent   260
T' undeck the pompous body of a king,
Made glory base ⟨and⟩ sovereignty a slave,
Proud majesty a subject, state a peasant.

NORTHUMBERLAND   My lord—

KING RICHARD
No lord of thine, thou haught insulting man,   265
Nor no man's lord. I have no name, no title,
No, not that name was given me at the font,
But 'tis usurped. Alack the heavy day,
That I have worn so many winters out
And know not now what name to call myself.   270
O, that I were a mockery king of snow
Standing before the sun of Bolingbroke,
To melt myself away in water drops.—
Good king, great king, and yet not greatly good,
An if my word be sterling yet in England,   275
Let it command a mirror hither straight,
That it may show me what a face I have
Since it is bankrupt of his majesty.

BOLINGBROKE
Go, some of you, and fetch a looking-glass.
                                        ⟨*An Attendant exits.*⟩

NORTHUMBERLAND
Read o'er this paper while the glass doth come.   280

KING RICHARD
Fiend, thou torments me ere I come to hell!

BOLINGBROKE
Urge it no more, my Lord Northumberland.

NORTHUMBERLAND
The commons will not then be satisfied.

KING RICHARD
They shall be satisfied. I'll read enough

286 SD. **glass:** i.e., looking **glass,** mirror

291. **in prosperity:** i.e., when I was prospering

292. **beguile:** deceive

295. **wink:** close their eyes

300. **shivers:** fragments, splinters

301. **Mark:** notice, pay attention to

303. **shadow of your sorrow:** i.e., the darkness cast by **your sorrow** (See lines 306–9.)

304. **shadow:** image

308. **manners of laments:** gestures and utterances of lamentation

309. **shadows to:** i.e., **shadows** of

311. **There:** i.e., **in the soul** (line 310)

A beadsman. (3.2.119)
From August Cassimir Redel, *Apophtegmata symbolica* (n.d.).

When I do see the very book indeed   285
Where all my sins are writ, and that's myself.

Enter one with a glass.

Give me that glass, and therein will I read.
⟨*He takes the mirror.*⟩
No deeper wrinkles yet? Hath sorrow struck
So many blows upon this face of mine
And made no deeper wounds? O flatt'ring glass,   290
Like to my followers in prosperity,
Thou dost beguile me. Was this face the face
That every day under his household roof
Did keep ten thousand men? Was this the face
That like the sun did make beholders wink?   295
Is this the face which faced so many follies,
That was at last outfaced by Bolingbroke?
A brittle glory shineth in this face.
As brittle as the glory is the face.
⟨*He breaks the mirror.*⟩
For there it is, cracked in an hundred shivers.—   300
Mark, silent king, the moral of this sport:
How soon my sorrow hath destroyed my face.
BOLINGBROKE
The shadow of your sorrow hath destroyed
The shadow of your face.
KING RICHARD   Say that again.   305
The shadow of my sorrow? Ha, let's see.
'Tis very true. My grief lies all within;
And these external ⟨manners⟩ of laments
Are merely shadows to the unseen grief
That swells with silence in the tortured soul.   310
There lies the substance. And I thank thee, king,
For thy great bounty, that not only giv'st
Me cause to wail but teachest me the way
How to lament the cause. I'll beg one boon

321. **to my:** i.e., as my

329. **Tower: Tower** of London, a fortress-prison (See page 222.)

330. **Conveyers:** i.e., thieves (The word **convey** was used as a euphemism for *steal*.)

332–33. **On Wednesday next ... prepare yourselves:** The early quartos print somewhat similar lines. We follow the Folio here in that the lines printed in the early quartos follow directly from the line which precedes them in the quarto (line 159 of our text). See longer note to 4.1.160–331, page 226. For the quarto reading, see the textual note for 4.1.332–33, page 234. **set down:** appoint

335 SP. CARLISLE: Arrested for capital treason, **Carlisle** was put in the hands of the abbot of Westminster (4.1.157–59). The two **clergymen** (line 337) now become the center of a plot against Henry.

And then be gone and trouble you no more.   315
Shall I obtain it?
BOLINGBROKE   Name it, fair cousin.
KING RICHARD
"Fair cousin"? I am greater than a king,
For when I was a king, my flatterers
Were then but subjects. Being now a subject,   320
I have a king here to my flatterer.
Being so great, I have no need to beg.
BOLINGBROKE   Yet ask.
KING RICHARD   And shall I have?
BOLINGBROKE   You shall.   325
KING RICHARD   Then give me leave to go.
BOLINGBROKE   Whither?
KING RICHARD
Whither you will, so I were from your sights.
BOLINGBROKE
Go, some of you, convey him to the Tower.
KING RICHARD
O, good! "Convey"? Conveyers are you all,   330
That rise thus nimbly by a true king's fall.
                    ⟨*Richard exits with Guards.*⟩
BOLINGBROKE
On Wednesday next, we solemnly set down
Our coronation. Lords, prepare yourselves.⌉
They exit. ⌈*The Abbot of* ⌉ *Westminster,* ⌈*the Bishop of*⌉
                    Carlisle, Aumerle remain.
ABBOT
A woeful pageant have we here beheld.
CARLISLE
The woe's to come. The children yet unborn   335
Shall feel this day as sharp to them as thorn.
AUMERLE
You holy clergymen, is there no plot
To rid the realm of this pernicious blot?

341–42. take the sacrament / To: i.e., receive the Eucharist as a vow to (See picture, page 192.)

342. bury my intents: keep my plans secret and hidden

346. lay: devise, contrive

The goddess Fortuna. (2.2.10)
From Charles de Bouelles,
Que hoc volumine continentur [1510].

ABBOT   My lord,
Before I freely speak my mind herein,   340
You shall not only take the sacrament
To bury mine intents, but also to effect
Whatever I shall happen to devise.
I see your brows are full of discontent,
Your hearts of sorrow, and your eyes of tears.   345
Come home with me to supper. I'll lay
A plot shall show us all a merry day.

They exit.

The Tragedy of

RICHARD II

ACT 5

5.1   Richard and his queen say their farewells, she to be sent to France, he to Pomfret Castle.

---

2. **Julius Caesar's . . . tower:** The Tower of London was said by many chroniclers to have been built by **Julius Caesar.** The Queen calls it **ill-erected** because of its use as an evil (**ill**) prison. (See picture, page 222.)

4. **doomed:** sentenced

7. **soft:** an exclamation meaning "wait a minute" (This line and the following three lines are addressed to herself.)

11. **the model . . . stand:** Richard is here compared to the ruins of the city of **Troy,** a desolate reminder of what he once was. (See picture, page 214.) The term **old Troy** may be distinguishing that city from "New Troy," the legendary name for London.   **model:** image, likeness

12. **map:** i.e., mere outline

13–15. **Thou most beauteous . . . guest:** Richard and Bolingbroke are set in contrast, the first a beautiful **inn** inhabited by **grief,** the second an **alehouse** with **triumph** as its **guest.**

⌜Scene 1⌝
Enter the Queen with her Attendants.

QUEEN
This way the King will come. This is the way
To Julius Caesar's ill-erected tower,
To whose flint bosom my condemnèd lord
Is doomed a prisoner by proud Bolingbroke.
Here let us rest, if this rebellious earth   5
Have any resting for her true king's queen.

Enter Richard ⌜and Guard.⌝

But soft, but see—or rather do not see
My fair rose wither; yet look up, behold,
That you in pity may dissolve to dew
And wash him fresh again with true-love tears.—   10
Ah, thou, the model where old Troy did stand,
Thou map of honor, thou King Richard's tomb,
And not King Richard! Thou most beauteous inn,
Why should hard-favored grief be lodged in thee
When triumph is become an alehouse guest?   15
KING RICHARD
Join not with grief, fair woman, do not so,
To make my end too sudden. Learn, good soul,
To think our former state a happy dream,
From which awaked, the truth of what we are

20. **sworn brother:** i.e., best friend (as if we were knights who had vowed to stand by each other like brothers)

22. **league:** covenant, compact

23. **religious house:** convent

24. **new world's crown:** See 2 Timothy 4.8: "For henceforth is laid up for me the **crown** of righteousness which the Lord the righteous judge shall give me at that day. . . ."

25. **profane:** worldly

28. **been in thy heart:** i.e., stolen your courage (The **heart** was considered the seat of courage and hence was synonymous with it.)

31. **To be o'er-powered:** i.e., at being overpowered

32. **correction:** punishment; **kiss the rod:** proverbial for "accept punishment meekly"

33. **rage:** violence; **base:** cowardly

34. **Which art a lion:** See note to 1.1.180 and picture, page 184.

35. **A king of beasts:** i.e., a ruler over beastly men; **If aught but:** i.e., had they been something other than

37. **sometime:** former; **prepare thee hence: prepare** to depart

43. **long ago betid:** i.e., that happened **long ago**

44. **quite:** repay, reward; **griefs:** (tales of) suffering

47. **Forwhy:** because (of your sad tale); **senseless:** insensate; **brands:** pieces of burning wood; **sympathize:** answer or correspond to, accord with

48. **heavy:** sorrowful

50. **some:** i.e., **some** of the brands

Shows us but this: I am sworn brother, sweet,   20
To grim necessity, and he and I
Will keep a league till death. Hie thee to France
And cloister thee in some religious house.
Our holy lives must win a new world's crown,
Which our profane hours here have thrown down.   25

QUEEN
What, is my Richard both in shape and mind
Transformed and weakened? Hath Bolingbroke
Deposed thine intellect? Hath he been in thy heart?
The lion dying thrusteth forth his paw
And wounds the earth, if nothing else, with rage   30
To be o'er-powered; and wilt thou, pupil-like,
Take the correction, mildly kiss the rod,
And fawn on rage with base humility,
Which art a lion and the king of beasts?

KING RICHARD
A king of beasts indeed. If aught but beasts,   35
I had been still a happy king of men.
Good sometime queen, prepare thee hence for
    France.
Think I am dead and that even here thou takest,
As from my deathbed, thy last living leave.   40
In winter's tedious nights sit by the fire
With good old folks, and let them tell thee tales
Of woeful ages long ago betid;
And, ere thou bid good night, to quite their griefs,
Tell thou the lamentable tale of me,   45
And send the hearers weeping to their beds.
Forwhy the senseless brands will sympathize
The heavy accent of thy moving tongue,
And in compassion weep the fire out,
And some will mourn in ashes, some coal-black,   50
For the deposing of a rightful king.

Enter Northumberland.

53. **Pomfret:** Pontefract Castle (in the northern county of Yorkshire)

54. **there is order ta'en:** i.e., arrangements have been made

56. **wherewithal:** by means of which

59. **gathering head:** reaching culmination or crisis (The image is from the maturing of a boil or abscess just before it breaks.)

62. **helping him:** i.e., since you helped him

65. **ne'er so little:** i.e., ever **so little,** even a **little** bit

67. **love of:** perhaps, **love** between; or, perhaps, (the king's) **love of; converts:** changes

68. **That fear:** i.e., **that fear** changes; **one or both:** perhaps, the **unrightful** king (line 64) or his supporter, or both of them

69. **worthy:** well-deserved

70. **there an end:** a phrase signaling that a topic of conversation is concluded

71. **Take leave:** i.e., say farewell; **and part:** and separate; **must part:** must depart

75. **unkiss:** i.e., undo with a kiss

79. **pines the clime:** afflicts the region

82. **Hallowmas:** i.e., November 1; **short'st of day:** i.e., the winter solstice (which occurs in December)

NORTHUMBERLAND
My lord, the mind of Bolingbroke is changed.
You must to Pomfret, not unto the Tower.—
And madam, there is order ta'en for you.
With all swift speed you must away to France. 55

KING RICHARD
Northumberland, thou ladder wherewithal
The mounting Bolingbroke ascends my throne,
The time shall not be many hours of age
More than it is ere foul sin, gathering head,
Shall break into corruption. Thou shalt think, 60
Though he divide the realm and give thee half,
It is too little, helping him to all.
He shall think that thou, which knowest the way
To plant unrightful kings, wilt know again,
Being ne'er so little urged another way, 65
To pluck him headlong from the usurped throne.
The love of wicked men converts to fear,
That fear to hate, and hate turns one or both
To worthy danger and deservèd death.

NORTHUMBERLAND
My guilt be on my head, and there an end. 70
Take leave and part, for you must part forthwith.

KING RICHARD
Doubly divorced! Bad men, you violate
A twofold marriage—twixt my crown and me,
And then betwixt me and my married wife.
⌜*To Queen.*⌝ Let me unkiss the oath twixt thee and 75
me;
And yet not so, for with a kiss 'twas made.—
Part us, Northumberland, I towards the north,
Where shivering cold and sickness pines the clime;
My wife to France, from whence set forth in pomp 80
She came adornèd hither like sweet May,
Sent back like Hallowmas or short'st of day.

86. **little policy:** i.e., bad politics

90. **Better far off:** i.e., it is **better** to be **far** apart; **ne'er the near:** a proverbial expression, "never the nearer," that means "no closer to achieving the good desired"

94. **piece the way out:** i.e., make the journey seem longer

97. **dumbly:** silently

99–100. **'Twere ... me:** i.e., it would not be a **good part** for **me** to play

100. **keep and kill thy heart:** i.e., **keep** your **heart** and (through my grief) **to kill** it

103. **make woe wanton:** perhaps, we luxuriate in **woe; fond:** (1) loving; (2) foolish, pointless

"A lion and the king of beasts." (5.1.34)

From John Speed, *A prospect of the most famous parts of the world* ... (1631).

QUEEN
　And must we be divided? Must we part?
KING RICHARD
　Ay, hand from hand, my love, and heart from heart.
QUEEN, ⌜*to Northumberland*⌝
　Banish us both, and send the King with me.　　　　85
⌜**NORTHUMBERLAND**⌝
　That were some love, but little policy.
QUEEN
　Then whither he goes, thither let me go.
KING RICHARD
　So two together weeping make one woe.
　Weep thou for me in France, I for thee here;
　Better far off than, near, be ne'er the near.　　　　90
　Go, count thy way with sighs, I mine with groans.
QUEEN
　So longest way shall have the longest moans.
KING RICHARD
　Twice for one step I'll groan, the way being short,
　And piece the way out with a heavy heart.
　Come, come, in wooing sorrow let's be brief,　　　　95
　Since, wedding it, there is such length in grief.
　One kiss shall stop our mouths, and dumbly part.
　Thus give I mine, and thus take I thy heart.
　　　　　　　　　　　　　　　　　⌜*They kiss.*⌝
QUEEN
　Give me mine own again. 'Twere no good part
　To take on me to keep and kill thy heart.　　　　100
　　　　　　　　　　　　　　　　　⌜*They kiss.*⌝
　So, now I have mine own again, begone,
　That I may strive to kill it with a groan.
KING RICHARD
　We make woe wanton with this fond delay.
　Once more, adieu! The rest let sorrow say.
　　　　　　　　　　　　　　　　　They exit.

5.2 The duke of York expresses his sympathy for Richard but declares his allegiance to King Henry. When York discovers that his son Aumerle is part of a conspiracy to kill Henry, York rides off to inform on his son. Aumerle and his mother also set off for the court to beg Henry's mercy.

----

3. **cousins:** kinsmen
4. **leave:** i.e., **leave** off
5. **stop:** pause, breaking off
6. **rude:** rough, violent; **windows' tops:** upper windows
10. **Which . . . know:** i.e., **which seemed to know** its **aspiring rider**
18. **painted imagery:** "The faces in the windows are compared to a **painted** cloth or mural, like those that sometimes graced civic pageantry" (Dawson and Yachnin). **at once:** all together
21. **Bareheaded, lower than:** i.e., with his hat removed and bowing even **lower than**
22. **Bespake:** addressed
23. **still:** continually
26. **well-graced:** i.e., popular; charming
27. **idly:** carelessly, indifferently

⌜Scene 2⌝
Enter Duke of York and the Duchess.

DUCHESS
My lord, you told me you would tell the rest,
When weeping made you break the story off
Of our two cousins coming into London.

YORK
Where did I leave?

DUCHESS   At that sad stop, my lord,   5
Where rude misgoverned hands from windows' tops
Threw dust and rubbish on King Richard's head.

YORK
Then, as I said, the Duke, great Bolingbroke,
Mounted upon a hot and fiery steed,
Which his aspiring rider seemed to know,   10
With slow but stately pace kept on his course,
Whilst all tongues cried "God save thee,
    Bolingbroke!"
You would have thought the very windows spake,
So many greedy looks of young and old   15
Through casements darted their desiring eyes
Upon his visage, and that all the walls
With painted imagery had said at once
"Jesu preserve thee! Welcome, Bolingbroke!"
Whilst he, from the one side to the other turning,   20
Bareheaded, lower than his proud steed's neck,
Bespake them thus: "I thank you, countrymen."
And thus still doing, thus he passed along.

DUCHESS
Alack, poor Richard! Where rode he the whilst?

YORK
As in a theater the eyes of men,   25
After a well-graced actor leaves the stage,
Are idly bent on him that enters next,
Thinking his prattle to be tedious,

35. **combating:** pronounced **còmbating**

36. **badges:** insignia (his **tears** signifying his **grief,** his **smiles** signifying his **patience,** his willingness to accept suffering)

38. **perforce:** necessarily

39. **barbarism itself have:** i.e., even savages would **have**

41. **bound:** made fast, tied

43. **state:** position; greatness; **for aye:** forever; **allow:** accept; or, approve

45. **Aumerle that was:** According to Holinshed, the duke of York's son was stripped of his title as duke of Aumerle on Bolingbroke's accession. He retained his title as earl of **Rutland.**

48. **truth:** loyalty

50. **violets:** i.e., favorites; or, newly created nobles

51. **new-come spring:** i.e., new king

53. **had as lief be none as one:** i.e., would just as soon not **be one** of them

54. **bear you:** i.e., conduct yourself (with a pun on **bear** [bring forth leaves or fruit] that, along with the words **cropped** [cut] and **prime** [full bloom], continues the imagery of growth in the new springtime)

56–57. **jousts and triumphs:** tournaments and pageants (See longer note, page 227.)

Even so, or with much more contempt, men's eyes
Did scowl on gentle Richard. No man cried "God   30
  save him!"
No joyful tongue gave him his welcome home,
But dust was thrown upon his sacred head,
Which with such gentle sorrow he shook off,
His face still combating with tears and smiles,   35
The badges of his grief and patience,
That had not God for some strong purpose steeled
The hearts of men, they must perforce have melted,
And barbarism itself have pitied him.
But heaven hath a hand in these events,   40
To whose high will we bound our calm contents.
To Bolingbroke are we sworn subjects now,
Whose state and honor I for aye allow.

⌜*Enter Aumerle.*⌝

DUCHESS
  Here comes my son Aumerle.
YORK   Aumerle that was;   45
  But that is lost for being Richard's friend,
  And, madam, you must call him Rutland now.
  I am in parliament pledge for his truth
  And lasting fealty to the new-made king.
DUCHESS
  Welcome, my son. Who are the violets now   50
  That strew the green lap of the new-come spring?
AUMERLE
  Madam, I know not, nor I greatly care not.
  God knows I had as lief be none as one.
YORK
  Well, bear you well in this new spring of time,
  Lest you be cropped before you come to prime.   55
  What news from Oxford? Do these jousts and
    triumphs hold?
AUMERLE   For aught I know, my lord, they do.

61. **seal:** i.e., the wax **seal** attached to a document; **without:** outside of; **bosom:** i.e., pocket (literally, receptacle for money and papers over the breast)

66. **to pardon me:** i.e., to excuse me (from showing it)

67. **a matter:** something

68. **would not have seen:** i.e., wish no one to see

72. **bond that he is entered into:** i.e., document he has signed promising to pay (a certain amount of money)

73. **gay apparel:** fine clothes; **'gainst:** in preparation for

74. **Bound to himself:** i.e., why would he have signed a bond with himself; **What doth he with:** i.e., why would he be in possession of

YORK You will be there, I know.

AUMERLE If God prevent not, I purpose so.   60

YORK
  What seal is that that hangs without thy bosom?
  Yea, lookst thou pale? Let me see the writing.

AUMERLE
  My lord, 'tis nothing.

YORK   No matter, then, who see it.
  I will be satisfied. Let me see the writing.   65

AUMERLE
  I do beseech your Grace to pardon me.
  It is a matter of small consequence,
  Which for some reasons I would not have seen.

YORK
  Which for some reasons, sir, I mean to see.
  I fear, I fear—   70

DUCHESS   What should you fear?
  'Tis nothing but some bond that he is entered into
  For gay apparel 'gainst the triumph day.

YORK
  Bound to himself? What doth he with a bond
  That he is bound to? Wife, thou art a fool.—   75
  Boy, let me see the writing.

AUMERLE
  I do beseech you, pardon me. I may not show it.

YORK
  I will be satisfied. Let me see it, I say.
            He plucks it out of his bosom and reads it.

YORK
  Treason! Foul treason! Villain, traitor, slave!

DUCHESS What is the matter, my lord?   80

YORK, ⌈*calling offstage*⌉
  Ho, who is within there? Saddle my horse!—
  God for his mercy, what treachery is here!

DUCHESS Why, what is it, my lord?

86. **appeach:** accuse, inform against

91. **answer:** i.e., **answer** for

93. **will:** i.e., **will** go

93 SD. **man:** servant

94. **him:** i.e., the servant; **amazed:** dumbfounded

99. **like:** likely

100. **teeming date:** childbearing period; **drunk up with:** i.e., swallowed up completely by, exhausted by

101. **mine age:** i.e., me in my old **age**

104. **fond:** foolish

106. **ta'en the sacrament:** received the Eucharist (See picture, below.)

107. **interchangeably set down their hands:** reciprocally signed their names (legal terminology)

109. **be none:** i.e., not be one of them

Taking "the sacrament." (4.1.341; 5.2.106)
From [Richard Day,] *A booke of christian prayers . . .* (1578).

YORK, ⌜*calling offstage*⌝
  Give me my boots, I say! Saddle my horse!—
  Now by mine honor, by my life, by my troth,   85
  I will appeach the villain.
DUCHESS   What is the matter?
YORK   Peace, foolish woman.
DUCHESS
  I will not peace!—What is the matter, Aumerle?
AUMERLE
  Good mother, be content. It is no more   90
  Than my poor life must answer.
DUCHESS   Thy life answer?
YORK, ⌜*calling offstage*⌝
  Bring me my boots!—I will unto the King.

     His man enters with his boots.

DUCHESS
  Strike him, Aumerle! Poor boy, thou art amazed.—
  Hence, villain, never more come in my sight.   95
YORK   Give me my boots, I say.
  ⌜*His man helps him on with his boots, then exits.*⌝
DUCHESS   Why, York, what wilt thou do?
  Wilt thou not hide the trespass of thine own?
  Have we more sons? Or are we like to have?
  Is not my teeming date drunk up with time?   100
  And wilt thou pluck my fair son from mine age
  And rob me of a happy mother's name?
  Is he not like thee? Is he not thine own?
YORK   Thou fond mad woman,
  Wilt thou conceal this dark conspiracy?   105
  A dozen of them here have ta'en the sacrament
  And interchangeably set down their hands
  To kill the King at Oxford.
DUCHESS
  He shall be none. We'll keep him here.
  Then what is that to him?   110

114. **pitiful:** compassionate

123. **his horse:** i.e., one of York's horses

124. **Spur post:** ride using relays of post-horses (According to the various chronicles, it was "riding **post**" that enabled Aumerle to outride his father and reach the court before him.)

125. **thy pardon:** i.e., **pardon** for yourself

5.3 Aumerle reaches King Henry and begs a pardon for an unnamed offence. The duke of York arrives and reveals the plot at Oxford and Aumerle's part in it. The duchess arrives, and the three kneel to Henry, York begging for Aumerle's death and the duchess and Aumerle begging the king's mercy. The king pardons Aumerle and sends out forces to capture the other conspirators.

1. **unthrifty:** dissolute; **son:** i.e., Prince Hal, who becomes King Henry V

2. **full:** fully

3. **us:** i.e., me (the royal "we," which King Henry uses off and on throughout this scene)

6. **frequent:** resort, visit (Accent on second syllable.)

YORK
Away, fond woman! Were he twenty times my son,
I would appeach him.

DUCHESS
Hadst thou groaned for him as I have done,
Thou wouldst be more pitiful.
But now I know thy mind: thou dost suspect   115
That I have been disloyal to thy bed
And that he is a bastard, not thy son.
Sweet York, sweet husband, be not of that mind!
He is as like thee as a man may be,
Not like to me or any of my kin,   120
And yet I love him.

YORK   Make way, unruly woman!
He exits.

DUCHESS
After, Aumerle! Mount thee upon his horse,
Spur post, and get before him to the King,
And beg thy pardon ere he do accuse thee.   125
I'll not be long behind. Though I be old,
I doubt not but to ride as fast as York.
And never will I rise up from the ground
Till Bolingbroke have pardoned thee. Away, begone!
⌜*They exit.*⌝

⌜Scene 3⌝
Enter the King with his Nobles.

KING HENRY
Can no man tell me of my unthrifty son?
'Tis full three months since I did see him last.
If any plague hang over us, 'tis he.
I would to God, my lords, he might be found.
Inquire at London, 'mongst the taverns there,   5
For there, they say, he daily doth frequent

7. **loose:** unprincipled, immoral; **companions:** fellows (a term of contempt)

9. **watch:** watchmen, guards; **passengers:** passersby

10. **wanton:** spoiled, rebellious; **effeminate:** rebellious; self-indulgent

11. **on the point:** i.e., as a **point**

14. **held:** i.e., to be **held**

15. **gallant:** fine gentleman

16. **would unto:** i.e., **would** go into; **stews:** brothels

17. **common'st creature:** i.e., most disreputable whore

18. **favor:** i.e., token of her **favor**

19. **lustiest:** most vigorous

22. **happily:** i.e., with good fortune

22 SD. **amazed:** i.e., looking panic-stricken

27. **conference:** conversation

32. **Unless a pardon:** i.e., **unless** you grant **a pardon**

With unrestrainèd loose companions,
Even such, they say, as stand in narrow lanes
And beat our watch and rob our passengers,
⌜While⌝ he, young wanton and effeminate boy,   10
Takes on the point of honor to support
So dissolute a crew.

PERCY
My lord, some two days since I saw the Prince,
And told him of those triumphs held at Oxford.

KING HENRY   And what said the gallant?   15

PERCY
His answer was, he would unto the stews,
And from the common'st creature pluck a glove
And wear it as a favor, and with that
He would unhorse the lustiest challenger.

KING HENRY
As dissolute as desperate. Yet through both   20
I see some sparks of better hope, which elder years
May happily bring forth. But who comes here?

Enter Aumerle amazed.

AUMERLE   Where is the King?

KING HENRY
What means our cousin, that he stares and looks so
    wildly?   25

AUMERLE
God save your Grace. I do beseech your Majesty
To have some conference with your Grace alone.

KING HENRY, ⌜*to his Nobles*⌝
Withdraw yourselves, and leave us here alone.
                              ⌜*The Nobles exit.*⌝
What is the matter with our cousin now?

AUMERLE, ⌜*kneeling*⌝
Forever may my knees grow to the earth,   30
My tongue cleave to my roof within my mouth,
Unless a pardon ere I rise or speak.

34. **on the first:** i.e., of **the first** kind (of **fault**)
39. **to:** after
41. **make thee safe:** render you harmless
42. **Stay:** hold
43. **secure:** careless, overconfident
50. **my haste:** i.e., my breathlessness (from riding so fast); **forbids me show:** keeps me from revealing
51. **thy promise passed:** i.e., the **promise** of a pardon that you made
53. **hand:** signature (with wordplay in line 54)
55. **bosom:** See note to 5.2.61.

Henry IV.
From John Speed, *A prospect of the most famous parts of the world* (1631).

KING HENRY
 Intended or committed was this fault?
 If on the first, how heinous e'er it be,
 To win thy after-love I pardon thee.   35
AUMERLE, ⌐*standing*¬
 Then give me leave that ⌐I¬ may turn the key
 That no man enter till my tale be done.
KING HENRY   Have thy desire. ⌐*Aumerle locks the door.*¬
     The Duke of York knocks at the door and crieth.
YORK, ⌐*within*¬
 My liege, beware! Look to thyself!
 Thou hast a traitor in thy presence there.   40
KING HENRY, ⌐*to Aumerle*¬   Villain, I'll make thee safe.
     ⌐*He draws his sword.*¬
AUMERLE
 Stay thy revengeful hand. Thou hast no cause to fear.
YORK, ⌐*within*¬
 Open the door, secure, foolhardy king!
 Shall I for love speak treason to thy face?
 Open the door, or I will break it open.   45
     ⌐*King Henry unlocks the door.*¬

     ⌐*Enter York.*¬

KING HENRY   What is the matter, uncle? Speak.
 Recover breath. Tell us how near is danger
 That we may arm us to encounter it.
YORK, ⌐*giving King Henry a paper*¬
 Peruse this writing here, and thou shalt know
 The treason that my haste forbids me show.   50
AUMERLE, ⌐*to King Henry*¬
 Remember, as thou read'st, thy promise passed.
 I do repent me. Read not my name there.
 My heart is not confederate with my hand.
YORK
 It was, villain, ere thy hand did set it down.—
 I tore it from the traitor's bosom, king.   55

57. **Forget:** i.e., **forget** your promise
61. **sheer:** clear, pure
62. **this stream:** i.e., Aumerle
64. **overflow:** i.e., excess; **converts:** changes (in Aumerle)
66. **digressing:** transgressing
67. **bawd:** procurer, go-between (in serving his wickedness)
69. **scraping:** frugal
72. **in his life:** i.e., in allowing him to live
73. **true:** loyal, honorable
79. **scene:** performance
80. **The Beggar . . . King:** probably an allusion to the title of a familiar ballad, "**King** Cophetua and **the Beggar** Maid"

A cormorant. (2.1.43)
From Ulisse Aldrovandi, . . . *Ornithologiae* . . . (1599–1603).

Fear, and not love, begets his penitence.
Forget to pity him, lest thy pity prove
A serpent that will sting thee to the heart.

KING HENRY
O heinous, strong, and bold conspiracy!
O loyal father of a treacherous son,   60
Thou sheer, immaculate, and silver fountain
From whence this stream, through muddy passages,
Hath held his current and defiled himself,
Thy overflow of good converts to bad,
And thy abundant goodness shall excuse   65
This deadly blot in thy digressing son.

YORK
So shall my virtue be his vice's bawd,
And he shall spend mine honor with his shame,
As thriftless sons their scraping fathers' gold.
Mine honor lives when his dishonor dies,   70
Or my shamed life in his dishonor lies.
Thou kill'st me in his life: giving him breath,
The traitor lives, the true man's put to death.

DUCHESS, ⌐within¬
What ho, my liege! For God's sake, let me in!

KING HENRY
What ⌐shrill-voiced¬ suppliant makes this eager cry?   75

DUCHESS, ⌐within¬
A woman and thy aunt, great king. 'Tis I.
Speak with me, pity me. Open the door!
A beggar begs that never begged before.

KING HENRY
Our scene is altered from a serious thing
And now changed to "The Beggar and the King."—   80
My dangerous cousin, let your mother in.
I know she is come to pray for your foul sin.
                                ⌐*Aumerle opens the door.*¬

          ⌐*Duchess of York enters and kneels.*¬

83. **whosoever pray:** i.e., whoever begs you for pardon

84. **for this:** i.e., because of **this**

85–86. **This festered joint ... confound:** See Matthew 5.30: "... if thy right hand make thee to offend, cut it off and cast it from thee. For better it is for thee that one of thy members perish than that thy whole body should be cast into hell." **let alone:** left untreated, or left in place **confound:** destroy

88. **none other can:** i.e., **can** love no one else

89. **frantic:** mad; **make:** i.e., do

90. **rear:** foster, nourish

105. **faintly:** feebly; **would be:** wishes to be

108. **still:** continue to

A pattern for planting a garden knot. (3.4.49)
From Charles Estienne, *Maison rustique . . .* (1606).

YORK
  If thou do pardon whosoever pray,
  More sins for this forgiveness prosper may.
  This festered joint cut off, the rest rest sound.   85
  This let alone will all the rest confound.

DUCHESS
  O king, believe not this hard-hearted man.
  Love loving not itself, none other can.

YORK
  Thou frantic woman, what dost thou make here?
  Shall thy old dugs once more a traitor rear?   90

DUCHESS
  Sweet York, be patient.—Hear me, gentle liege.

KING HENRY
  Rise up, good aunt.

DUCHESS   Not yet, I thee beseech.
  Forever will I walk upon my knees
  And never see day that the happy sees,   95
  Till thou give joy, until thou bid me joy
  By pardoning Rutland, my transgressing boy.

AUMERLE, ⌈*kneeling*⌉
  Unto my mother's prayers I bend my knee.

YORK, ⌈*kneeling*⌉
  Against them both my true joints bended be.
  Ill mayst thou thrive if thou grant any grace.   100

DUCHESS
  Pleads he in earnest? Look upon his face.
  His eyes do drop no tears, his prayers are in jest;
  His words come from his mouth, ours from our
    breast.
  He prays but faintly and would be denied.   105
  We pray with heart and soul and all beside.
  His weary joints would gladly rise, I know.
  Our knees still kneel till to the ground they grow.
  His prayers are full of false hypocrisy,
  Ours of true zeal and deep integrity.   110

116. **An if:** i.e., **if; nurse . . . teach:** i.e., nurse-maid, teaching you to speak

121. **meet:** fitting, suitable

122. **pardonne moy:** i.e., *pardonnez-moi* (a courteous form of refusal)

128. **chopping:** jerky, broken

133. **rehearse:** repeat

135. **sue:** petition

138. **happy vantage:** fortunate advantage

139. **Yet:** still

140. **pardon twain:** divide a **pardon** in two

Garden Rue.

Rue, or "herb of grace." (3.4.112)
From John Gerard, *The herball or generall historie of plantes . . .* (1597).

Our prayers do outpray his. Then let them have
That mercy which true prayer ought to have.
⌜KING HENRY⌝
Good aunt, stand up.
DUCHESS   Nay, do not say "stand up."
Say "pardon" first and afterwards "stand up."   115
An if I were thy nurse, thy tongue to teach,
"Pardon" should be the first word of thy speech.
I never longed to hear a word till now.
Say "pardon," king; let pity teach thee how.
The word is short, but not so short as sweet.   120
No word like "pardon" for kings' mouths so meet.
YORK
Speak it in French, king. Say "pardonne moy."
DUCHESS
Dost thou teach pardon pardon to destroy?
Ah, my sour husband, my hard-hearted lord,
That sets the word itself against the word!   125
⌜*To King Henry.*⌝ Speak "pardon" as 'tis current in
    our land;
The chopping French we do not understand.
Thine eye begins to speak; set thy tongue there,
Or in thy piteous heart plant thou thine ear,   130
That, hearing how our plaints and prayers do
    pierce,
Pity may move thee "pardon" to rehearse.
KING HENRY
Good aunt, stand up.
DUCHESS   I do not sue to stand.   135
Pardon is all the suit I have in hand.
KING HENRY
I pardon him, as God shall pardon me.
DUCHESS
O, happy vantage of a kneeling knee!
Yet am I sick for fear. Speak it again.
Twice saying "pardon" doth not pardon twain,   140
But makes one pardon strong.

144. **But for:** i.e., as for; **brother-in-law:** the duke of Exeter, married to Bolingbroke's sister Elizabeth; **the Abbot:** i.e., abbot of Westminster (See 4.1.334–47.)

145. **consorted crew:** i.e., gang in league together
146. **straight:** straightway, immediately
147. **powers:** forces
152. **true:** loyal

5.4 Sir Pierce Exton, reflecting on King Henry's wish that Richard be removed, decides to carry out that wish.

————————

1. **mark:** hear, note
8. **wishtly:** intently
12. **rid:** get rid of, destroy

Torture by pressing (3.4.78)
From *The life and death of Griffin Flood informer* . . . (1623).

206

KING HENRY   I pardon him with all my heart.
DUCHESS   A god on Earth thou art.
⌜*They all stand.*⌝
KING HENRY
But for our trusty brother-in-law and the Abbot,
With all the rest of that consorted crew,   145
Destruction straight shall dog them at the heels.
Good uncle, help to order several powers
To Oxford or where'er these traitors are.
They shall not live within this world, I swear,
But I will have them, if I once know where.   150
Uncle, farewell,—and cousin, adieu.
Your mother well hath prayed; and prove you true.
DUCHESS, ⌜*to Aumerle*⌝
Come, my old son. I pray God make thee new.
They exit.

⌜Scene 4⌝
⌜*Enter*⌝ Sir Pierce Exton and ⌜*Servants.*⌝

EXTON
Didst thou not mark the King, what words he spake,
"Have I no friend will rid me of this living fear?"
Was it not so?
SERVINGMAN   These were his very words.
EXTON
"Have I no friend?" quoth he. He spake it twice   5
And urged it twice together, did he not?
SERVINGMAN   He did.
EXTON
And speaking it, he wishtly looked on me,
As who should say "I would thou wert the man
That would divorce this terror from my heart"—   10
Meaning the king at Pomfret. Come, let's go.
I am the King's friend and will rid his foe.
⌜*They exit.*⌝

5.5 Richard, imprisoned at Pontefract Castle, is visited by a former groom of his stable and then by the prison Keeper. Exton and his men enter with weapons. Richard kills several of the men before Exton kills him.

---

2. **unto:** i.e., to, with

3. **for because:** i.e., **because**

5. **hammer it out:** work **it out**

6–8. **My brain . . . thoughts:** As begetters of **thoughts, my brain** will play **the female** role and **my soul** the male. **prove:** show to be **still-breeding thoughts:** i.e., **thoughts** that will continue to breed more **thoughts**

9. **people this little world:** i.e., will **people this prison where I live** (line 2)

10. **humors:** dispositions, temperaments; **this world:** i.e., the real **world**

11. **sort:** i.e., class (of thought)

12. **As:** i.e., for example

13. **scruples:** doubts

14. **Come, little ones:** See Matthew 19.14: "Suffer the little children . . . to come to me. . . ."

16–17. **It is . . . eye:** See Matthew 19.24. "It is easier for a camel to go through the eye of a needle, than for a rich man to enter into the kingdom of God." **postern:** narrow gate

19. **vain:** worthless

20. **flinty ribs:** i.e., stone **walls** (line 21)

21. **ragged:** rough

22. **for they:** because the nails; **die:** i.e., the ambitious thoughts **die**

(continued)

⌜Scene 5⌝
Enter Richard alone.

RICHARD
　I have been studying how I may compare
　This prison where I live unto the world,
　And for because the world is populous
　And here is not a creature but myself,
　I cannot do it. Yet I'll hammer it out.   5
　My brain I'll prove the female to my soul,
　My soul the father, and these two beget
　A generation of still-breeding thoughts,
　And these same thoughts people this little world,
　In humors like the people of this world,   10
　For no thought is contented. The better sort,
　As thoughts of things divine, are intermixed
　With scruples, and do set the word itself
　Against the word, as thus: "Come, little ones,"
　And then again,   15
　"It is as hard to come as for a camel
　To thread the postern of a small needle's eye."
　Thoughts tending to ambition, they do plot
　Unlikely wonders: how these vain weak nails
　May tear a passage through the flinty ribs   20
　Of this hard world, my ragged prison walls,
　And, for they cannot, die in their own pride.
　Thoughts tending to content flatter themselves
　That they are not the first of fortune's slaves,
　Nor shall not be the last—like silly beggars   25
　Who, sitting in the stocks, refuge their shame
　That many have and others must ⌜sit⌝ there,
　And in this thought they find a kind of ease,
　Bearing their own misfortunes on the back
　Of such as have before endured the like.   30
　Thus play I in one person many people,
　And none contented. Sometimes am I king.

24. **of fortune's slaves:** i.e., to become **slaves** to fortune

25. **silly:** simpleminded

26. **stocks:** an instrument of punishment in which the feet of the person being punished were clamped into a heavy timber frame (See picture, page 216.) **refuge their shame:** i.e., find refuge for **their shame** (in the thought)

38. **straight:** straightway, immediately

39. **Nor . . . nor:** neither . . . **nor**

41. **With being nothing:** i.e., with death

44. **time is broke:** i.e., rhythm is faulty

46. **daintiness:** delicacy, refinement

47. **check time broke:** i.e., rebuke faulty rhythm; **string:** i.e., stringed instrument

48. **concord:** harmony

51. **numb'ring clock:** i.e., **clock** with which **time** numbers the hours

52–53. **with . . . watch:** i.e., by means of **sighs**, which occur at regular intervals, **my thoughts** are impelled, as units of time (**watches**), to my eyes, which are like the face of a clock   **outward watch:** i.e., the face of the clock

54. **dial's point:** hand of the clock

55. **still:** continually

60. **posting:** hurrying

61. **jack of the clock:** i.e., figure that strikes the bell on the outside of a **clock** (See picture, page 212.)

62. **mads:** i.e., maddens

63. **have holp:** i.e., has helped

65. **gives it me:** i.e., **gives it** to **me**

67. **strange brooch:** rare jewel

Then treasons make me wish myself a beggar,
And so I am; then crushing penury
Persuades me I was better when a king.   35
Then am I kinged again, and by and by
Think that I am unkinged by Bolingbroke,
And straight am nothing. But whate'er I be,
Nor I nor any man that but man is
With nothing shall be pleased till he be eased   40
With being nothing. (*The music plays.*) Music do I
    hear?
Ha, ha, keep time! How sour sweet music is
When time is broke and no proportion kept.
So is it in the music of men's lives.   45
And here have I the daintiness of ear
To check time broke in a disordered string;
But for the concord of my state and time
Had not an ear to hear my true time broke.
I wasted time, and now doth time waste me;   50
For now hath time made me his numb'ring clock.
My thoughts are minutes, and with sighs they jar
Their watches on unto mine eyes, the outward watch,
Whereto my finger, like a dial's point,
Is pointing still in cleansing them from tears.   55
Now, sir, the sound that tells what hour it is
Are clamorous groans which strike upon my heart,
Which is the bell. So sighs and tears and groans
Show minutes, times, and hours. But my time
Runs posting on in Bolingbroke's proud joy,   60
While I stand fooling here, his jack of the clock.
This music mads me. Let it sound no more,
For though it have holp madmen to their wits,
In me it seems it will make wise men mad.
Yet blessing on his heart that gives it me,   65
For 'tis a sign of love, and love to Richard
Is a strange brooch in this all-hating world.

Enter a Groom of the stable.

69–70. noble ... dear: Richard responds to being called **royal prince** by claiming the Groom as his equal (**peer**), and by playing with the fact that a **royal** (a coin worth ten shillings) exceeded a **noble** (a coin worth about seven shillings) by about **ten groats**. **dear:** expensive, precious, costly

71. how ... hither: i.e., **how** did you gain access

76. ado: trouble, fuss

78. earned: grieved

82. dressed: groomed

84. went he: i.e., did the horse go; **him:** Bolingbroke

88. clapping: patting

90. pride ... fall: proverbial

96. jauncing: prancing

96 SD. meat: food

Two "jack[s] of the clock." (5.5.61)
From Angelo Rocca, *De campanis commentarius* ... (1612).

GROOM   Hail, royal prince!
RICHARD   Thanks, noble peer.
  The cheapest of us is ten groats too dear.   70
  What art thou, and how comest thou hither,
  Where no man never comes but that sad dog
  That brings me food to make misfortune live?
GROOM
  I was a poor groom of thy stable, king,
  When thou wert king; who, traveling towards York,   75
  With much ado at length have gotten leave
  To look upon my sometime royal master's face.
  O, how it earned my heart when I beheld
  In London streets, that coronation day,
  When Bolingbroke rode on roan Barbary,   80
  That horse that thou so often hast bestrid,
  That horse that I so carefully have dressed.
RICHARD
  Rode he on Barbary? Tell me, gentle friend,
  How went he under him?
GROOM
  So proudly as if he disdained the ground.   85
RICHARD
  So proud that Bolingbroke was on his back!
  That jade hath eat bread from my royal hand;
  This hand hath made him proud with clapping him.
  Would he not stumble? Would he not fall down
  (Since pride must have a fall) and break the neck   90
  Of that proud man that did usurp his back?
  Forgiveness, horse! Why do I rail on thee,
  Since thou, created to be awed by man,
  Wast born to bear? I was not made a horse,
  And yet I bear a burden like an ass,   95
  Spurred, galled, and tired by jauncing Bolingbroke.

    Enter one, ⌐the Keeper,¬ to Richard with meat.

97. **give place:** yield your **place** (to me)

101. **Taste of it first:** Part of the duty of the person serving food to a king was to **taste it first** to make sure it was not poisoned. **wont:** accustomed

110 SD. **kills another:** According to Holinshed, "Sir Piers entered the chamber, well armed, with eight tall men likewise armed, every of them having a bill in his hand. King Richard . . . stepping to the foremost man, wrung the bill out of his hands and so valiantly defended himself that he slew four of those that thus came to assail him." (A bill was a long-handled pointed and bladed weapon.)

112. **staggers thus my person:** i.e., thus knocks me down (literally, causes me to stagger)

115. **seat:** throne

116. **gross:** i.e., mortal (literally, material, perceptible to the senses)

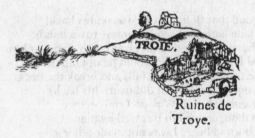

Ruins of Troy. (5.1.11)
From Pierre Belon, *Les observations . . .* (1588).

KEEPER, ⌜*to Groom*⌝
   Fellow, give place. Here is no longer stay.
RICHARD, ⌜*to Groom*⌝
   If thou love me, 'tis time thou wert away.
GROOM
   What my tongue dares not, that my heart shall say.
                                         Groom exits.
KEEPER   My lord, will 't please you to fall to?   100
RICHARD
   Taste of it first as thou art wont to do.
KEEPER
   My lord, I dare not. Sir Pierce of Exton,
   Who lately came from the King, commands the
      contrary.
RICHARD, ⌜*attacking the Keeper*⌝
   The devil take Henry of Lancaster and thee!   105
   Patience is stale, and I am weary of it.
KEEPER   Help, help, help!

      The Murderers ⌜*Exton and his men*⌝ *rush in.*

RICHARD
   How now, what means death in this rude assault?
   Villain, thy own hand yields thy death's instrument.
                   ⌜*Richard seizes a weapon from a Murderer*
                              and kills him with it.⌝
   Go thou and fill another room in hell.   110
                   ⌜*He kills another Murderer.*⌝
                   Here Exton strikes him down.
   That hand shall burn in never-quenching fire
   That staggers thus my person. Exton, thy fierce hand
   Hath with the King's blood stained the King's own
      land.
   Mount, mount, my soul. Thy seat is up on high,   115
   Whilst my gross flesh sinks downward, here to die.
                              ⌜*He dies.*⌝

5.6 News is brought to Henry about the capture and punishment of rebel leaders. Henry pardons the bishop of Carlisle. Exton enters with Richard's body and is banished for the murder. Henry vows to launch a crusade to the Holy Land to wash off his own guilt.

---

2. **rebels:** See 5.3.144–50.
3. **Ciceter:** i.e., Cirencester
4. **they:** i.e., the rebels
9. **taking:** capture
10. **At large discoursèd:** explained in full
11. **Percy:** The earl of Northumberland was named Henry **Percy.**

A man "sitting in the stocks." (5.5.26)
From August Casimir Redel, *Apophtegmata symbolica* . . . (n.d.).

EXTON
　As full of valor as of royal blood.
　Both have I spilled. O, would the deed were good!
　For now the devil that told me I did well
　Says that this deed is chronicled in hell.   120
　This dead king to the living king I'll bear.
　Take hence the rest and give them burial here.
　　　　　　　　　　　⌜*They exit with the bodies.*⌝

　　　　　　　　⌜Scene 6⌝
　　　Enter ⌜*King Henry,*⌝ *with the Duke of York.*

KING HENRY
　Kind uncle York, the latest news we hear
　Is that the rebels have consumed with fire
　Our town of Ciceter in Gloucestershire,
　But whether they be ta'en or slain we hear not.

　　　　　　Enter Northumberland.

　Welcome, my lord. What is the news?   5
NORTHUMBERLAND
　First, to thy sacred state wish I all happiness.
　The next news is: I have to London sent
　The heads of Oxford, Salisbury, Blunt, and Kent.
　The manner of their taking may appear
　At large discoursèd in this paper here.   10
　　　　　　　⌜*He gives King Henry a paper.*⌝

KING HENRY
　We thank thee, gentle Percy, for thy pains,
　And to thy worth will add right worthy gains.

　　　　　　Enter Lord Fitzwater.

FITZWATER
　My lord, I have from Oxford sent to London
　The heads of Brocas and Sir Bennet Seely,

15. **consorted:** i.e., conspiring (See 5.3.145.)

18. **wot:** know

19. **Abbot of Westminster:** See 4.1.334–47.

20. **clog:** See note to 1.3.204 and picture, below.

22. **abide:** submissively await

23. **doom and sentence of:** judgment **and sentence** on

25. **some reverend room:** i.e., a place suitable for the religious life or religious retirement

35. **deed of slander:** i.e., **deed** that will bring disgrace

38. **They love . . . need:** Compare the proverb, "to **love** the treason but hate the traitor."

Burdened with a clog. (1.3.204; 5.6.20)
From Geoffrey Whitney, *A choice of emblemes . . .* (1586).

Two of the dangerous consorted traitors   15
That sought at Oxford thy dire overthrow.

KING HENRY
Thy pains, Fitzwater, shall not be forgot.
Right noble is thy merit, well I wot.

Enter ⌈*Harry*⌉ *Percy* ⌈*with the Bishop of Carlisle.*⌉

PERCY
The grand conspirator, Abbot of Westminster,
With clog of conscience and sour melancholy   20
Hath yielded up his body to the grave.
But here is Carlisle living, to abide
Thy kingly doom and sentence of his pride.

KING HENRY   Carlisle, this is your doom:
Choose out some secret place, some reverend room,   25
More than thou hast, and with it joy thy life.
So, as thou liv'st in peace, die free from strife;
For, though mine enemy thou hast ever been,
High sparks of honor in thee have I seen.

Enter Exton ⌈*and Servingmen*⌉ *with the coffin.*

EXTON
Great king, within this coffin I present   30
Thy buried fear. Herein all breathless lies
The mightiest of thy greatest enemies,
Richard of Bourdeaux, by me hither brought.

KING HENRY
Exton, I thank thee not, for thou hast wrought
A deed of slander with thy fatal hand   35
Upon my head and all this famous land.

EXTON
From your own mouth, my lord, did I this deed.

KING HENRY
They love not poison that do poison need,
Nor do I thee. Though I did wish him dead,
I hate the murderer, love him murderèd.   40

43. **with Cain go wander:** See note to 1.1.108–10 for Cain's killing of Abel. For Cain's punishment, see Genesis 4.11–12, where God says to Cain, "Now therefore thou art cursed from the earth. . . . A vagabond . . . shalt thou be in the earth."

45. **protest:** say to you that

48. **sullen black:** i.e., melancholy **black** clothing; **incontinent:** immediately

49. **make a voyage to the Holy Land:** i.e., launch a crusade (See note to 2.1.59–62; see also the opening scene of Shakespeare's *Henry IV, Part 1*.)

51. **Grace:** do honor to

Map of the Holy Land. (5.6.49)
From the Geneva Bible (1562).

The guilt of conscience take thou for thy labor,
But neither my good word nor princely favor.
With Cain go wander through shades of night,
And never show thy head by day nor light.

⌐*Exton exits.*¬

Lords, I protest my soul is full of woe   45
That blood should sprinkle me to make me grow.
Come mourn with me for what I do lament,
And put on sullen black incontinent.
I'll make a voyage to the Holy Land
To wash this blood off from my guilty hand.   50

⌐*Servingmen lift the coffin to carry it out.*¬

March sadly after. Grace my mournings here
In weeping after this untimely bier.

⌐*They exit, following the coffin.*¬

The Tower of London. (5.1.2, 53)
From John Seller, *A book of . . . London . . .* (c. 1700?).

Longer Notes

1.1.103. Duke of Gloucester: Shakespeare would have read in Holinshed's *Chronicles* that in 1397 the duke of Gloucester entered into a conspiracy with several lords of the realm to capture and imprison King Richard and the dukes of Lancaster and York, and to kill the remaining lords of the king's council. The conspiracy was revealed to the king, who had Gloucester arrested and sent to Calais. According to Holinshed (who notes that he took this story "out of an old French pamphlet"), the king ordered "Thomas Mowbray, Earl Marshall" to kill the duke of Gloucester secretly. When "the earl prolonged time for the executing of the king's commandment, though the king would have had it done with all expedition, . . . the king conceived no small displeasure, and swore that it should cost the earl his life if he quickly obeyed not his commandment. The earl thus as it seemed in manner enforced, called out the duke at midnight, as if he should have taken ship to pass over into England, and there in the lodging called the Princes Inn, he caused his servants to cast featherbeds upon him, and so smother him to death, or otherwise to strangle him with towels (as some write)."

1.1.201. face: Many editors insert after this word the Folio's stage direction *"Exit Gaunt."* (This exit does not appear in the First Quarto.) They do so because Gaunt begins the next scene onstage, and rarely in the drama of Shakespeare's time does a character appear onstage at the end of one scene *and* at the beginning of the next. But there are reasons for not including this stage direction from the Folio: (1) since no motive is presented for an exit by Gaunt, his leaving may puzzle an audience or a reader and thus provide a distraction from King Richard's speech; (2) it is most uncommon in the drama of Shakespeare's time for a noble to leave a king's presence without being formally dismissed or excused.

1.3.197. so far as to mine enemy: In the early printed texts, the word **far** is spelled "fare"—a variant spelling of *far* at the time; some editors print "fare," thus linking the line to the journey on which Mowbray will "fare" or travel.

1.3.255–56. Cousin . . . show: Some editors add an exit for Aumerle after this farewell couplet. There is something to be said for this decision, since Aumerle is again onstage at the beginning of the next scene, and, as observed in the longer note to 1.1.201, it is unusual for a character to be onstage at the end of one scene *and* the beginning of the next. Other editors choose not to introduce a stage direction on the grounds that Aumerle in 1.4 describes going with Bolingbroke on the first leg of his journey into exile; to give Aumerle a formal farewell and exit here would set up a contradiction with the dialogue in 1.4. Given this uncertainty, we have chosen not to add a stage direction calling for Aumerle's exit.

1.4.46. farm our royal realm: Holinshed's *Chronicles* reads, "The common bruit ran, that the king had set to farm the realm of England, unto Sir William Scroop, earl of Wiltshire, and then treasurer of England, to Sir John Bushy, Sir John Bagot, and Sir Henry Green, knights." The comment in the margin reads: "The realm let to farm by the king."

1.4.49–51. substitutes . . . sums of gold: These lines appear to be based on the following passage in Holinshed: "Many blank charters were devised and brought into the city [of London], which many of the substantial and wealthy citizens were fain [happy] to seal [in modern terms, to sign], to their great charge [expense] as in the end appeared. And the like [the same sort of] charters were sent abroad into all shires within the realm, whereby great grudge and murmuring arose among the people: for when they were so sealed, the king's officers wrote in the same, what liked them, as well for charging the parties with payment of money, as otherwise." None of these alleged "blank charters" survives among the well-preserved financial records of Richard's reign. Whether or not such documents ever existed, the ambiguity of Holinshed's language ("what liked them . . . otherwise") makes it hard to know with certainty the details of the extortion alleged against Richard in Holinshed and Shakespeare's *Richard II.* Hence the uncertainty expressed in our commentary on lines 49–51.

2.1.211–13. Call in the letters patents that he hath / By his attorneys general to sue / His livery: Holinshed's *Chronicles* records that at the death of the duke of Lancaster, Richard "seized into his hands all the goods that belonged to him [i.e., Lancaster], and also received all the rents and revenues of his lands which ought to have descended unto the duke of Hereford by lawful inheritance, in revoking his letters patents, which he had granted to him before, by virtue whereof he [i.e., Hereford] might make his attorneys general to sue livery for him of any manner of inheritances or possessions that might from thenceforth fall unto him, and that his homage might be respited [remitted] with making reasonable fine: whereby it was evident that the king meant his [Hereford's] utter undoing."

2.1.291. That late broke: Because the *Richard II* text wrongly attributes the escape from Exeter to Lord Cobham, editors assume that a line has been dropped from the text, perhaps cut by the censor. Queen Elizabeth I was hostile toward the earl of Arundel of her own time, whom she had executed in 1595, and she sought to deprive his son of his title and his inheritance; thus references to "the son of the Earl of Arundel" might have seemed inflammatory when *Richard II* was printed in 1597. It was Edmond Malone who, in 1790, added the line that reads in many texts "The son of Richard Earl of Arundel." The addition also affects line 292, since the former archbishop of Canterbury, Thomas Arundel, was, in fact, the brother of Richard, earl of Arundel. Since Malone's line is only a guess (though a plausible one), we have chosen not to add it to the text.

3.1.46. Glendower: Owen Glendower was a Welsh nobleman with connections to both Richard II and Henry IV; he was famous historically for leading a rebellion—"the Welsh Revolt"—against the English. In *Henry IV, Part 1*, Shakespeare presents him as a powerful military leader who claims supernatural powers. In *Richard II*, Glendower's name occurs only in this one line (3.1.46), and it comes in so unexpectedly, so inconsequentially, interrupting what would otherwise have been a scene-closing couplet (away/holiday), that some scholars suspect the line was inserted to connect the play more noticeably to *Henry IV, Part 1*.

3.3.18. mistake: In the quarto there is no punctuation after this word. Acknowledged meanings of the word and Bolingbroke's response suggest that a new sentence begins with "The heavens."

4.1.160–331. May it please you . . . true king's fall: No way has as yet been found to determine whether the "Deposition Scene" was written c. 1608 for insertion into 4.1 of the play or whether it was present in the original play and cut, presumably by censors, before the publication of Q1 in 1597. Highly respected scholars have argued both sides of the question. In the 2011 Oxford World's Classics edition of *Richard II*, editors Antony Dawson and Paul Yachnin summarize the claims and themselves argue persuasively that it is "likely that the full text as we have it was written all at the same time (late 1595)—i.e., that it was not extensively revised some ten years after it was originally written—and that it was performed more or less intact throughout its history, though in the print version the deposition scene was excised" (pp. 9–11). We agree with Dawson and Yachnin that this claim cannot be proved, but we also agree that the evidence they put forward about the passage's poetic style vis-a-vis Shakespeare's lyric and late styles and about the shape of 4.1 with and without the deposition scene strongly suggests that the passage was there from the beginning. Their argument that the full text was played onstage, with censorship falling only on the printed text, is equally persuasive. It also seems likely, as they argue, that the acting company would not have conserved for a decade a piece of text that had not been performed. Dawson and Yachnin draw on important recent scholarship—some of which links the play intriguingly to royal and parliamentary politics of the 1590s—to make a persuasive case for press censorship of *Richard II*, 4.1, in the late 1590s. See especially pp. 9–16 of their edition.

5.2.56–57. jousts and triumphs: Holinshed reports: "By the advice of the Earl of Huntington, it was devised that they should take upon them a solemn jousts to be enterprised [plotted, planned] between him [i.e., the earl of Huntington] and twenty on his part, and the earl of Salisbury and twenty with him at Oxford, to the which triumph King Henry should be desired [invited], and when he should be most busily marking [paying attention to] the martial pastime he suddenly should be slain and destroyed, and so by that means King Richard . . . might be restored to liberty, and have his former estate and dignity."

Textual Notes

The reading of the present text appears to the left of the square bracket. This edition is based on the earliest extant printing of the play, the First Quarto of 1597, cited below as **Q1**. There are four copies of **Q1** in existence, the Capell copy at Trinity College, Cambridge (referred to below as **C**); the Kemble-Devonshire copy at the Huntington Library, San Marino, California (**D**); the Huth copy at the British Library, London, England (**H**); and the Petworth copy, privately owned, at Petworth House (**P**). The earliest sources of readings not in **Q1** are indicated as follows: **Q2** is the Second Quarto of 1598; **Q3** is the Third Quarto of 1598; **Q4** is the Fourth Quarto of 1608; **Q5** is the Fifth Quarto of 1615; **Q6** is the Sixth Quarto of 1634; **F** is the Shakespeare First Folio of 1623, in which *Richard II* is largely a reprint of one of the later quartos (**Q5**, or, it has been speculated, **Q3** supplemented by **Q5**) but in which the so-called Deposition Scene (4.1.160–331) seems to be based on a manuscript. **Ed.** is an earlier editor of Shakespeare, from the editor(s) of the Second Folio of 1632 to the present. No sources are given for emendations of punctuation or for correction of obvious typographical errors, like turned letters that produce no known word. **SD** means stage direction; **SP** means speech prefix; ~ refers to a word already quoted; ∧ indicates the omission of a punctuation mark.

1.1. 8 *and hereafter to the end of Act 3.* SP KING RICHARD] Ed.; *King.* Q1   15–16. presence. Face] ~∧ ~ Q1   17. hear∧] ~, Q1   21. befall∧] ~, Q1   51. tongues,] ~∧ Q1   55. hushed] Q1 (huisht)   98. land∧] ~: Q1   105. traitor] taitour Q1   106. Sluiced] Q1 (Slucte)

229

122. my] F; *omit* Q1   130. Calais] Q1 (Callice)   134. account∧] ~: Q1   143. But] Q1 (H); Ah but Q1 (CDP)   156. gentlemen] F; gentleman Q1   167. When, Harry, when?] ~∧ ~? ~∧ Q1   167–68. when? / Obedience bids] Ed.; when obedience bids, / Obedience bids Q1   179. must] ɯɯust Q1   182. gage.] ~, Q1   184. reputation;] ~∧ Q1   195–96. height∧ . . . dastard?] ~, . . . ~? Q1 (CDH); ~? . . . ~, Q1 (P)   198. parle] F; parlee Q1   207. hate.] ~, Q1

1.2.   39. quarrel;] ~∧ Q1   44. then, alas] Q1 (DP then alas); then Q1 (CH)   49. sit] F; set Q1   50. butcher . . . breast] Q1 (DP); butchers . . . brest Q1 (CH)   56. sometime] Q1 (sometimes)   60. it] Q2; is Q1   61. empty] Q1 (DP emptie); emptines Q1 (CH)   62. begun] Q1 (begone)   72. hear] Q1 (DP heare); cheere Q1 (CH)   74. everywhere.] ~, Q1

1.3.   6 SD, 25 SD. *with a Herald*] F *only* (*and Harrold*)   11. art∧] ~. Q1   15. thee] Q1 (the)   31. hither,] ~? Q1   32. lists?] ~, Q1   33. comest] Q1 (comes)   43. daring-hardy] Q1 (daring, hardy)   58. thee] Q1 (the)   75. coat∧] ~, Q1   76. o'] Q1 (a)   81. casque] Q1 (caske)   92. adversary.] ~, Q1   94. years.] ~, Q1   104. SP FIRST HERALD] Q1 (*Herald*)   108. his God] Q1 (DP); God Q1 (CH)   110. Duke] Q1 (D)   129. civil] Q1 (DP ciuill); cruell Q1 (CH)   132. rival-hating] Q1 (DP riuall-hating); riuall hating Q1 (CH)   134. Draws . . . sleep,] Drawes . . . sleepe∧ Q1 (DP); Draw . . . sleepe, Q1 (CH)   138. wrathful iron] Q1 (DP wrathfull yron); harsh resounding Q1 (CH)   153. exile.] ~, Q1   154. hopeless] Q1 (hoplesse)   157. Highness'] Hɪghnesse Q1   157. mouth.] ~, Q1   169. portcullised] portcullist Q1 (DP); portculist Q1 (CH)   174. then but] F; but Q1   184. you owe] F; y' owe Q1   191. louring] Q1 (lowring)   197. far] Q1 (fare)   201. land.] ~, Q1   202. realm.] ~, Q1   210. stray;] ~, Q1   228. extinct] Q1 (extint)   228.

night] Q4; nightes Q1   241. lour] Q1 (lowre)   245.
had it] Q1 (had 't)   247. partial . . . sought] Q1 (DH);
partiall . . . ought   Q1   (CP)   254.   SD *Flourish.*] F
only   254. SD. *exits*] Q1 (DH *Exit*); omit Q1 (CP)   275.
world∧] ~: Q1   296. strewed] Q1 (strowd)   314. yet.]
~, Q1   315. Where'er] Q1 (Where eare)

1.4   0. SD *Green and Bagot*] F; *Bushie &c.* Q1   13.
word, . . . craft∧] ~∧ . . . ~, Q1   21. our cousin] F; our
Coosens Q1   24. Bushy, Bagot here, and Green] Q6;
Bushy Q1; *Bushy:* heere *Bagot* and *Greene* F   28.
What] Q1 (DH); With Q1 (CP)   29. smiles∧] ~. Q1   31.
him.] ~, Q1   33. bid∧ . . . well∧] bid∧ . . . well, Q1 (CP);
bid, . . . wel, Q1 (DH)   48. hand.] ~∧ Q1   53. SD] F;
Enter Bushie with newes. Q1   54. Bushy, what news?]
F *only* 65–66. late. | ALL Amen!] Ed.; late, | Amen Q1

2.1   0. SD *and Attendants*] *&c.* Q1   1. last∧] ~?
Q1   18. life's] Q1 (liues)   21. fond;] Ed.; found∧ Q1
41. betimes;] ~∧ Q1   53. as a] Q4; as Q1   74. SD *2
lines later in* Q1; *Aumerle . . . Willoughby*] F *only*   76.
reined] Ed.; ragde Q1   91. No,] ~∧ Q1   108. encagèd]
F; inraged Q1   119. now, not king] Ed.; now not, not
King Q1   131. brother] Q2; brothers Q1   132. son!]
~, Q1   152. his;] ~∧ Q1   153. SD F *only*   164. kern]
Q1 (CDP kerne); kernes Q1 (H)   169. coin] Q1 (CDH
coine); coines Q1 (P)   176. my own] Q1 (CDH my
owne); his owne Q1 (P)   180. first.] ~∧ Q1   185. the]
F; a Q1   194–95. KING RICHARD Why . . . matter? | YORK
O, my] Q1 (CDH *King* Why Vnckle whats the matter?
| *Yorke* Oh my); My Q1 (P)   209. say] Q1 (CDP); lay
Q1 (H) This can be only an inking variant, although it
is misreported as a press variant by Ure (Arden), Gurr
(Cambridge), Wells and Taylor (Oxford).   218. seize]
Q1 (cease)   232. SD *Northumberland . . . remain*] Q1
(*Manet North.*), F (*Manet North. Willoughby, & Ross*)
238. Ere 't] Q1 (Eart)   261. i'] Q1 (a)   272. kinsman.]

~∧ Q1   281. say∧] ~, Q1   287. Blanc] Ed.; Blan Q1
289. Lord] Q1 (L.)   291. Exeter,] ~∧ Q1   295. Coint]
Q1 (Coines)

2.2.   12. With] Q1 (CDH); At Q1 (P)   19. Show]
Q1 (CDH Shew); Shews Q1 (P)   24. Then, thrice-gra-
cious queen,] ~∧ ~ (~ ~) Q1   34. BUSHY 'Tis . . . lady.]
Q1 (DCH *Bush*. . . . Lady.); *omit* Q1 (P)   41. SD F *only*
54. worse,] ~: Q1   55. Harry] Q1 (H.)   57. Lords] Q1
(DCH lords); lord Q1 (P)   76. SD F *only*   82. on the]
Q1 (DCH); in the Q1 (P)   89. SD F *only* (*seruant*)   91.
He was? Why,] ~ ~; ~∧ Q1   126 *and hereafter.* Berkeley]
Q1 (Barckly *or* Barkly)   134. Besides,] ~∧ Q1   142.
Bristow] Q1 (Brist.)   149. Farewell.] ~∧ Q1   157. SD
F (*Exit*)

2.3.   24 *and hereafter* (*except in* 4.1 *and* 5.6). SP
PERCY] Ed.; *H. Per.* Q1   32. Lordship] Q1 (Lo:)   33.
lord] Q1 (Lo:)   38. Hereford] Q3; Herefords Q1   39.
lord] Q1 (Lo:)   40. remember.] ~, Q1   43. lord] Q1
(Lo:)   56. three hundred] Q1 (300.)   59. SD F *only*
70. SD F *only*   79. lord . . . lord] Q1 (Lo: . . . Lo:)   81.
York,] ~: Q1   83. SD F *only*   85. person.] ~, Q1   102.
power.] ~, Q1   105. men,] ~. Q1   113. treason.] ~, Q1
129. cousin.] ~, Q1   174. foes,] ~∧ Q1

2.4   1, 7. SP WELSH CAPTAIN] Ed.; *Welch* Q1   17. SD
F *only*   24. SD F *only*

3.1.   3. bodies,] ~∧ Q1   25. imprese] Q1 (impreese)
46. Glendower] Q1 (Glendor)

3.2.   0. SD *Drums . . . colors.*] F *only*   0. SD *and
Soldiers*] F; &c. Q1   17. thee.] ~, Q1   18. enemies,]
~: Q1   31. not— . . . offer∧] ~, . . . ~, Q1   32. suc-
cor] Q1 (succors)   33. lord] Q1 (Lo:)   40. boldly] Q1
(bouldy)   61. Richard] Q1 (Ric.)   63. SD *Salisbury*]
Q1 (*Salisb.*)   64, 65, 68. lord] Q1 (Lo:)   77. twenty
thousand] Q1 (20000.)   87. name! . . . strikes∧] ~∧ . . .
~, Q1   99. we?] ~, Q1   100. be.] ~, Q1   107. calamity.]
~, Q1   128. steps?] ~, Q1   130. Bolingbroke] Q1 (Bull-

ing) 140–41. hate. Again∧] ~, ~, Q1   157. death∧] ~:
Q1   167. antic] Q1 (antique)   184. wail.] ~, Q1   193.
well.] ~, Q1   202. say.] ~, Q1

3.3   0. SD *with Drum and Colors*] F *only*;   0.
SD *Bolingbroke, . , . Northumberland*] Q1 (*Bull., . . .
North.*);   0. SD *with Soldiers and Attendants*] F
(*Attendants*)   5. good,]   ~∧   Q1   18. mistake.]   ~∧
Q1   24. Royally?] ~, Q1   32. lord] F; Lords Q1   35.
deliver] delịuer Q1   36. Henry Bolingbroke] Q1 (H.
Bull.)   47. Bolingbroke] Q1 (Bulling.)   49. land,] ~:
Q1   61. rain] Q1 (raigne)   62. waters—on . . . him.]
~ ∧ ~ . . . ~, Q1   64. See] Q1 (*Bull.* See)   102. pastures']
Q1 (pastors)   103. forbid∧] ~: Q   103. lord] Q1 (Lo:)
121. a prince and] Ed.; princesse Q1   123. thus∧] ~,
Q1   129. We] Q1 (*King* We)   134. No, good] ~∧ ~ Q
134. lord] Q1 (Lo:)   151. I'] Q1 (a)

3.4.   0. SD *Ladies-in-waiting*] Q1 (*attendants*)   11.
joy] Ed.; griefe Q1   24. weep, . . . good.] ~; . . . ~? Q1
26. SD *a Gardener and two Servingmen*] F (*Seruants*);
Gardeners Q1   29. pins] F (Pinnes); pines Q1   30–31.
so∧ . . . change.] ~, . . . ~∧ Q1   32. apricokes] Q1 (Aph-
ricokes)   37. too] F; two Q1   52. hath] htah Q1   63.
garden! We at] Ed.; garden at Q1   87. Cam'st] Q2 (Cam-
est); Canst Q1   87. tidings?] ~∧ Q1   91. weighed.] ~∧
Q1   92. lord's] Q1 (Lo.)

4.1   0. SD *Aumerle . . . Officers*] F *only* (*Aumerle,
Northumberland, Percie, Fitz-Water, Surrey, Carlile,
Abbot of Westminster, Herauld, Officers*)   14, 86. Cal-
ais] Q1 (Callice)   24. him] Q3; them Q1   43. forgèd,]
~∧ Q1   46. Fitzwater] Q1 (Fitzwaters)   47. SP PERCY]
Q1 (*L. Per.*)   57. As may] Ed.; As it may Q1   58. sun
to sun] Ed.; sinne to sinne Q   58. pawn.] ~∧ Q1   65.
true.] ~∧ Q1   80. my] Q3; *omit* Q1   87. gage.] ~, Q1
101. And,] ~∧ Q1   106. bishop] Q1 (B.)   115. thee]
Q1 (the)   118. Henry,]   ~∧ Q1   121–22. speak, . . .
truth.] ~. . . . ~, Q1   137. deed!] ~∧ Q1   151. you] Q2;

yon Q1 160–331. F; *not in* Q1 170 *and hereafter in this scene.* SP KING RICHARD] Ed.; *Rich.* F 174. tutor] F (tuture) 262. and] Q4; a F 266. Nor no] Q4; No, nor no F 271. mockery . . . snow∧] ~, . . . ~, F 308. manners] Q4; manner F 332–33. BOLINGBROKE On . . . yourselves.] F; *Bull.* Let it be so, and loe on wednesday next, | We solemnly proclaime our Coronation, | Lords be ready all. Q1 333. SD *Westminster . . . Carlisle*] Q1 (*West. Caleil*) 339. lord] Q1 (Lo.)

5.1. 3. whose] wohse Q1 6. SD F; *Enter Ric.* Q1 16. SP KING RICHARD] Ed.; *Rich.* Q1 35 *and hereafter in this scene.* SP KING RICHARD] Ed.; *King.* Q1 35. indeed.] ~, Q1 37. sometime] Q1 (sometimes) 42. thee] Q1 (the) 51. SD *Northumberland*] Q1 (*Northum.*) 72. divorced! . . . men,] ~ (. . . ~) Q1 86. SP NORTHUMBERLAND] F; *King* Q1 93. groan, . . . short,] ~∧ . . . ~∧ Q1

5.2. 2. off] Q1 (of) 12. thee] Q1 (the) 14. spake,] ~: Q1 19. thee! Welcome, Bolingbroke!] Q1 (the welcome Bullingbrooke,) 30. Richard] Q1 (Ric.) 43. SD F; *1 line later in* Q4 72. bond] Q1 (band) 103. thee] Q1 (the) 115. thy] rhy Q1 119. a man] Q1 (CDP); any man Q1 (H) 120. or any] Q1 (CDP); or a Q1 (H) 126. behind.] ~, Q1 128. And] Q1 (An)

5.3. 19, 24, 75, 92, 134, 142, 144 SP KING HENRY] Ed.; *King H.* Q1 10. While] Ed.; Which Q1 13. PERCY] Q1 (*H. Percie*) 15, 28, *and then hereafter, except lines 19, 24, 75, 92, 134, 143, 144.* SP KING HENRY] Ed.; *King.* Q1 36. I may] Q2; May Q1 43. foolhardy king] Q1 (foole, hardie King) 45. SD *Enter York.*] F *only* 49. writing] writtng Q1 68. And] Q1 (An) 72. life:] ~∧ Q1 75. shrill-voiced] Q3; shril voice Q1 82. SD F (*Enter Dutchesse*) *4 lines later* 103. mouth] Q2; month Q1 113. SP KING HENRY] Q2 (*Bol.*); *yorke* Q1 130. thy piteous] Q1 (CDP); this piteous Q1 (H) 148. are.] ~, Q1

5.4 0. SD] Q1 (*Manet sir Pierce Exton, &c.*); *Enter*

Exton and Seruants. F 1. King] Q1 (K.) 4, 7. SP
SERVINGMAN] This ed.; *Man* Q1 5. twice∧] ~. Q1 12.
SD] Q4

5.5 6. prove∧] ~, Q1 12. divine,] ~∧ Q1 18.
ambition, . . . plot∧] ~∧ . . . ~, Q1 22. And, . . . cannot, . . . pride.] ~∧ . . . ~∧ . . . ~, Q1 27. sit] Q3; set Q1
41. SD *one-half line later in* Q1 53. eyes,] ~∧ Q1 65.
blessing] blessiing Q1 77. sometime] Q1 (sometimes)
91. proud] prond Q1 100. will 't] Q1 (wilt) 111.
That] Q1 (*Rich.* That) 122. SD F (*Exit.*)

5.6. 0. SD *King Henry*] Ed.; *Bullingbrooke* Q1 1.
SP KING HENRY] Ed.; *King* Q1 12. SD *Fitzwater*] Q1
(*Fitzwaters*) 17. Fitzwater] Q1 (Fitz.) 17. not] nor
Q1 18. SD *Harry*] Q1 (*H*) 25. reverend] Q1 (reuerent)
37. lord] Q1 (Lo.) 52. SD] F *only* (*Exeunt*)

Richard II:
A Modern Perspective

Harry Berger, Jr.

Can a king possess the divine charisma of his office as his own personal quality, or power, or protection? Can the personal wickedness of a bad ruler contaminate the office?[1] These are the questions taken up by modern interpreters of *Richard II*, who focus—not surprisingly—on the relation between Richard's view of the king's divine right and his problematic behavior. Proponents of the view that the play treats skeptically the Tudor doctrine of the divinely appointed king often identify the force of the critique with the unflattering characterization of Richard. For example, John Halverson claims that Richard "is never aware" of his contribution to the play's mockery of divine right; "he does sincerely believe in the divinity of his kingship, sincerely believes his downfall to be solely the work of traitors, and is sincerely sorry for himself"; his unintended exposure of "royal pretensions and royal ambitions" is thus, ironically, "a *self*-exposure," and this is what makes the play a "lamentable comedy" rather than tragedy.[2] Richard is not only a mean-spirited knave but also a fool "who has cast himself in the role of tragic hero, a role that no one else in the play takes seriously," and whose "fall is directly due to his own folly" (352, 362).

It is easy to concur with the claim that if Richard is an advocate of divine right he is unconvincing. But *is* he an advocate? What if it can be shown that the play represents him not as an advocate but as a critic, not as one who means simply to assert the ideology but as one who mocks and undermines it? To go back a step, what would it take to show this? What shift of interpretive perspective is required to refocus Richard as not only the object but also the chief source of the play's mockery? We might begin by thinking about the play and its primary source, Holinshed's *Chronicles*,[3] and by considering the most obvious distinction between narrative and theater, Holinshed's medium and Shakespeare's: the dramatist represents characters only through the words they speak to and about each other. That would seem to be a severe restraint, a challenge for the playwright to overcome. Unlike the chronicler, the playwright can't represent himself describing actions, commenting on character, and sympathizing or criticizing in his own voice. Characters can only be represented in and performed by their speech. But by the same token the playwright can represent characters representing themselves in a much more sustained and consistent manner than in poetry or prose mediated by a narrator. If the functions or powers of description, representation, and interpretation are to survive the passage from narrative to theater, they must be transferred to and wholly vested in dramatic speakers.

One of the ways Shakespeare met this challenge was to develop the art of representing self-representation, that is, the art of representing speakers who seem aware that in their words and actions they represent themselves to others, speakers who try to control the effects of their self-representation and who thus use their language the way actors do in an effort to impose on their auditors a particular interpretation of the persons they pretend to be. How, then, would a reading of *Richard II* that takes into account the emphasis on self-representation be affected by it? What would happen, in other words, if we tried to keep our attention consistently focused on the interpretation of himself that Richard performs for the benefit of his auditors—and, I add, for his own benefit, since I assume that a performer can't represent himself to others without at the same time representing himself to himself. My answer is that it would make it much more difficult to accept the prevailing view illustrated by Halverson's reading of Richard as a politically incompetent knave who is undone by his own folly and who is the butt of the play's irony. On the contrary, such a shift of perspective would show that, from the beginning of the play, Richard performs the role of the Bad Richard, bad both as a person and as a king, and that he does it with wry "in your face" gusto that shows him—again, from the beginning of the play—asking for trouble.

Before trying to support this reading I would like to suggest what I think is at stake in rejecting the view of Richard as a king committed to the doctrine of the divine right of kings. In spite of all the Shakespearean innovations and departures by which Halverson distinguishes Shakespeare's Richard from Holinshed's— the rhetorical extravagance, the irritating tendency to strike poses and hog the stage, the shift of emphasis from politically justified to gratuitously aggressive behavior—this insistence that the play's Richard is the *unwitting* victim of his own folly reinscribes him in the traditional chronicle portrait but without the occasional sympathy that made Holinshed's view of Richard interestingly ambivalent. Holinshed also represents Richard as the victim of his own folly but shuttles back and forth between sympathizing with or apologizing for him and lambasting his "insolent misgovernance" and loose living. The chronicle keeps its reader in touch with a prelapsarian Richard, the anointed king who "knew his title just, true, and infallible; and his conscience cleane, pure, and without spot of envie or malice," and who was "a right noble and woorthie prince" before succumbing to "the frailtie of wanton youth" and the influence of evil counselors. Compared with this, Halverson's essay illustrates a tendency to be—and to find Shakespeare—more judgmental and to expose beneath Richard's showy exterior the stereotypical core of a morality figure, the example of a bad king. This is what may be called a voyeuristic reduction. It implies that critic, playwright, and audience see and know the character better than he sees and knows himself; it elevates their moral power at his expense.

I propose to begin instead with the hypothesis that Shakespeare took up Holinshed's unthematized and unfocused ambivalence, sharpened its focus, and transferred it to Richard as the attitude—or set of attitudes—his language shows him to perform not only before others but also before himself. This hypothesis allows us to treat all assessments of reactions to Richard by his auditors (onstage or off) as mirrors or echoes of his reaction to himself. So, for example, Phyllis Rackin's account of the way the play's opening scenes work "to make Richard contemptible in the eyes of the audience" becomes a clue to the way Richard works to make himself appear contemptible to his onstage audience by treating them with a degree of contempt guaranteed to alienate them and weaken his position.[4] In fact, by the time Gaunt warns him that he is "possessed now to depose [himself]" (2.1.114), we have begun to wonder whether he is not daring—or perhaps begging—his interlocutors to check him, soliciting punishment even as he tries to see how much he can get away with. However flippant his utterances are in these scenes, they are edged with anger that seems directed as much toward himself as toward his interlocutors.

This verbal aggressiveness may be illustrated by Richard's very first words:

> Old John of Gaunt, time-honored Lancaster,
> Hast thou, according to thy oath and band,
> Brought hither Henry Hereford, thy bold son,
> Here to make good the boist'rous late appeal,
> Which then our leisure would not let us hear,
> Against the Duke of Norfolk, Thomas Mowbray?
> (1.1.1–6)

Richard begins with a string of blunt monosyllables that identify the addressee by place of birth ("Old John of Gaunt," that is, John *from* Gaunt, or Ghent). These are rhythmically organized to accentuate "Old . . . Gaunt," so that they lean on the association of age with weakness or impotence. They are followed by the resonant polysyllables of the first qualifier, the ducal title, "time-honored Lancaster." The shift upward from "Old" to "time-honored" gives the expression of respect for seniority a wicked bite—makes it puffier, more suspect as a mystifying euphemism, because it appears to countervail the snide allusion to senility. Richard's second qualifier, "according to thy oath and band," quietly turns a purely rhetorical and ceremonial question into an admonitory nudge: "have you lived up to your promise?" Young Bolingbroke has been troubling the king's peace, and old Gaunt will be held responsible for his boisterous boy's good behavior. Finally, Richard's explanation for ignoring Hereford's "boist'rous late appeal" is so bizarre that editors have in effect rewritten it: they have insisted that "our leisure" in line 5 must mean want or lack of leisure. But given his obvious pleasure in what may be characterized as a kind of ceremonial trash-talking, Richard may well mean what he says—that is, "I chose not to let official business or unruly youngsters interrupt my leisure, my playtime." I find this both plausible and hilarious as a sequel to his insistence on the promptness, the obedience, he expects from Gaunt: "We expect you to hop to it when we give an order. We, on the other hand, will attend to these matters when we aren't busy doing something less important." In short, "Look how Bad we are. And what are you going to do about it?"

These lines foreshadow what will soon become evident: Richard is a tart and witty practitioner of the politics of oratory whose occasional mimicry of the way his interlocutors deploy the resources of the genre suggests more than a touch of cynicism. He goes out of his way to offend those by whom he has cause to suspect he is threatened, and indeed his obvious contempt for Gaunt seems linked to the latter's refusal to stand up to Richard's bullying. Richard goes on pushing and bullying until he finally succeeds in arousing organized resistance to his conspicuously arbitrary displays of power and violations of his subjects' rights. In current parlance, he "has an attitude": whatever trouble he gets is trouble he asks for. To recognize this is to view his apparently radical change of behavior in 3.2 with suspicion. If after returning from Ireland the "new Richard" is "hysterically indecisive" and "more embarrassing than sympathetic" (Halverson 355), if he refuses to take action and instead flaunts his helplessness and luxuriates in self-pity, the thought that he is a knowing accomplice in his undoing (even as he loudly proclaims himself an innocent victim) makes it difficult to take his self-representation as a betrayed Christ-figure at face value.

The consequence of assuming he "sincerely believes his downfall to be solely the work of traitors, and is sincerely sorry for himself" (Halverson 360) is the conviction that he must be remarkably stupid. We can save him from this by imagining that the speaker of Richard's words in 3.2 remembers no less than we remember about the same speaker's performances in 1.1, 1.3, 1.4, and 2.1. Then it will be easier to read or hear the royal victim's protestations of outrage as acts of parody, easier to imagine that he glories not only in expressing self-pity but also in displaying it, and by "it" I mean not the self-pity per se but its expression.

Once we grant Richard the minimal self-awareness of his seemingly calculated campaign to *get* himself victimized, it becomes obvious that his hyperarticulate flights of menace and lament in 3.2 and after are self-discrediting provocations, that is, rhetorical outbursts intended to embarrass those who are foolish enough to continue encouraging him to stay the course when he and they know it is a course he has thoroughly discredited. At least from the moment in which he directs them to "Mock not my senseless conjuration" (3.2.23), he seems obsessed, exhilarated, by a histrionic project guaranteed to try their dignity as well as their patience: he throws himself into a high-decibel mimicry and mockery of a bad-faith role we are all familiar with because it is a cultural readymade, a well-formed strategy of self-representation anyone can perform, the victim's discourse pithily expressed in Lear's self-pitying rationalization, "I am a man / More sinned against than sinning."[5] This rationalization obviously defends against the speaker's apprehension that he may be more sinning than sinned against. Various versions of the victim's discourse are utilized by Gaunt and York, and Richard's parody may be directed against all those who have countenanced his crimes and disclaimed responsibility for their passivity or nonresistance. On another level, the parody may be directed against the hapless, helpless figure of Poor Richard one finds in the chronicles, as if Shakespeare's Richard is making fun of Holinshed's Richard. For anyone who finds allusions to—and not merely echoes of—the chronicle account in the play, this could contribute to a critique of the simplistic morality, the absence of any narrative penetration into (or interpretation of) the motivational infrastructure of events, that characterizes Richard's story in the chronicles.

This critical relation to the chronicle is evident in the most important of Shakespeare's departures. Richard doesn't have much to say for himself in Holinshed.[6] *Richard II* corrects this in a way that suggests a correlation between haplessness and inadequate opportunities for self-representation. Shakespeare's Richard "does nothing but talk and talk and talk," Halverson complains (352), but he goes on to make a striking suggestion: the "astonishing eloquence [that] seems to have been Shakespeare's invention" is "the verbal equivalent of Richard's beautiful physical appearance"; "none of his sources credits the king with a reputation for fine speech, although they do regularly mention his handsome features and dress" (360). More forcefully, there is not only equivalence but also displacement, as if Shakespeare saw in the narcissism of fine appearance a less sensitive and nuanced medium of self-expression than the narcissism of fine speech—as if the performer's dressing himself up in speech can do more justice to the complex erotic charge of his investment in the visual and verbal media that represent him to himself and others. Critics have always observed that Richard is in love with the sound of his own speech—is a Poet King as well as a Player King—and I have been trying to bring out the elements of self-parody, self-critique, and self-loathing that constitute the richness of such love. In this connection I find it significant that the play virtually ignores a side of Richard that Holinshed associates with his fine appearance—that is, his participation in "the filthie sinne of leacherie and fornication" that "reigned abundantlie" in his court.[7] It redirects attention from Richard's pleasures in sex to his pleasures in speech and from sexual aggression to verbal aggression. Where the chronicle associates Richard's misgovernance and fall with luxurious self-indulgence, the play associates it with luxurious self-representation.

Shakespeare thus replaces Holinshed's royal victim with a more complicated figure who seems to go out of his way to get himself victimized and then blames his victimization on others. It is as if the author of *Richard II*, trying to give an old story a new twist, decided to do this by having the character himself give the story of his decline and fall a new twist; as if Richard enters the play already knowing he had been—would be— deposed and decides to rewrite his story by preemptively taking his deposition into his own hands.[8] This is not to deny that Bolingbroke is a usurper and regicide. But if Richard is actively complicit in his own undoing, if he is the usurper's silent partner or—to put it more forcefully—his seducer, if he contributes more aggressively to his deposition than Bolingbroke knows, then the portrayal of Bolingbroke is also radically altered. Bolingbroke remains a usurper and regicide, but he also, in a strange way, becomes Richard's victim.

In the discussion that follows I shall try to show that Richard entertains the idea of getting deposed well before deposition becomes a clear and definite option for Bolingbroke, who is neither consistently nor decisively committed to usurpation until Richard forces him in 3.3 to commit himself (see 206–7 and 214–18). Though Richard doesn't move to abdicate until 4.1, when he adopts Bolingbroke as his heir (112–18), he drops hints from the very beginning that suggest he finds his cousin impressively qualified to serve as his usurper, and he proceeds to goad and in effect seduce him into performing that service.

Richard's contrariness is evident in the episode that opens the play. His cousin Henry Bolingbroke has accused Thomas Mowbray, the duke of Norfolk, of treason and requested that the king let him justify the charge in trial by combat, a judicial ritual in which God supposedly is the umpire who picks the winner and thus reveals the truth. Richard at first tries to persuade the participants to back off, and when they refuse, he schedules it for a later date. On the second occasion he again intervenes and prevents the duel, but only after acting as if he will let it happen. Then he chastises the would-be combatants as prideful and envious disturbers of the peace, and banishes them, Mowbray for life and Bolingbroke for ten years, subsequently reduced to six. What does he stand to gain by stopping the duel and banishing the combatants?

According to the specific conventions of trial by combat, if Bolingbroke were to win it would be God's way of declaring Mowbray guilty. As we learn later, Richard's guilt and Mowbray's complicity in the murder of Gloucester are already assumed (see 1.2); they don't have to be made evident to Gaunt, the duchess of Gloucester, the duke of York, or, presumably, Bolingbroke. Bolingbroke's accusation sends a message to Richard and others, but were Mowbray to be defeated he would, dead or alive, officially carry the blame he unofficially shared with Richard. On the other hand, were Mowbray to win, he would redeem his honor by "proving" Bolingbroke a liar, and he would thus protect Richard.[9] Richard, then, stops a fight by which he would be protected, officially "cleared," no matter who won. That he stops it in a manner calculated to anger and dishonor the two combatants hardly seems motivated by political self-interest. Furthermore, Bolingbroke, the appellant, is on the face of it the more dangerous of the two. Why, then, does Richard banish Mowbray for good but give Bolingbroke some encouragement to return from exile? These moves reveal Richard's interest in *not* being protected either by Mowbray's victory

or by Mowbray's judicial assumption of guilt if Bolingbroke won. In short, Richard seems to want to keep
open the possibility—and maintain control—of his
self-destruction. But why? Richard's actions in 1.1 and
1.3 are as Holinshed reports them, but Shakespeare
makes it clear through Richard's language, especially
in 1.4 and 2.1, that Richard's abuse of his royal office,
while unconscionable, is not unconscious. He knows
very well what he is doing when he milks the "royal
domain" to support not only his Irish war but also his
extravagance (1.4.44–53), and when he expropriates
Bolingbroke's inheritance (2.1.167–219). He knows, in
short, that he has abused and slandered the office as
well as the idea of kingship; if he accepts the dogma
that the king is God's deputy, he knows very well that
God did not choose—or lacked the power—to prevent
him from using his divine office to commit "murders,
treasons, and detested sins" (3.2.44). Indeed, even as
he uses these words to characterize those who, like
"this thief, this traitor Bolingbroke," will be exposed
and guiltily "self-affrighted" by the light of the returning sun-king (3.2.36–54), his terms of accusation apply
to himself. This diatribe against Bolingbroke is rhetori-
cally excessive and self-delighting, savage and bitter in
tone, as it wickedly flashes a lining of mockery mixed
with self-mockery. For Richard has already shown
himself to be—and heard himself called—a thief of
his subjects' property (and his uncle's life). It is as if he
enjoys hinting to his supporters and sycophants that
he is speaking of his depravity and theirs, and that the
God who lets his deputy do what Richard does and
speak as he now speaks must be willing to let him get
away with murder. Thus if he ever *was* wedded to the
idea that the occupant of the throne was morally con-
strained or uplifted by the sanctity of divine kingship,
he has already divorced himself from it. The energy

with which he mocks the rhetoric of sanctification testifies less to cynicism than to the bitterness of an apostate, an ex-believer.

When, for example, he invokes the assistance of stones and angels, Richard's utterance vibrates with a range of parodic and sarcastic tones, as in the statements following the diatribe against Bolingbroke:

> Not all the water in the rough rude sea
> Can wash the balm off from an anointed king.
> The breath of worldly men cannot depose
> The deputy elected by the Lord.
> For every man that Bolingbroke hath pressed
> To lift shrewd steel against our golden crown,
> God for His Richard hath in heavenly pay
> A glorious angel. Then, if angels fight,
> Weak men must fall, for heaven still guards the right.
> (3.2.55–63)

Broadly parodied in lines 57–58 is a well-known principle of nonresistance to the ruler—even a bad ruler—promulgated by the Elizabethan government: the idea that the ruler's subjects should not resist is here replaced by the idea that they couldn't possibly do so. The lines leave open the possibility that although only the Lord has the authority to depose an anointed king, He may delegate that to his deputy—who may bring it about by his own nonresistance, as Richard suggests when, in lines 59–63, he reduces the bishop of Carlisle's plea for action (27–32) to an argument for remaining inactive and leaving the good fight to heaven.[10]

By such mordant utterances Richard conveys the sense that if he was once convinced of the dogma that the monarch is the Lord's deputy and therefore secure from "worldly men," he no longer believes it and now condemns himself for having believed it. The more pressing question for Richard is whether it is by divine will that he has been able to get away with all he has been accused of, and, if so, what this says about the power of that divine will or about his relation to it. Since at several points in the first two acts he cheerfully demonstrates his lawlessness (1.4.44–53 and 60–65; 2.1.161–70 and 218–19), his subsequent appeals to the rhetoric of divinely ordained kingship in Acts 3 and 4 can hardly be accepted at face value. There are not enough clues in his language to enable us to determine whether he is defying or slandering God, trying to prove that God is helpless to stop him or that God legitimizes knavery. But there are many clues that, although he may deem himself beyond forgiveness, he is interested in punishment, and that he is prepared to subject any conviction of invulnerability to earthly powers to a serious test. In Ernst Kantorowicz's political reading of the play, Richard becomes "a traitor to his own immortal body politic and to kingship such as it had been to his day"; therefore he is complicit in the destruction not only of his "body natural" but also of "the indelible character of the king's body politic, godlike or angel-like."[11] My point is that awareness of the betrayal is inscribed in Richard's language, that it is the source of his self-contempt and of his often sarcastic use of Christian rhetoric.

I want to emphasize that it is not merely poetic effusion we hear in such utterances as the diatribe against Bolingbroke discussed above, and it is not merely arrogance; rather it is a diffuse contempt aimed both at the ideology of kingship and at his performance as king. It is a contempt inscribed in the mocking irony of his setting himself up as Christ (4.1.177–80, 248–53), coming down as Phaëton the usurper of the sun-god's chariot (3.3.183–84), and playing the role of a Faustus forced to stage-manage his own secular damnation. He shows contempt for an ideology of sacralized kingship powerless to restrain his abuses; contempt for those around him who, if they don't actually believe in the ideology, continue to invoke it, especially when they want to excuse or justify the inaction that lets him go on abusing and slandering it. His conspicuous disregard and rejection of defensive measures, indeed, his going out of his way to antagonize powerful enemies and give them the advantage, is the familiar symptom or index of a desire to seek the punishment one feels one deserves. The advantage of inducing others to cut him down to size is that he can blame them while enjoying the savor of his victimage. The disadvantage is that such a strategy can only increase his self-contempt.

This spiraling oscillation—between contempt for self and contempt for others, between the impulse to aggression against oneself and the impulse to aggression against others—is inscribed in Richard's rhetoric and politics. It patterns the course of his behavior and the trajectory of his career. It motivates his perverse, skillfully managed project: to begin the process of getting himself deposed, choose a likely candidate for the job, give him the motive and the cue to action, reward him with the title of usurper, and leave him with a discredited crown. The first item in this schedule is announced early in the play by Gaunt: "[thou] art possessed now to depose thyself" (2.1.114). But Richard's appreciation of Bolingbroke's qualifications has already found its way into his language in the play's opening scene:

> How high a pitch his resolution soars!
> . . . .
> Were he my brother, nay, my kingdom's heir,
> As he is but my father's brother's son,
> Now by my scepter's awe I make a vow:
> Such neighbor nearness to our sacred blood
> Should nothing privilege him. . . .
>
> (113, 120–24)

This display of evenhandedness has another side to it, a side that appears when Richard first calls Mowbray and Bolingbroke "to our presence" in words that momentarily suggest the opposing knights will confront him rather than each other:

> Face to face
> And frowning brow to brow, ourselves will hear
> The accuser and the accusèd freely speak.
>
> (1.1.16–18)

Like the nefarious dangling participle that manuals of style always warn about, the parallel adverbial phrases unsettle the meaning because they are attracted as modifiers to "ourselves will hear" before they reach their rightful destination as descriptions of the way the opponents will speak. The oddly pluralized royal plural ("ourselves" rather than "ourself") encourages this diversion: if only for a second, it depicts Richard self-divided into two opponents before the image is twice recomposed, successively modulating into phantasms of Richard vs. the others and of Bolingbroke vs. Mowbray. The central scenario of the play is epitomized in the oscillation between Richard against himself and against the others, and the wonderfully apt syntactical confusion in the utterance registers the scenario as—at this point—no more than a pressure on language, a sequence of accidental flickers, nothing so clear as an intention of the speaker.

The scenario moves a little closer toward the intentional status of a possible (and nasty) pun in 1.3 during the preliminaries to the duel. Richard concludes his response to Bolingbroke's ceremonial leave-taking with a smartly turned couplet, "Farewell, my blood—which, if today thou shed, / Lament we may but not revenge thee dead" (57–58). The obvious message is that if Bolingbroke loses he will have unjustly—by the logic of judicial combat—shed the lineal blood his kinsman shares, so that there can be no royal redress. But the statement also lets "my blood—which, if today thou shed" be heard as "if you kill me," and this subversive hint is generated by the lines preceding the couplet:

> We will descend and fold him in our arms.
> Cousin of Hereford, as thy cause is right,
> So be thy fortune in this royal fight. (54–56)

The speech rhythm accentuates the *will* to descend; the image of embrace, reinforced by the odd reference to "royal fight," darkly figures the desire coupling Richard and Bolingbroke in their dance toward deposition and regicide—and toward the subsequent regime of Henry IV, during which the usurper gradually comes to feel the embrace as a moral stranglehold. Of course the compelling power of these insinuations can be felt only by readers and auditors who know the whole story of Henry IV's reign. But since this story was enshrined in Tudor historiography, it is plausible to assume some familiarity with it on the part of at least some of the audiences for whom the plays were written. Or, to put it a little more rigorously, the plays presuppose and therefore construct—and will most richly reward—such an audience.

This effect of retrospective foreboding is again produced by Richard's language after he stops the fight and pronounces the sentences of banishment. In a puzzlingly gratuitous gesture, he commands both nobles to perform the following ritual:

> Lay on our royal sword your banished hands.
> Swear by the duty that you owe to God—
> Our part therein we banish with yourselves—
> To keep the oath that we administer:
> You never shall, so help you truth and God,

> Embrace each other's love in banishment,
> Nor never look upon each other's face,
> . . . .
> Nor never by advisèd purpose meet
> To plot, contrive, or complot any ill
> 'Gainst us, our state, our subjects, or our land.
>   (1.3.182–94)

At this point nobody expects Bolingbroke and Mowbray, sworn enemies, to form an alliance. Why, then,
does Richard so carefully give specific instructions
about the sorts of things the exiles are not to do? More
than a display of apprehensiveness, the speech carries
the weight of an insult; it seems intended to rankle, as
does the order that joins the two together in a sym-
bolic tableau of cooperation. But it also actualizes and
stabilizes the flickering image, evoked at 1.1.16–18, of
Richard and the two nobles "frowning brow to brow"
as if the latter were in league against him.

Richard's parade of prohibitions winds eerily, risk-
ily, toward the status of an invitation: as he lists the
sorts of things they might well do were they willing
to overcome their scruples and homebred hate when
abroad, the prohibitions begin to sound like sugges-
tions, proposals, or dares. "Our part therein we banish
with yourselves"—that is, "you are now free to dissociate us from God; if you are dishonorable enough
to join forces, no obligation to our part in the divine
kingship need stand in the way of your returning to lay
banished hands on our royal sword, crown, and body."
My paraphrase is intended to accentuate what I detect
as a wry acridity of tone in Richard's utterance, a histrionic pleasure in flaunting his control of ritual speech
and action to the point of frustrating and antagonizing
the participants, and ultimately—one already begins
to suspect—of arousing resistance to his high-handed

exploitation of sovereign privilege. Richard brings this self-subverting strategy to a first climax in 2.1 when he noisily seizes Bolingbroke's inheritance, dismisses in one airy couplet the duke of York's long, impassioned protest against this move, then blithely announces that he is placing the country in the shaky hands of that very protester while he himself dashes off to Ireland (161–232). All this is staged for the benefit of Northumberland and the other peers who are standing by, as if to invite and incite the uprising that is already in motion and that only (as he seems to expect) awaits "[t]he first departing of the King for Ireland" (301). When he returns from Ireland in 3.2 his success in mobilizing aggression against himself enables him to step comfortably into the victim's role he has solicited.

Someone else is also standing by in 2.1 and quietly watching Richard behave as if possessed to depose himself—so quietly, indeed, that critics often ignore her presence. The queen speaks one line at her entrance and is addressed once just before leaving when Richard briskly bids her be merry as he marches her offstage (2.1.231–32). Critics who puzzle over her strange and haunting rhetoric in 2.2 often write as if this is where she makes her first appearance, even though Bushy begins the scene by reminding her— and therefore the audience—of Richard's parting injunction in 2.1 that she should "Be merry," saying that she promised the king she would "lay aside life-harming heaviness" (2.2.2–3). We should take this as a cue to try to imagine what she may have observed or felt or thought in 2.1. Her foreboding in 2.2, her presentiment of giving birth to the monster, the "nothing" with which her "inward soul . . . trembles," is expressed in language so dense and tortured as to be conspicuously evasive.

What is it that she simultaneously hints at and

resists? What does she flinch from as if trying not to
acknowledge the (no)thing she knows, not to utter the
name of the woe she bears? It must be more than the
bad news Green brings (47–64), even though she calls
Green "the midwife" who helps her soul bring "forth
her prodigy" (65, 67). Following the uncanny force of
the words that express her anxiety, the news of political danger seems anticlimactic. For if Bolingbroke is
her "sorrow's dismal heir," the sorrow she gives birth to
must be Richard. But what could that mean? In what
sense is Richard the "woe" that she so tortuously insists
is "nameless," the "grief" that haunts and impregnates
her speech, the "unborn sorrow" she would like, perhaps, to abort? Lines 6–9 suggest an answer:

> . . . I know no cause
> Why I should welcome such a guest as grief,
> Save bidding farewell to so sweet a guest
> As my sweet Richard.

That wistful and wishful—and perhaps already
nostalgic—"sweet" may register her continuing loyalty
and love in the face and against the grain of what she
has just observed in 2.1. Richard's departure for Ireland
troubles her less than the exchange of guests in which
the sweet Richard has been displaced in her "inward
soul" by the bitter Richard whom she now knows has
willed to get rid of himself because he is possessed by
and reduced to the self-loathing of despair. The queen
balks at calling her "prodigy" Richard's child, for the
nothing she grieves over is the void produced by his
refusal to confront or let her share his "life-harming
heaviness." Instead she speaks of an "unborn sorrow
ripe in Fortune's womb" (10) and thence transferred to
hers. The name of the "nothing [that] hath begot my
something grief" and of the "something [that] hath the

nothing that I grieve" (37–38) is the bitter Richard, and she can receive it as his child only "in reversion"—that is, she cannot inherit as her own the despair Richard withholds until his intercourse with Fortune produces the "dismal heir" (2.2.66) who will finally help him fulfill his deepest wish: to "be eased / With being nothing" (5.5.40–41).

> What, is my Richard both in shape and mind
> Transformed and weakened? Hath Bolingbroke
> Deposed thine intellect? Hath he been in thy heart?
> The lion dying thrusteth forth his paw
> And wounds the earth, if nothing else, with rage
> To be o'er-powered; and wilt thou, pupil-like,
> Take the correction, mildly kiss the rod,
> And fawn on rage with base humility,
> Which art a lion and the king of beasts?
>
> (5.1.26–34)

With these words of spirited chastisement the queen finally has her say. But her words say more than she perhaps intends. She intends to rebuke Richard for being a cowardly lion who doesn't even put up a show of angry resistance to being overpowered. But since "rage / To be o'er-powered" can mean "desire to be overpowered," the rebuke also describes the self-flagellation of the lion who flatters his rage by treating his downfall as his "correction." And whatever she intends by her questions about Bolingbroke, "Hath he been in thy heart?" suggests between Richard and his adopted son the kind of intimate attachment she has been denied. Bolingbroke has replaced her as his partner. And when she, in her final words, refuses to take responsibility for killing Richard's heart or letting him kill hers (5.1.99–102), she signals her reluctance to let him do to her what he is doing to Bolingbroke and himself.

Richard's passive-aggressive scenario of self-deposition is more consistent and decisive than his partner's answering scenario of usurpation. Of the two protagonists, Bolingbroke initially shows more respect for the ideology of kingship than does Richard. Whatever happens later, he enters the judicial process in 1.1 as a reformer intent on making those who wield or influence authority clean up their act. Though his three accusations clearly have Richard for their target, he has enough respect for the protocols of deference and piety to redirect them toward Mowbray. There is no reason to doubt that when, in 2.3 and 3.1, he claims to be weeding out the sycophantic "caterpillars of the commonwealth" (2.3.170), he is at least in part genuinely concerned to preserve the kingship from corrupt practices that jeopardize respect for the system of lineal inheritance on which all the major players—kings of England and dukes of Lancaster alike—depend. The guilt and remorse that haunt him from the end of this play until his death in *Henry IV, Part 2* are hardly those of the hard-edged Machiavel that Bolingbroke has sometimes been taken to be; they are the signs of a tender conscience. He is aware that the trials he undergoes as king and as father may be God's punishment for his "mistreadings." [12] In this he understands his predicament in traditional terms. That is, he is an orthodox reader of his story; he speaks and behaves as if he were in Holinshed's chronicle. The irony is that unbeknownst to himself he is in a very different kind of story in which the royal victim has in effect selected his victimizer, appointed his usurper, and coopted him into seizing a discredited crown. In this story, Bolingbroke plays the part of a character who at first isn't sure—or doesn't want to know—where he is going. Until Richard actively maneuvers him—and all but locks him—into the project of usurpation, he vacillates between gestures that threaten rebellion and gestures of restraint, loyalty, and obeisance. From the end of 1.3 through 3.3 he seems diffusely aggressive, ready for anything, but inconsistent as to the precise course he will choose. He jumps abruptly forward with imperious gestures, then nervously backtracks into deferential postures.

Some critics sensitive to the complexity of Shakespeare's portrayal have described Bolingbroke as the prototypical political climber: "the man who will go further than his rivals because he never allows himself to know where he is going"; the exemplar of the "tacit vice" of opportunism, the duplicitous ability to induce others to clarify and fulfill the purposes of which one keeps oneself only "vaguely aware."[13] Bolingbroke's language represents a speaker who sometimes betrays anxiety about where he is going—where he finds himself desiring or tempted to go. To Gaunt's advice that he dull the pain of exile with idyllic rationalizations and fantasies, he protests, "O no, the apprehension of the good / Gives but the greater feeling to the worse" (1.3.307–8). The words gesture toward meanings beyond the rejection of Gaunt's half-baked recipes for grief-management. To imagine the good one desires but can't have, Bolingbroke remonstrates, only makes one feel worse. What if the good is kingship? Or what if it is virtue—loyalty, piety, respect for legitimate authority? What if "apprehension" means not only the imagination of the good but also the act of reaching for it, apprehending it, taking it ("here, cousin, seize the crown" [4.1.190])? And, since "to apprehend" means not only "to imagine" and "to take" but also "to fear," what if one fears the desire to reach for the good, and fears the consequences of taking it? On the other hand, if one is fearful of the desire to take the good, will one feel worse for having suppressed the desire? I am far from claiming that Bolingbroke audits the full range of meanings that resonate discordantly in the suspension of his utterance. Rather, my claim is that all these meanings are relevant to and revealing of desires and anxieties that obtrude themselves again and again in his language. They betray a moral irritability, a desire for justification, a fear of his own susceptibility to the very opportunism critics accuse him of. In this respect, the resonance of "the apprehension of the good / Gives but the greater feeling to the worse" echoes through the long corridor of the plays about Henry's reign as a prophetic motto of Bolingbroke's ever more precarious journey through the declivities of his own conscience.

The first unguarded manifestation of apprehensive desire occurs in one of the play's cloudier moments. In 2.1, after Richard has laid claim to Bolingbroke's patrimony and departed, Northumberland confides to Willoughby and Ross that Bolingbroke is on his way home from Brittany with several peers and a small army in "eight tall ships" (289–99). In 2.3, shortly after he lands, Bolingbroke insists to Berkeley and York that the reason for his illegal reentry is "personally" to "lay my claim / To my inheritance" (139–40), since he has been denied the normal channels of legal representation by which an heir reclaims property that reverts to the crown. At 2.1.210–17 York warned Richard not to violate this procedure, but Bolingbroke's complaint at 2.3.117–40 shows that Richard ignored the warning. The problem is that according to Northumberland's announcement, Bolingbroke set sail from Brittany before the events in 2.1 transpired. Perhaps, as Peter Ure suggests, Shakespeare may have "telescoped the various events" in this episode "in the interests of dramatic timing";[14] perhaps readers and auditors are not expected to grasp legal complexities that are only hinted at in passing;[15] perhaps they aren't being asked to worry about the inconsistency between Bolingbroke's asserted motive for returning and the fact that he couldn't have had that motive when he mustered his forces and left Brittany (since Gaunt had not yet died); perhaps, if they do notice the inconsistency, they will chalk it up to Bolingbroke's hypocrisy and opportunism.

My own view is that in 2.3 Bolingbroke behaves as if *he* worries about the inconsistency and about a moment in which "the apprehension of the good" led to a brief and diffuse act of opportunism.[16] For in spite of the aggressive embarkation Northumberland reports, Bolingbroke seems careful, even diffident, in his dealings with those who greet him on his return. His response to Northumberland's windy sweet talk (2.3.2–18) is curt. He shows himself to be concerned with the way he is perceived, addressed, and flattered or criticized. In thanking the nobles for their support, he is careful to keep his promises vague. He seems to resist—without entirely discouraging—the push of an incipient rebellion of nobles who would obviously like to see him go all the way and who thus, ironically, have the same designs on Bolingbroke that Richard has—an unwitting complicity that will, with Bolingbroke's help, turn against him in *Henry IV, Part 1*, after he has become king. Above all, he takes the opportunity offered by Berkeley's cool and York's censorious remarks to back away from any appearance of ambition greater than the desire to recover his rightful inheritance. However wild or undefined his intention may have been on setting sail before Richard seized his patrimony, the seizure gives him a defined ground of defiance and grievance.[17] Against York's double charge that Bolingbroke is "a banished man" who has returned "Before the expiration of [his] time, / In braving arms against [his] sovereign" (2.3.114–16), Bolingbroke's demand for legal justice actually reproduces the logic of York's earlier protest against the seizure. York warned that Richard jeopardizes his own position as well as his cousin Bolingbroke's in violating the principle of lineal succession; Bolingbroke agrees: "If that my cousin king be king in England, / It must be granted I am Duke of Lancaster" (127–28). Within these limits, Bolingbroke's sense of grievance is morally justified, and he can represent himself to himself as a man more sinned against than sinning. Richard's problem, then, given what I take to be his agenda, will be to make Bolingbroke transgress those limits and reach for more than his own.

My response to Bolingbroke's language coincides with the opinion of one critic that throughout the play Bolingbroke "is genuinely trying to say what he means."[18] But what he means, what he intends to do, is often far from obvious—is marked by moments of confusion and indecisiveness that suggest it is not always obvious to him. When he sentences Richard's friends to death in 3.1, he goes back, in effect, to square one and blames them for all royal misdeeds, just as he had blamed Mowbray in 1.1. This time, however, he is more careful to dissociate the misdeeds from Richard and represent the king himself as the victim of the flatterers' corrupt practices. He is equally careful to control public reaction to the death sentences by a painstaking explanation, most of which is devoted to Bushy's and Green's victimization of him. Thus, according to this argument, he and Richard are in the same position, so that whatever he does on his own behalf he also does on Richard's, preserving both the king and the crown from the sources of corruption. However, the pressure behind this strenuous exercise in self-exculpation betrays itself in the introductory comment with which he justifies the death penalty: "to wash your blood / From off my hands, here in the view of men / I will unfold some causes of your deaths" (3.1.5–7). As Rackin points out, "Richard's association [in 4.1] of his betrayers with Pilate, the biblical archetype for a futile attempt to deny guilt . . . is prefigured here" (*Stages* 129). But in Bolingbroke's case (as opposed to Richard's flamboyant assumption of the divine victim's role), the allusion slips out against the grain of the speaker's stated intention and hints at the futility of his attempt to persuade himself he is not guilty of an action aimed at weakening rather than—as he claims—safeguarding Richard's position. The solicitude he shows for the queen (38–42) immediately after his indictment of Bushy and Green is part of the same pattern. It may be dismissed as another politic gesture intended to impress or placate his audience, but that does not prevent it from being at the same time a gesture of good faith he performs for his own benefit—or, more darkly, a preemptive washing of the hands by one who, like Macbeth, may be shaken by his apprehension of the good.

It is an apprehension he struggles to control in 3.3 against the mounting pressure of Richard's disturbing acquiescence. Even the impatient Northumberland tries to slow down the process and lower the stakes when Richard accuses him of backing an effort to seize the crown (3.3.74–122), but Richard sardonically and melodramatically persists in offering the lure of deposition (148–80). Bolingbroke's one long speech early in the scene (32–63) registers his uncertainty. It begins with a calculated alternation between reassurance and threat expressly confined to the demand that his banishment be repealed and his lands restored. But as he continues he momentarily loses control of his imagery and has to rein it back in:

> Be he the fire, I'll be the yielding water;
> The rage be his, whilst on the Earth I rain
> My waters—on the Earth, and not on him. (60–62)

The runover line pausing on, then passing through, its ear-pun (rain/reign) enacts a loss of balance, but stumbles awkwardly back on its feet. Two lines later, after Richard shows himself on the battlements, Bolingbroke is still stumbling: Richard appears, says Bolingbroke,

> As doth the blushing discontented sun
> From out the fiery portal of the east
> When he perceives the envious clouds are bent
> To dim his glory and to stain the track
> Of his bright passage to the occident. (65–69)

As Bolingbroke continues to develop the figure of elemental warfare, his words attribute questionable motives to the envious clouds that represent *him*, but it is unclear from his phrasing whether the dimming and the staining are Richard's (mis)perceptions or are motives the speaker acknowledges.

The parley between Richard and Northumberland that follows goes on for more than a hundred lines before Bolingbroke speaks again, and during the remainder of the scene, which Richard monopolizes, Bolingbroke is allowed only five brief utterances. In the second of these he commands obeisance to the king, and in the third he protests once more that "I come but for mine own" (206). But Richard immediately denies him this fallback position: "Your own is yours, and I am yours, and all" (207). Bolingbroke still resists: "So far be mine, my most redoubted lord, / As my true service shall deserve your love" (208–9). Richard will brook no further resistance. He pushes Bolingbroke into a corner and forces him to take all:

> Cousin, I am too young to be your father,
> Though you are old enough to be my heir.
> What you will have I'll give, and willing too,
> For do we must what force will have us do.
> Set on towards London, cousin, is it so? (214–18)

That is, "what I will give you'll have, for do *you* must what force will have *you* do: convey me to London to prepare for the next phase of deposition." Bolingbroke surrenders: "Yea, my good lord" (219). This is the turning point of the play. The die has been cast—by Richard—and Bolingbroke has lost the moral struggle, and now commence the "inward wars" of the future King Henry IV.

"Here, cousin, seize the crown" (4.1.190): like this duplicitous speech act, the inverted rite of discoronation shows Richard having it both ways. He formally reenacts the self-deposition he has helped bring about, thereby publicly demonstrating his active relinquishment of the crown. At the same time he forces Bolingbroke to reenact the usurpation, thereby publicly dramatizing the act of illegal seizure while Richard presents himself to his audience as the usurper's Christ-like victim (4.1.190–253). But shortly after this, he begins to shift from the victim's pose to the sinner's and to perform an act of degradation aimed as much at the crown as at himself. Thus what he proposes to remove from his person and offer Bolingbroke is a debased crown, a gift that has poison in it. Perversely staging and savoring both the pathos of victimization and the power of the self-deposing sinner, he stigmatizes Bolingbroke as a usurper even as he denies him the manly pleasure of being able to claim that he won the throne without Richard's help.

Bolingbroke's disadvantage in his competition with Richard had been established at the beginning of 4.1, before Richard's entry, with the play's return to the question of Gloucester's murder. The scene invites a contrast with Richard's brash management of the trial by combat in the opening scenes, producing the battle of the gages as a comic and soured replay. The contrast reflects poorly on Bolingbroke, who sits quietly through

most of the scene and—unlike Richard—doesn't intervene in the volatile factionalism that bodes ill for future
stability. The epidemic of gage-throwing reaches a
thudding climax when, first, Aumerle runs out of gages
and, second, Bolingbroke is once again—as in 1.1 and
1.3—frustrated, this time by the shadow of Mowbray,
the news of whose holy death abroad prevents another
attempt to resolve the Gloucester question.

At the end of 5.3, after having pardoned Aumerle for
his part in the conspiracy planned by Richard's supporters (see 4.1.334–47), Bolingbroke threatens "the
rest of that consorted crew" with death, but, as he
twice suggests (5.3.148, 150), carrying out the threat is
contingent on finding the conspirators. The next scene
begins with Sir Pierce Exton quoting words uttered in
his direction by Bolingbroke—"Have I no friend will
rid me of this living fear?" (5.4.2)—and deciding that
he has just been invited to kill Richard. The quarto
(though not the Folio) suggests that Exton may have
been onstage when, at the end of 5.3, Bolingbroke
issues his threats against the traitors; such a suggestion
has a substantial impact on our response to Exton's
decision, which is expressly voiced as *his* interpretation of Bolingbroke's words:

> . . . he wishtly looked on me,
> As who should say "I would thou wert the man
> That would divorce this terror from my heart"—
> Meaning the king at Pomfret.   (5.4.8–11)

Other accounts of this episode—those of Hall, Holinshed, and Samuel Daniel—clearly signal Bolingbroke's
intention to have Richard secretly put to death so that,
in Daniel's words, he would not "seeme to wil the act."[19]
But Shakespeare muddies things by placing Exton's
remarks in the immediate vicinity of Bolingbroke's

worry about the conspirators, and then appointing Exton the sole interpreter of Bolingbroke's "ambiguous instigation."[20] This juxtaposition makes it more plausible that Exton may have misconstrued a request to get rid of the conspirators (who are at liberty while Richard is safely in prison).[21]

Nevertheless, the instigation remains ambiguous, and the question is how to interpret the ambiguity. Some see the episode as consistent with the representation of the character's "deviousness": "without explicitly avowing his intention," Bolingbroke gets someone else not only to do his dirty work for him but also to articulate the purpose he leaves unexpressed, another example of his refusal to allow himself "to know where he is going."[22] Making a slight but significant change in this strong reading, I add that for Bolingbroke such a refusal is no longer possible. After Richard has denied him the fallback position in 3.3 and teased him in 4.1 with "Here, cousin, seize the crown," he knows where he is going and where he has gone. The words with which he pardons Aumerle in 5.3 poignantly betray his own sense of moral precariousness ("I pardon him, as God shall pardon me," 137). Thus the motivational haziness or terseness characteristic of his language after 3.3 is indicative less of political deviousness or even of moral self-protection than of his fear of where he finds himself going.

"Have I no friend will rid me of this living fear?": whatever Bolingbroke intends to say, the living fear of danger from others has come by this time to mirror the living fear of danger from himself. Were Bolingbroke to utter the wish Exton extrapolates from his glance— "I would thou wert the man / That would divorce this terror from my heart"—the mood would be counterfactual (that is, "if only you could; but you can't"), for nobody else, least of all a political supernumerary like

Exton, could alleviate the terror or assure him that
"God shall pardon me." And whatever he may have
intended Exton to hear or do, the upshot in 5.6 is that
he seems once again to lose control of the situation.
The effort to wrap things up and assume high moral
ground signified by the parade of rhymed couplets with
which he pardons Carlisle in the final scene (5.6.24–29)
is rudely interrupted by Exton's melodramatic entry
and announcement: "Great king, within this coffin
I present / Thy buried fear. Herein," he adds, angling
for his gratuity, "all breathless lies / The mightiest of
thy greatest enemies, / Richard of Bourdeaux, by me
hither brought" (30–33). He gets no thanks from the
great king, who oddly identifies Richard's plight with
his own when he blames Exton for having "wrought /
A deed of slander with thy fatal hand / Upon my head"
(34–36). This is uncanny: it is as if Richard has pene-
trated Bolingbroke's conscience, possesses it, and now
speaks through him. To hear this ghostly intrusion is to
hear something startling in Exton's simple and direct
reply, for it voices precisely the protest Bolingbroke
would be justified in making to Richard: "From your
own mouth, my lord, did I this deed" (37).

Perhaps, surrounded as he is by supporters,
Bolingbroke is not politically embarrassed by Exton's
entrance. Yet perhaps even the supporters who brought
in a harvest of rebel heads would shy away from the
ultimate crime of regicide. The evidence on this score is
not decisive because the play's emphasis is elsewhere.
In Bolingbroke's rejoinder to Exton it remains fixed
on the continuing intrusion of the uncanny Ricardian
overtones:

> They love not poison that do poison need,
> Nor do I thee. Though I did wish him dead,
> I hate the murderer, love him murderèd.

The guilt of conscience take thou for thy labor,
But neither my good word nor princely favor.
With Cain go wander through shades of night,
And never show thy head by day nor light.   (38–44)

As we listen to this bitter reproach we may hear Bolingbroke's malediction on himself as well as on Exton.
Sending Exton off with Cain recalls Bolingbroke's comparison of Gloucester's murder to that of sacrificing
Abel in 1.1; Bolingbroke's words suggest that he now
finds himself involved in the same kind of kin-murder
as he had accused Richard of. But it is Richard whose
voice usurps the grammatical first person and it is his
despair that speaks through Bolingbroke's words, con-
demning both himself and Bolingbroke. "Here, cousin,
seize the crown": and so Bolingbroke did, and now
he resurrects his buried fear and receives his reward,
or sentence. "Hath Richard / Deposed thine intellect?
Hath he been in thy heart?"

------

1. These questions were raised in the early Middle
Ages in terms of the effect of a priest's personal wickedness on his ritual efficacy. For the classic discussion of
the doctrine of the two "bodies" of the king, see Ernst
Kantorowicz, *The King's Two Bodies: A Study in Medieval Political Theology* (Princeton: Princeton University
Press, 1957). Kantorowicz quotes Elizabethan lawyers
who state, "What the King does in his Body politic cannot be invalidated or frustrated by any disability in his
natural Body" (Kantorowicz 7). For an important revi-
sionary account of the use of the doctrine during and
after Elizabeth's regime, see Marie Axton, *The Queen's
Two Bodies: Drama and the English Succession* (London: The Royal Historical Society, 1977). It is interesting to note that one Elizabethan law case for which the

two-bodies doctrine was elaborated concerned the very duchy of Lancaster of which John of Gaunt was the first owner and which the three kings descended from him owned as private property—held "in their Body natural." See Kantorowicz 7–10 and Axton 16–17 and 29. For an attempt to explore "the clash of person and office" in the play, see Wolfgang Iser, *Staging Politics: The Lasting Impact of Shakespeare's Histories*, trans. David Henry Wilson (New York: Columbia University Press, 1993), 71–84.

2. John Halverson, "The Lamentable Comedy of Richard II," *English Literary Renaissance* 24 (1994): 366, 360, 368–69.

3. Raphael Holinshed, *Chronicles of England, Scotland, and Ireland* (1587; rpt. London: J. Johnson et al., 1808). See also Geoffrey Bullough, *Narrative and Dramatic Sources of Shakespeare*, vol. 2 (1960; rpt. New York: Columbia University Press, 1975), 9–15, and Peter Saccio, *Shakespeare's English Kings: History, Chronicle, and Drama* (New York: Oxford University Press, 1977), 17–35.

4. See Phyllis Rackin, "The Role of the Audience in Shakespeare's *Richard II*," *Shakespeare Quarterly* 36 (1985): 262–81, esp. 264–65. See also Rackin's *Stages of History: Shakespeare's English Chronicles* (Ithaca: Cornell University Press, 1990), 117–30.

5. *King Lear* 3.2.62–63 (New Folger Edition). For a more detailed account of Richard's language in 3.2, see my *Imaginary Audition: Shakespeare on Stage and Page* (Berkeley: University of California Press, 1989), 79–83, 88–93, and 104–33.

6. Richard reads aloud the articles of resignation and is directly quoted in a few occasions restricted to brief public utterances, but is otherwise represented through and controlled by the narrator's voicing in indirect discourse.

7. Holinshed 2:868. This omission is noted by Halverson (362), who also reminds us that Holinshed partly dissociates himself from this opinion, ascribing it to the hostility and ungratefulness of Richard's subjects (2:869). In the play there is one vague reference to the "sinful hours" Richard spent with his evil counselors (3.1.11–15), but this doesn't come across as information about Richard because it is part of Bolingbroke's grievance against the counselors and it contributes to his public justification for putting them to death.

8. In making this suggestion I am applying to Richard II an interpretation of Shakespeare's Richard III first advanced by Nicholas Brooke in 1968 and later taken up in some brilliant general comments by Patricia Parker and an impressively detailed analysis by Linda Charnes: Brooke, *Shakespeare's Early Tragedies* (1968; rpt. London: Methuen, 1973), 48–79, especially 55–58 and 77–79; Parker, "Preposterous Events," *Shakespeare Quarterly* 43 (1992): 201–4; Charnes, *Notorious Identity: Materializing the Subject in Shakespeare* (Cambridge, Mass.: Harvard University Press, 1993), 20–69.

The idea that Richard collaborates in his own downfall is obvious and has often been noted. For a compact statement of the thesis, see Richard Wheeler, *Shakespeare's Development and the Problem Comedies: Turn and Counter-Turn* (Berkeley: University of California Press, 1981), 158–59. My variation on the thesis is to treat it as a project consistently sustained by the language assigned to the name, or speech prefix, "Richard." I put it this way to emphasize that I am not concerned with what an imaginary person named Richard might actually have been aware of or intended at any moment. Rather my concern is with a pattern of motivation that can be traced in his language throughout the play. It is entirely conceivable that two actors preparing to perform the role of Richard could agree that this project, this pattern, is discernible in the language and yet disagree as to whether at any particular moment Richard should be played as a speaker clearly aware, vaguely aware, or unaware that he is engaged in a scenario and discourse of self-deposition.

9. Andrew Gurr, in his edition of the play, has included the suggestion that, if he won, Mowbray could blackmail Richard (Cambridge, Mass.: Cambridge University Press, 1984), 22, but I do not find this suggestion persuasive.

10. For the more detailed account of these lines from which the present comments are drawn, see *Imaginary Audition*, 88–93.

11. Kantorowicz, *The King's Two Bodies*, 38, 27.

12. *Henry IV, Part 1*, 3.2.12 (New Folger Edition).

13. John Palmer, *Political Characters of Shakespeare* (London: Macmillan, 1945), 130; Brents Stirling, *Unity in Shakespearian Tragedy: The Interplay of Theme and Character* (New York: Columbia University Press, 1956), 32.

14. Peter Ure, ed., *King Richard II*, 5th ed. (1961; rpt. London: Methuen, 1966), 68.

15. We read or hear just enough about the complex legal conventions to suspect that Richard's seizure involved more than brute force; it required manipulations of property law that set up obstructions to Bolingbroke's ability to claim his inheritance. For details, see Jack Hexter, "Property, Monopoly, and Shakespeare's *Richard II*," in *Culture and Politics from Puritanism to the Enlightenment*, ed. Perez Zagorin (Berkeley: University of California Press, 1980), 1–24.

16. "Diffuse" in the sense that there are several possible answers to why Bolingbroke would return before he knew his property was jeopardized: to mobilize noble and popular hostility to Richard, to continue his

effort to purge the court and crown of corrupt influences, to pursue the project of avenging Gloucester's death, and to do the work his father should have been doing. These aims have been established in the previous scenes. Another concern an exile might be expected to entertain before the situation arose is indicated by the references to the legal procedures necessary to claim an inheritance.

17. Hexter, "Property," 9–10, 11.

18. Lois Potter, "The Antic Disposition of Richard II." *Shakespeare Survey* 27 (1974): 33–41, esp. 35.

19. Samuel Daniel, *The First Fowre Bookes of the civile wars between the two houses of lancaster and York*, 3:58, in *The Complete Works in Verse and Prose of Samuel Daniel*, ed. A. B. Grosart, vol. 2 (1885; rpt. New York: Russell and Russell, 1963), 121.

20. The phrase is John Palmer's: *Political Characters*, 173.

21. The quarto stage direction—*Manet sir Pierce Exton, &c.*—makes it impossible to determine whether Bolingbroke's words to Exton were uttered specifically and secretly to him (and on an occasion different from the one in 5.3) or were part of a more general request to the nobles who—according to both Q and F stage directions—were present at the beginning of 5.3 (though dismissed by the king partway through the scene).

22. Stirling, *Unity in Shakespearian Tragedy*, 38; Palmer, *Political Characters*, 173, 134.

Further Reading

In addition to the following books and articles,
see *www.folger.edu/shakespeare* and
www.folger.edu/online-resources.

Richard II

Abbreviations: ESC = English Shakespeare Company,
1 and *2H4* = *Henry IV, Parts 1* and *2*, *H5* = *Henry V*,
R2 = *Richard II*, *R3* = *Richard III*, RSC = Royal
Shakespeare Company

Barroll, Leeds. "A New History for Shakespeare and
His Time." *Shakespeare Quarterly* 39 (1988): 441–64.

As a way of focusing his concerns with "some of the
confusions plaguing" the critical movements known as
new historicism and cultural materialism, Barroll discusses the performance of *R2* at the Globe on the eve of
the Essex rebellion in 1601. He specifically faults political readings that, by failing to take into account all the
available evidence, mistakenly posit the play's essential subversiveness. An investigation of primary documents reveals that the commissioning of *R2* by Essex's
supporters "was not a severely punishable offense in
itself," and thus suggests that Elizabethan authorities
did not consider the play a dangerous piece of subversive propaganda. Furthermore, Elizabeth's famous
retort that "I am Richard II" may have been precipi-
tated not by the drama but by John Hayward's prose
Life of Henry IV (printed in 1599), which emphasized
Richard's deposition and killing. For the Privy Council
and Elizabeth, the story of Richard as told in the print
medium seems to have presented more of a political

threat than did the dramatic version. Barroll also discusses "the myth" of a suppressed or censored deposition scene from the pre-1608 quartos, expanding on the theory of David Bergeron ("The Deposition Scene in *Richard II*," *Renaissance Papers* 1974 [1975]: 31–37) that the formal abdication may have been written for a revision of the play—"and not necessarily for purposes of subversion." [Barroll's essay is reprinted in Farrell, below.]

Berger, Harry, Jr. *Harrying: Skills of Offense in Shakespeare's Henriad.* New York: Fordham University Press, 2015.

As part of his continuing efforts to practice a "reconstructed old New Criticism," Berger reads *R3*, *R2*, *1* and *2H4*, and *H5* in terms of a verbal feature he calls "harrying." By this he means that "[t]he language Shakespeare's characters speak always says more than they mean to say. They try to say one thing. Their language says other things that often question the speakers' motives or intentions." Included among the book's thirteen chapters are two dealing with *R2*: "'Here, Cousin, Seize the Crown': The Triumphant Fall of Richard, the Self-Harrier" (pp. 20–47) and "Richard's Soliloquy: *Richard II*, Act 5, Scene 5, Lines 1–66" (pp. 48–54). In the first, Berger explores the effects of *harrying*'s "linguistic mischief" on the "self-representation" that Richard "performs for the benefit of his auditors . . . [a]nd . . . for his own benefit as well." Berger rejects the common reading of Richard as a staunch believer in and defender of "divine right" theory (the doctrine positing the monarch as God's anointed minister on Earth, rebellion against whom would be tantamount to rebellion against God), proposing instead that the play represents him "as a critic, . . . as one who mocks and undermines [this theory]." Richard thus emerges

as both the object and the source of the play's mockery, playing from beginning to end "the Bad Richard
with wry 'in your face' gusto as if he is asking for
trouble." As evidence, Berger discusses Richard's "ceremonial trash-talking" to "old . . . and time-honored"
Gaunt (1.1.1–6), his "push[ing] Bolingbroke . . . to
take all" (3.3.199–205), and the "duplicitous speech
act" whereby Richard "reenacts the self-deposition he
has helped bring about" and simultaneously "forces
Bolingbroke to reenact his usurpation" (4.1.190). [The
chapter is a slight revision of Berger's 1996 "Modern
Perspective," which is reprinted in this updated New
Folger *Richard II* (see pp. 236–71).]

The chapter "Richard's Soliloquy," a close reading
of Richard's only soliloquy, focuses on the performative implications of the stage direction "Enter Richard
alone," which "teasingly runs up the question of the
[speech's addressee] like a flag in his statement that
'here is not a creature but myself'" (line 4). Answering those who claim that Richard is now replacing a
missing audience of flatterers or adversaries with
himself—"postur[ing] for his own approval or disap-
proval as if checking his performance in a mirror"—
Berger contends that that is precisely what Richard has
been doing all along. In fact, everything that he has said
up to this point is "a variation or illustration of what
he says in this soliloquy." The major discovery now,
however, is that he "cannot escape himself even when
alone." [This chapter first appeared in Russ McDonald,
Nicholas D. Nace, and Travis D. Williams, eds., *Shakespeare Up Close: Reading Early Modern Texts* (London:
Bloomsbury Arden Shakespeare, 2012), pp. 225–33.]

Farrell, Kirby, ed. *Critical Essays on Shakespeare's Richard II.* New York: G. K. Hall, 1999.

The anthology consists of an introduction by the
editor ("Play, Death, and History in *Richard II*) and thir-

teen essays: R. Morgan Griffin, "The Critical History of *Richard II*"; Samuel Schoenbaum, "*Richard II* and the Realities of Power"; F. W. Brownlow, "*Richard II* and the Testing of Legitimacy"; David M. Bergeron, "*Richard II* and Carnival Politics"; Leeds Barroll, "A New History for Shakespeare and His Time"; David Norbrook, " 'A Liberal Tongue': Language and Rebellion in *Richard II*"; Cyndia Susan Clegg, " 'By the choise and inuitation of al the realme': *Richard II* and Elizabethan Press Censorship"; Sharon Cadman Seelig, "Loyal Fathers and Treacherous Sons: Familial Politics in *Richard II*"; Sheldon P. Zitner, "Aumerle's Conspiracy"; James Calderwood, "*Richard II*: The Fall of Speech"; John W. Blanpied, "Sacrificial Energy in *Richard II*"; Harry Berger, Jr., "Ars Moriendi in Progress, or John of Gaunt and the Practice of Strategic Dying"; and John Halverson, "The Lamentable Comedy of *Richard II*." In his introductory essay, Farrell argues that *R2* "dramatizes some of the processes by which imaginations [both the playwright's and the audience's] adapted to the psychic stress" of the early modern period's traumatic sociopolitical and cultural changes: "The [play's] mood of civic crisis . . . is structured like the psychic crisis associated with the collapse of belief in traditional, ritualistic monarchy. . . . An older mentality structured around polarized opposites—king, beggar; heaven, hell; life, death—is developing toward a structure emphasizing multiplicity, strategy, and dynamic equilibrium." The critical afterlife of *R2* is a "story of increasing freedom to recognize the disturbing openness in its conception of history," as the criticism of recent decades manifests a greater tolerance "of the play's peculiar fractures and ambiguities."

Fletcher, Christopher. *Richard II: Manhood, Youth, and Politics 1377–99*. Oxford: Oxford University Press, 2008.

Observing that Richard's "unmanly reputation"—as willful, inconstant, extravagant, susceptible to poor counsel, obsessed with courtly culture, and averse to warfare—is rooted in contemporary accounts that even revisionist studies over the last forty years have been unable to shake, Fletcher sets Richard's life and the politics of his court in the cultural and sociolinguistic context of late medieval assumptions about the nature of manhood and youth. He finds that while Richard's traditional reputation does not accurately represent his character, "it is not unrelated to the events of his reign. It is a political phenomenon in itself, created by the interaction between late medieval cultural commonplace and the politics of 1377–99." Fletcher devotes three chapters to exploring how the words "manhood" and "manly" and the expression "as a man" were used and understood at the time: "The Language of Manhood I: Strength, Violence, and Honour" addresses martial and chivalric virtues; "The Language of Manhood II: 'Humanitas,' Decorum, and Largesse" considers qualities associated with the splendor and "magnificent action" deemed appropriate to maintaining one's rank; and "Medico-Moral Theories of Manhood, Strength, Constancy, and Reason" examines the moral standpoints used to define "correct masculinity" as found in late medieval medical and didactic texts. The remaining eight chapters, arranged chronologically, deal specifically with Richard and the Ricardian court: "The Royal Authority and the King's Childhood, 1376–82," "The Emergence of the King's Firm Purpose, 1382–84," "The Pursuit of Manhood, 1384–86," "The Return of the King's Youth, 1386–88," "The Establishment of a Conciliar Regime, 1388–90," "Majesty and Restriction, 1390–97," "The Drift to Power, c. 1390–97," and "A Boy Not a Man? 1397–99." Fletcher concludes that "far from being the effeminate tyrant of historical imagination, Richard was a typical young noble-man trying to establish his manhood—and hence his authority to rule—by thoroughly conventional means: first through a military campaign, and then, fatally, through violent revenge against those who attempted to restrain him."

Grady, Hugh. "The Discourse of Princes in *Richard 2:* From Machiavelli to Montaigne." In *Shakespeare, Machiavelli, and Montaigne: Power and Subjectivity from Richard II to Hamlet*, pp. 58–108. Oxford: Oxford University Press, 2002.

Taken together, Machiavelli and Montaigne "form [in *R2*] an intertextuality which opens up in turn into central issues of power, identity, and subjectivity." Grady divides his examination of this dialectic into two parts: (1) "The Machiavellian World of *R2*" (pp. 58–82) and (2) "Modern Subjectivity in *R2*" (pp. 82–108). Despite Act 1's "ceremonious" feudalism with all of its chivalric rites, the world of *R2* is ruled by "Machiavellian reduction" and Machiavellian tenets as articulated in *The Prince* (1513), chief among them the pragmatics of "instrumental reason" and the assumption that "in a world of bad men, it is folly to be good." In Grady's reading, there are two Machiavels but only Henry is a true Machiavellian: Richard's downfall "unfolds . . . in large measure by his own political incompetence, and the dramatic dynamic around which the play is built—the confrontation between skilled and unskilled Machiavellians." This political strand dominates the dramatic action until the mirror sequence in the deposition scene, when a new strand, reflective of Montaigne's *Essays*, introduces the issue of selfhood and "the flux of subjectivity," a shift in emphasis nowhere more pronounced than in the interiority of Richard's prison soliloquy (5.5.1–67). Within the confines of a prison cell and of his own mind, the conception of "unfixed, modern subjectivity" achieves a "new level of conceptualization," as Richard, stripped of the social life and self-identity he has known, "find[s] a kind of ease" (line 28) in the "flux of his own emotional experience" and in the "remarkable and (Montaignean) view of the possibilities of multiple identities within subjectivity" (lines 31–41). By way of its "Montaignean turn in [the] second half," *R2* becomes one of the first of Shakespeare's plays to explore "modern subjectivity as at once the outcome and the antithesis of Machiavellian dynamics." [For a different approach to Richard's failure as a monarch, see Phillips, below.] [The chapter incorporates Grady's article "Shakespeare's Links to Machiavelli and Montaigne: Constructing Intellectual Modernity in Early Modern Europe," *Comparative Literature* 52 (2000): 119–42.]

Hammer, Paul E. J. "Shakespeare's *Richard II*, the Play of 7 February 1601, and the Essex Rising." *Shakespeare Quarterly* 59 (2008): 1–35.

Hammer's discussion of the context and nature of the Essex Rising and of the identity of the play chosen for performance at the Globe on February 7, 1601, leads him to offer both a "new interpretation" of the events of February 8 and "new insights into how [*R2*] might have functioned politically in the last years of Elizabeth's rule," thereby confirming the special place it holds in Shakespeare scholarship as "the most conspicuous and famous example of a Shakespearean play transcending the confines of theatrical production to enter into real-life political drama during the playwright's own lifetime." The author argues that the royal authorities, led by the earl of Essex's enemies, misrepresented the events of February 8 as a "bungled *coup d'état*" aimed at seizing the queen and at destroying Essex's "personal enemies and reward[ing] his friends, and, one way or another, mak[ing] himself King 'Robert the First.'" While most scholars accept this "official" version of Essex's actions, Hammer contends that the earl was actually planning "to stage an aristocratic intervention at court," where he and fellow lords would "humbly petition . . . [the Queen] for the arrest of the earl's enemies on charges of treason and corruption"; "any risk of violence in the vicinity of the queen" was to be reduced and proper reverence for the sovereign maintained. As to the play performed on February 7, Hammer states that it had "no direct connection with what happened the following day because those events were unforeseen on Saturday afternoon, let alone a day or so earlier when the performance was commissioned." The aristocrats who arranged for and attended the performance of *R2* found in it the "perfect fit" for their "personal and political needs": they would "watch a play that featured their own ancestors and that seemed [in its first three acts, with the royal banishment of Bolingbroke and the denial of his titular claim to the duchy of Lancaster] to offer striking parallels with the fortunes of their leader, the earl of Essex." Moreover, in the play's final two acts, they would find "a salutary reminder of the need for special care" in the intervention being planned for the following week. "By seeing and knowing the outcome of 1399, they could avoid a fresh tragedy in 1601"; unlike Bolingbroke, Essex would "*properly*" remove the "caterpillars of the commonwealth" (2.3.170), ensuring that "Elizabeth [would] not become another Richard II." Ironically, because of the unexpected events of the next day, "Essex never got to become a more virtuous version of Bolingbroke but found himself consigned to the tragic role of a figure, like Richard II, whose enemies got to write the script."

Hibbard, G. R. "Making a Virtue of Virtuosity: *Love's Labour's Lost* and *Richard II.*" In *The Making of Shakespeare's Dramatic Poetry*, pp. 104–19 (esp. pp. 113–19). Toronto: University of Toronto Press, 1981.

    Calling *R2* a transitional/experimental play, Hibbard focuses on Richard's self-conscious language from 3.2 through 5.5, praising it as a brilliant advance in Shakespeare's search for a style that harmonizes poetic conceits and lyricism with theatrical demands for action and character. By allowing Richard the liberty to indulge in fanciful verbal extravagance, Shakespeare writes beautiful poetry that simultaneously reveals and criticizes his protagonist as a man who, instead of attempting to understand his experience, is all too ready to "descant" on it as a spectator seeking "a refuge in words." Lyrical expression that describes both the situation and the speaker's own consciousness of that situation is thereby rendered dramatic. The prison soliloquy at the beginning of 5.5 represents the culmination of Richard's self-conscious, self-critical discourse. In *R2*, Shakespeare writes "the poetry he wants to write . . . [while making] his own critical attitude to that poetry serve also as a criticism of his hero."

Holderness, Graham. "'A Woman's War': A Feminist Reading of *Richard II.*" In *Shakespeare Left and Right*, edited by Ivo Kamps, pp. 167–83. New York: Routledge, 1991.

    Noting Mowbray's distinction between masculine and feminine identity at 1.1.49–53 (hot blood versus cold words, heated battles versus scolding matches), Holderness examines *R2* through "a strategic conjuncture of feminism, historicism and the politics of gender." He focuses on the play's three female characters—the Duchess of Gloucester, the Queen, and the Duchess of York—all of whom are defined by their relationships with men as exclusively wives and mothers. Holderness identifies "sadness and melancholy" as the "natural fate" of females in this play, Richard's Queen being essentially a figure of pathos as she passively watches her husband's downfall. Unlike the other women, the Duchess of York "affects a success-story, precisely because she accepts and embraces the subjected and marginal role of women." The marginalization of women in *R2*, Holderness concludes, functions most importantly as a historical reality of the past, foregrounding the fundamental injustice at the core of patriarchy, a system the play "interrogates . . . and criticizes. Women may not be much in [*R2*], but femininity is." [For readings that challenge Holderness's view of the play's women, particularly that of the Queen as weak and powerless, see Laroche and Munroe, and Vaught, below.]

Hopkins, Lisa. "The King's Melting Body: *Richard II*." In *A Companion to Shakespeare's Works*, edited by Richard Dutton and Jean Howard, 2:395–411. Malden, Mass.: Blackwell, 2003.

"Despite its various chivalric trappings and its occasionally archaic feel," *R2* is "not medieval"; on the contrary, Hopkins contends, its roots lie in "its own, distinctively Elizabethan, historical moment," making *R2* "the most closely connected to [an Elizabethan audience] of all Shakespeare's history plays." Surprisingly, however, iconic medieval depictions of Richard (e.g., the Wilton diptych, the coronation portrait in Westminster Abbey, and the portrait effigy on his tomb) hold the key to *R2*'s "vitally contemporary concerns" (such as deposition, divine right, the king's two bodies, the "spectral presence" of the earl of Essex, colonialism, and national identity). Hopkins's examination of the tensions between the "visual protocols" of medieval portraiture and early modern practices of surveying and mapping leads her to conclude that "identity in the play is habitually fluid" and that boundaries—whether geographical (see 1.1.95–96 and 1.3.161–69) or sexual (see Richard's feminine self-imaging as a mother [3.2.8–10] and as Helen of Troy [4.1.292–94])—are "pointedly not inviolable." Awareness of the differences between "the shifting perspective of the itinerant surveyor and the single, fixed centrality of Richard II's coronation portrait" helps us see "how this play both evokes the world of the past and forces us, by adopting a modern perspective, to perceive it as such."

Laroche, Rebecca, and Jennifer Munroe. "On a Bank of Rue; Or Material Ecofeminist Inquiry and the Garden of *Richard II.*" *Shakespeare Studies* 42 (2014): 42–50.

Countering the traditional view of the garden scene (3.4) as solely metaphorical, i.e., as a trope for the body politic, Laroche and Munroe draw on the work of ecofeminists and food studies scholars to reveal the gender implications of the scene and, consequently, to argue for a reading that underscores the role of women in the play. When examined in terms of the materiality of plants and gardening practices, the Gardener's lines at 3.4.61–63 ("O, what pity is it / That he had not so trimmed and dressed his land / As we this garden!") highlight not the king's failure to imagine England in metaphoric terms but his failure to take "a cue from those who work outside with the land." Central to the authors' thesis are the gendered binaries of early modern gardening practices and garden spaces: orchards, typically associated with profit and pleasure, were considered to be a male domain; kitchen and herb gardens, essential for the nutritional and medical needs of the household, were regarded as a female province. The language of the scene—with references, on one hand, to arboreal practices (see lines 32, 37, 48, 62, and 64) and, on the other, to "noisome weeds," "wholesome" flowers, herbs, and plants such as rue (see lines

41, 42, 49, 112–13)—renders the garden "a composite of an orchard *and* a kitchen garden." For Shakespeare's audience, rue would have connoted not only an affective expression of grief but also (because of its rank aroma) the healing virtues of a bitter medicinal cure made by women: exactly what Richard's kingdom requires. Laroche and Munroe's emphasis both on the Queen's gendered association with female garden space and on the bank of rue that the Gardener will plant in soil fertilized by her tears causes them to assign the Queen a more influential presence than most critics concede (see, e.g., Holderness, above). In *R2*, "the dual nature of the material work of the garden"—the large-scale pruning of excess and the "more intimate" work of weeding—"points simultaneously to political righting of the realm and to the integral roles of men and women in material mending and healing, work that is not metaphoric and is essential to the larger healing that must take place."

Lopez, Jeremy, ed. *Richard II: New Critical Essays*. New York: Routledge, 2012.

In addition to a lengthy introduction (pp. 1–51), which includes an extensive bibliography, the volume contains eleven new essays: James Siemon, "Dead Men Talking: Elegiac Utterance, Monarchial Republicanism, and *Richard II*"; Roslyn L. Knutson, "The History Play, *Richard II*, and Repertorial Commerce"; Melissa E. Sanchez, "Bodies That Matter in *Richard II*"; Paul Menzer, "*c.f.* Marlowe"; Margaret Shewring, "Staging *Richard II* for a New Millennium"; Bridget Escolme, "Gendered Neurosis on Stage and Screen: Fiona Shaw's *Richard II*"; Brian Walsh, "The Dramaturgy of Discomfort in *Richard II*"; Mark Metzloff, "Insurgent Time: *Richard II* and the Periodization of Sovereignty"; Holger Schott Syme, " 'But, what euer you do, buy': *Richard II* as Popular Commodity"; Rebecca Lemon,

"Shakespeare's *Richard II* and Elizabethan Politics"; and Genevieve Love, "Going Back to That Well: *Richard II's* 'deposition scene.'" Lopez's introduction consists of four sections: (1) a survey of the play's critical afterlife in the last one hundred years and an "oblique perspective" on lesser-known, mostly regional North American productions after World War II; (2) a discussion of various kinds of historicist engagements with the play under the headings of source study, the bibliographical history of *R2*'s variant early texts, and historiographical criticism of the dramatic action "as . . . an interpretation of early modern or medieval history"; (3) an analysis of how thematic, generic, and character criticism of *R2* is "fundamentally informed by critical attitudes toward and questions about the efficacy of [poetic form]"; and (4) an overview of the volume's new critical essays. For the most part, the *R2* criticism of the past century has been historicist in character, focusing more on "what kind of king Richard is" rather than on "the kind of man the king is" (the focus of nineteenth-century scholarship, which examined the king as "independent . . . of history").

Phillips, James. "The Practicalities of the Absolute: Justice and Kingship in Shakespeare's *Richard II*." *ELH* 79 (2012): 161–77.

Phillips examines *R2* in terms of the "ethico-political history of the absolute," citing in particular the writings of such apologists for monarchical absolutism as the medieval Giles of Rome and the early modern Jean Bodin, both of whom viewed justice as the fundamental duty of a monarch, a claim reiterated in coronation oaths. "[S]ubject not to the law but to justice," the monarch is above the law only when the law itself is unjust or when "the mechanical application of even a good law would be unjust." The criterion, therefore, by which kingship—the "constitutionalization of an extraconstitutional power"—can itself be judged "is as the conduit of the justice that the laws in their formalism, archaicism, or conflict with one another fail to deliver." Since the king is the "terrestrial conduit" of justice, justice in turn must rule over him in his role as "the *deus ex machina* of the legal system." Phillips argues that Shakespeare's Richard fails as a monarch not because he is a "deficient Machiavellian" (Hugh Grady's claim; see above) but because (1) he does not understand the centrality of justice to his rule as a divine right king and (2) he fails to appreciate that the body politic accepts absolutist rule with "dissembling conditionality" as long as the commonwealth perceives the monarch to be just. "Richard's tragic fate is to expose the hypocrisy of a body politic that makes room for the absolute and yet expects the absolute to conduct itself in a moderate manner." The king's "pivotal infraction" in the play is his denial of Bolingbroke's rightful claim to the Duchy of Lancaster (2.1.168–70, 218–19), an act that causes the commonwealth to "muster...around [Bolingbroke] as the victim of expropriation" and to "call into question the justice of Richard's claim to kingship": "An unjust king invites deposition as the semblance of a king." As Phillips reads the play, the problem that Richard and his subjects face "is how to recognize justice, how to give its absoluteness room for operation in the body politic even as it defies institutionalization."

Potter, Lois. "The Antic Disposition of Richard II." *Shakespeare Survey* 27 (1974): 33–41.

Contrary to the traditional interpretation of Richard's highly rhetorical language as a sign of weakness, Potter reads it as a conscious attempt to assume a Hamlet-like antic disposition. In opting for verbal extravagance from the transitional 3.2 onward, Richard abandons the terse language that he had used to deflate the elaborate figuration of Bolingbroke, Mowbray,

Gaunt, and York in Acts 1 and 2; irony and the suggestion of duplicity, however, are present in Richard's language from beginning to end. In fact, irony serves as his major means of defense once he is deprived of political power. In the deposition scene, for example, where "a well-timed burst of hysterics" enables Richard to avoid reading aloud the list of charges brought against him, his verbal ambiguity forces Bolingbroke to declare his intentions publicly. By exploiting poetic conceits and using words to transform weakness into strength in 3.3 and 4.1, Richard shows his awareness of the evocative power of verbal theatrics and patriotic and religious sentiments to sway an audience. Throughout the latter half of the play the "ritualistic King of Sorrows" exists alongside a Richard who is "sharp-tongued, self-mocking and quite unresigned." Even from the coffin (5.6.29SD–52), Richard dominates the stage "in his silence as he had dominated it before with words."

Rackin, Phyllis. "The Role of the Audience in *Richard II*." *Shakespeare Quarterly* 36 (1985): 262–81.

By presenting history in *R2* not only as a quaint period piece (the perspective that emerges from the play's formal, ritualistic scenes) but also as current action, Shakespeare depicts "a living process that directly involves and implicates the audience in the theater." Rackin examines the trajectory of the audience's shifting responses in moving from the dilemma of conflicting loyalties—first to Bolingbroke's camp and then to Richard's; the deposition scene, she argues, marks "the crucial transfer" of audience sympathy. Richard's eloquence as the anointed king in 4.1, coupled with his several prophecies of divine retribution, intensifies the audience's feelings of guilt for having supported the rebels' cause. But Shakespeare goes on to present yet a third, explicitly theatrical, perspective on history in the Aumerle conspiracy scenes of Act 5, where the comedy distances or "alienates" audience members from the dramatic action, reminding them that they are simply attending a theatrical performance. The final transformation of York from sympathetic elder statesman to comic scapegoat releases the audience from complicity in the act of rebellion. [See also Rackin's full-length study of the history plays, *Stages of History: Shakespeare's English Chronicles* (Ithaca, N.Y.: Cornell University Press, 1990); the chapter on anachronism and nostalgia (especially pp. 117–37) incorporates much of the argument in this *Shakespeare Quarterly* essay.]

Saccio, Peter. "Richard II: The Fall of the King." In *Shakespeare's English Kings: History, Chronicle, and Drama*, pp. 17–35. 2nd ed. Oxford: Oxford University Press, 2000.

Saccio discusses the historical record and Shakespeare's creative use of it under four headings: the king's reign to 1397, the background of the Bolingbroke–Mowbray quarrel in 1398, the usurpation itself in 1399, and the earls' rebellion in 1400. Shakespeare's departures from his primary source, Holinshed's *Chronicles*, include the transformation of Richard's fractious uncles into well-intentioned senior statesmen, the depiction of Richard's Queen as a mature woman when in fact she was a child, the dramatic fabrication of the public deposition scene (a show that Bolingbroke would never have allowed), and the radical compression of the earls' rebellion in Act 5. The recurring question throughout Richard's reign was who would rule during his minority and who would advise and influence him when he came into his own. Although Richard reigned for twenty-two years, his accomplishments were dwarfed in the almost two hundred years following his death by one event: namely, his loss of the crown.

Scott, William O. " 'Like to a tenement': Landholding, Leasing, and Inheritance in *Richard II*." In *Law in Shakespeare*, edited by Constance Jordan, pp. 58–72. New York: Palgrave Macmillan, 2007.

Central to Scott's analysis of *R2* in light of medieval and early modern property law is Gaunt's charge that Richard leases out the nation "[l]ike to a tenement or pelting farm" (2.1.65–66). This passage—along with Gaunt's subsequent lines (115–20), York's warning to Richard (2.1.204–17), and Bolingbroke's argument for inheritance of the Duchy of Lancaster (2.3.117–40)—should be understood in the context of contemporary landholding practices, which involved "varieties of ownership": namely, freehold, copyhold, and leasehold (all of which Scott discusses at length, especially the differences in security between copyholds and leases). The nobles' criticism of Richard's "absolutist" conduct is voiced "not only through [the] argument about succession or inheritance but through an analogy with forms of property ownership and use that applied among commoners as well as among the nobility." Knowledge of the socioeconomic implications of early modern property law and of the secondary legal meanings of words such as "seize" (4.1.190), "convey" (4.1.330), and "waste" (5.5.50) enables us to tap into "other contests of ownership and power" with which an Elizabethan audience in the economy of the 1590s would have been familiar; for that audience, the play would have "renew[ed] questions of struggle and its customary modulation." In short, *R2* illustrates the threats to ownership and inheritance that a subject may suffer when the king misuses the "national property" and compromises his tenure as "hereditary monarch": by delegating the duties of royal stewardship of the kingdom and its material property "to favorites and tenants turned fee and rent collectors, Richard created a 'waste' of resources that the crown should have used to govern and sustain the people." As the essay concludes, Scott turns briefly to the "controversial notion of selfhood." Observing how Richard feels a loss of identity in the loss of his title and possessions, the author wonders whether selfhood "can be carefully defined for the sixteenth century through one's inherited or lawfully acquired status, possessions, and skills." [The essay is a condensed, updated version of "Landholding, Leasing, and Inheritance in *Richard II*," *Studies in English Literature 1500–1900* 42 (2002): 275–92.]

Sherman, Donovan. "'What more remains?': Messianic Performance in *Richard II*." *Shakespeare Quarterly* 65 (2014): 22–48.

Sherman reads *R2* as a play "littered with discarded objects" that, once having theatrically fulfilled a "prescribed ceremony," are cast aside as useless: a mirror, a scepter, gages, and, most prominent of all, the king himself. Rather than viewing the abundant theatricality in *R2* as "empty artifice," however, Sherman contends that the play's many episodes of "apparently failed enactments"—e.g., gages that fall "without fully initiating a duel" (1.1 and 4.1), a "seemingly seditious document [that] comically slips away into inconsequence" (5.3), and a deposition scene (4.1) in which Richard ends where he began, "in a public display of monarchical power transferring hands"—are in fact "successful instances" of what he calls "'messianic performance': a choreographed effacement and rendering irrelevant of action that must be executed *through* action." The first section of the essay ("Explicit Remnants") develops this concept by attending to two "resonant but seldom conversant" discourses: performance theory and the spirituality of St. Paul. In rethinking Richard's relationship to theater, Sherman focuses on the Richard of 4.1 who "vibrates somewhere between 'ay' and 'no,' which is to say 'nothing,' or more precisely 'no-no-thing,' performing himself into nearly quasi-substantial status" (see lines 210–11). By viewing Richard's "body natural" as a "performing" rather than "decaying body," Sherman counters the traditional critique of Richard's "unkinged body" as an "excessive, inefficacious use of theatricality"—i.e., as "a source of impotence." Noting how both Paul and performance studies evoke and are sensitive to "the insistent present," Sherman links Richard's "remains" to Paul's "remnant" (Rom. 11.5): neither is "just a physical leftover . . . but [rather] the wedge driven between self and self, between 'ay' and 'no,' the 'nothing' that must somehow 'be.'" The essay's second section ("Unpromising Gains") "maps the progression of messianic performances" in the play as a whole in order to "recover from its displays of seemingly hollow ritual a mode of performance that must, by its nature, appear to fail." Such mimetic "failure," Sherman argues, "does not indicate weakness or inefficacy but gestures powerfully at a form of logic beyond both the representational mechanics of the pageantry within the narrative and the play's own status as a work of staged action." Reading *R2* alongside St. Paul and in light of the tension in early modern theater between insubstantiality and materiality, Sherman concludes that the play's overall mode of "self-defeat" and the deposition scene, in particular, are "a theatrical detheatricalizing."

Shewring, Margaret. *King Richard II*. Shakespeare in Performance. Manchester: Manchester University Press, 1996.

The first part of this performance history devotes three chapters to the following topics: (1) the problematic structure of *R2*, (2) the concept of "state" as related to the issues of deposition and regicide, and (3) the "politics and aesthetics" of *R2*'s performance afterlife from the mid-seventeenth- to mid-nineteenth-century stage (with special attention paid to Nahum Tate's *The Sicilian Usurper* [1680], John Rich's Covent Garden production [1738], and the adaptations of Lewis Theobald [1719] and Richard Wroughton [1814/15]). The second part of the volume consists of five chapters that examine specific stage and television productions spanning the years 1857 to 1987: "The Spectacle of History: Charles Kean [1857] and Jeremy Irons / Barry Kyle [1986]," "A Play of Personality: Frank Benson [1896], John Gielgud [1929 and 1937], and Ian McKellen [1968]," "In the Context of English History: Anthony Quayle (1951); the RSC's Wars of the Roses (1964) and the ESC's Wars of the Roses (1986/89)," "Adjusting the Balance: John Barton (1973/74)," and "*Richard II* on Television: Maurice Evans (NBC [1951, 1954]) and Derek Jacobi (BBC [1978])." Turning to productions in cultural contexts outside of England and the United States, Shewring focuses the final chapter on the stagings of Jean Vilar (1947), Giorgio Strehler (1947), and Ariane Mnouchkine (1982). In an afterword titled "A *Richard II* for the 1990s," the author discusses Deborah Warner's 1995 revival for London's Royal National Theatre, with Fiona Shaw in the title role: "Warner's and Shaw's [*R2*] is a production devised for the 1990s, sensitive alike to the detachment of post-modernism and to a contradictory urge towards compassionate understanding. Whatever the ultimate judgment of scholars and critics, this compelling, essentially apolitical interpretation will earn its place in the collective memory of performance history." The volume concludes with a bibliography and three appendices relating, respectively, to the 1601 Lambarde Document, Charles Kean's 1857 elaborate staging of Bolingbroke's triumphant entry into London, and the names of major actors and staff for the productions discussed in the book. [See also Shewring's essay in Lopez, above.]

Siemon, James R. *Word Against Word: Shakespearean Utterance*. Massachusetts Studies in Early Modern Culture. Amherst: University of Massachusetts Press, 2002.

Working from the Bakhtinian circle's concept of art as a form of social utterance—and its "associated notions of social accent, dialogism, carnival, and heteroglossia"—Siemon uses *R2* to focus his examination of the "centripetal (homogenizing, hierarchizing) and centrifugal (dispersing, denormatizing) aspects" of Shakespeare's sociolinguistic environment: "despite its apparent thematic and formal unities," the play is "an arena marked by struggles among competing groups and orientations, with their socially defined languages and assumptions." While the book does not provide a complete reading of the play, Siemon attends throughout to the social implications of such formal features as tonality, diction, timing, gesture, and metaphor. Among the topics receiving chapter-length study are *R2's* place in contemporary debates on agrarian change, most notably, the enclosure movement (Chapter 3, "Landlord, Not King: Agrarian Change and Inter-articulation"); the play's construction of character and subject in the "highly-charged social space among utterances and languages" (Chapter 4, "'Subjected Thus': Utterance, Individuation, and Interlocution"); and *R2's* connection to the "tonality of lamentation and elegy" that was dominant in the literature of the 1590s (Chapter 5, "The Lamentable Tale of Me: Intonation, Politics, and Religion in *Richard II*"). In Siemon's reading, the character of Richard "emerges as a revealing example of a form of subjectivity constructed amid the demands of conflicting voices." To illustrate the "gains" to be had when one looks for "voices in everything and dialogic relationships among them," Siemon reconsiders Richard's soliloquy in 5.5; he concludes that it is "neither a simple revelation of a fatuous individual character nor the straightforward reiteration of a self-blinded ideology that ignores social differentiation. . . . [Richard's] subjective musings upon 'man' . . . turn out to have real political topicality for the realm of 'men' now constituting . . . his former kingdom." [See also Siemon's essay in Lopez, above.]

Syme, Holger Schott. *Theatre and Testimony in Shakespeare's England: A Culture of Mediation*. Cambridge: Cambridge University Press, 2012.

Contrary to "the influential view that the [early modern] period underwent a crisis of representation," Syme (drawing on archival research in the fields of law, demonology, historiography, and science) traces "a pervasive conviction that testimony and report," when delivered by proper figures of authority, "provided access to truth." Viewing early modern English culture as one of "mediation dominated by transactions in which one person stood for another, giving voice to absent speakers or bringing past events to life," Syme constructs "a revisionist account of the nature of representation on the early modern stage"; the result is "a radically new explanation for the theatre's importance in Shakespeare's time." The chapter on *R2* explores the play under six headings: "Paper Witnesses: Historiography and the Rhetoric of Testimony," "Holinshed's Richard: Authority by Deferral," "Bearing Witness: *Richard II* and the Repetition of the Past," "Depositions, Deferral, and the Fantasy of Presence," "Immanence vs. Reference: The Impossibility of Self-Deposition," and "Scripted Confession and Reading the Self: Acts of Representation." *R2*, Syme writes, "is not just a history play; it is a play about the making and telling of histories. Its main character is not merely a king, but also, in his own words, a historian" who "tell[s] sad stories of the death of kings" (3.2.161): Richard "inserts himself into an account, yet to be written, of personal suffering," and at the same time "conceives of himself as both allegorically linked to and the end product of a teleological trajectory of 'murdered' monarchs." As a whole, the play "can be said to shift back and forth from postures and claims of immanence ['the immediacy of the embodied'] to a system grounded in gestures of mediation and deferral." This movement between the two poles of presence and representation becomes particularly feverish and revealing in the deposition scene as the sequence moves first from Bolingbroke's faith in the testimonial force of Bagot's freely spoken word to York's report of Richard's resignation, and then from Carlisle's insistence on the king's presence to Richard's "proposed and realized performances of reading" (whether of the list of crimes he is to "ventriloquize" or of "his own reflected face" in the mirror passage). Syme's close reading of 4.1—along with the analogous description in Holinshed's *Chronicles*—reveals that both depict the deposition as "a scene of scripting, reading and reporting; an event made up of performative vocal acts, their written sources, and their ultimate reconstitution in and as writing," thereby making it history. In both the *Chronicles* and *R2*, the deposition "triggers an extended, if oblique, reflection on how strategies of deferral and substitution construct legal, historiographical and representational authority."

Vaught, Jennifer C. " 'Wise men ne'er sit and wail their woes': Woeful Rhetoric and Crocodile Tears in Shakespeare's *Richard II*." In *Masculinity and Emotion in Early Modern English Literature*, pp. 88–113. Aldershot, Eng.: Ashgate, 2008.

In the chapter on *R2*, Vaught argues that "emotions in general and tears in particular" serve as manipulative "avenues of agency," serving to empower rather than weaken Richard and the play's three female characters (the Duchess of Gloucester, the Queen, and the Duchess of York). The more that Richard allies himself with women and the emotional registers conventionally labeled "feminine," the stronger he becomes, his "grief and patience" (5.2.36) suggesting a heroism "bas[ed] . . . on emotionally persuasive, rather than militaristic factors." To buttress her argument, Vaught focuses on Richard's emotionally charged utterances in selected scenes: his return from Ireland (3.2), his histrionic "performance" at Flint Castle (3.3), his "theatrical" deposition (4.1), his poignant farewell to the Queen (5.1), and his solitary confinement at Pomfret Castle (5.5). The cumulative effect of these affective moments enables Richard in the second half of the play to "regain . . . a vital, if imaginary, sense of authority and agency": in control of a narrative that evokes sympathy for himself (as the legendary " 'lamentable' King" of chronicle and oral accounts) and disdain for Bolingbroke/Henry IV (as the "cold-hearted" usurper), Richard wields rhetorical power over his onstage and offstage audiences. In contrast, Bolingbroke's "sparse emotional displays make less of an impression" on those same audiences. A "compelling figure prone to affect," whose story escapes the coffin to be "continually retold and never finished," Shakespeare's Richard is a forerunner of the "man of feeling" who would dominate the eighteenth-century stage.

Shakespeare's Language

Abbott, E. A. *A Shakespearian Grammar.* New York: Haskell House, 1972.

This compact reference book, first published in 1870, helps with many difficulties in Shakespeare's language. It systematically accounts for a host of differences between Shakespeare's usage and sentence structure and our own.

Blake, Norman. *Shakespeare's Language: An Introduction.* New York: St. Martin's Press, 1983.

This general introduction to Elizabethan English discusses various aspects of the language of Shakespeare and his contemporaries, offering possible meanings for hundreds of ambiguous constructions.

Dobson, E. J. *English Pronunciation, 1500–1700.* 2 vols. Oxford: Clarendon Press, 1968.

This long and technical work includes chapters on spelling (and its reformation), phonetics, stressed vowels, and consonants in early modern English.

Hope, Jonathan. *Shakespeare's Grammar.* London: Arden Shakespeare, 2003.

Commissioned as a replacement for Abbott's *Shakespearian Grammar,* Hope's book is organized in terms of the two basic parts of speech, the noun and the verb. After extensive analysis of the noun phrase and the verb phrase come briefer discussions of subjects and agents, objects, complements, and adverbials.

Houston, John. *Shakespearean Sentences: A Study in Style and Syntax.* Baton Rouge: Louisiana State University Press, 1988.

Houston studies Shakespeare's stylistic choices,

considering matters such as sentence length and the relative positions of subject, verb, and direct object. Examining plays throughout the canon in a roughly chronological, developmental order, he analyzes how sentence structure is used in setting tone, in characterization, and for other dramatic purposes.

Onions, C. T. *A Shakespeare Glossary*. Oxford: Clarendon Press, 1986.
This revised edition updates Onions's standard, selective glossary of words and phrases in Shakespeare's plays that are now obsolete, archaic, or obscure.

Robinson, Randal. *Unlocking Shakespeare's Language: Help for the Teacher and Student*. Urbana, Ill.: National Council of Teachers of English and the ERIC Clearinghouse on Reading and Communication Skills, 1989.
Specifically designed for the high-school and undergraduate college teacher and student, Robinson's book addresses the problems that most often hinder present-day readers of Shakespeare. Through work with his own students, Robinson found that many readers today are particularly puzzled by such stylistic characteristics as subject-verb inversion, interrupted structures, and compression. He shows how our own colloquial language contains comparable structures, and thus helps students recognize such structures when they find them in Shakespeare's plays. This book supplies worksheets—with examples from major plays—to illuminate and remedy such problems as unusual sequences of words and the separation of related parts of sentences.

Williams, Gordon. *A Dictionary of Sexual Language and Imagery in Shakespearean and Stuart Literature*. 3 vols. London: Athlone Press, 1994.
Williams provides a comprehensive list of words to

which Shakespeare, his contemporaries, and later Stuart writers gave sexual meanings. He supports his identification of these meanings by extensive quotations.

Shakespeare's Life

Baldwin, T. W. *William Shakspere's Petty School.* Urbana: University of Illinois Press, 1943.

Baldwin here investigates the theory and practice of the petty school, the first level of education in Elizabethan England. He focuses on that educational system primarily as it is reflected in Shakespeare's art.

Baldwin, T. W. *William Shakspere's Small Latine and Lesse Greeke.* 2 vols. Urbana: University of Illinois Press, 1944.

Baldwin attacks the view that Shakespeare was an uneducated genius—a view that had been dominant among Shakespeareans since the eighteenth century. Instead, Baldwin shows, the educational system of Shakespeare's time would have given the playwright a strong background in the classics, and there is much in the plays that shows how Shakespeare benefited from such an education.

Beier, A. L., and Roger Finlay, eds. *London 1500–1700: The Making of the Metropolis.* New York: Longman, 1986.

Focusing on the economic and social history of early modern London, these collected essays probe aspects of metropolitan life, including "Population and Disease," "Commerce and Manufacture," and "Society and Change."

Chambers, E. K. *William Shakespeare: A Study of Facts and Problems.* 2 vols. Oxford: Clarendon Press, 1930.

Analyzing in great detail the scant historical data, Chambers's complex, scholarly study considers the nature of the texts in which Shakespeare's work is preserved.

Cressy, David. *Education in Tudor and Stuart England.* London: Edward Arnold, 1975.
This volume collects sixteenth-, seventeenth-, and early eighteenth-century documents detailing aspects of formal education in England, such as the curriculum, the control and organization of education, and the education of women.

Duncan-Jones, Katherine. *Shakespeare: An Ungentle Life.* London: Arden Shakespeare, 2010.
This biography, first published in 2001 under the title *Ungentle Shakespeare: Scenes from His Life,* sets out to look into the documents from Shakespeare's personal life—especially legal and financial records—and it finds there a man very different from the one portrayed in more traditional biographies. He is "ungentle" in being born to a lower social class and in being a bit ruthless and more than a bit stingy. As the author notes, "three topics were formerly taboo both in polite society and in Shakespearean biography: social class, sex and money. I have been indelicate enough to give a good deal of attention to all three." She examines "Shakespeare's uphill struggle to achieve, or purchase, 'gentle' status." She finds that "Shakespeare was strongly interested in intense relationships with well-born young men." And she shows that he was "reluctant to divert much, if any, of his considerable wealth towards charitable, neighbourly, or altruistic ends." She insists that his plays and poems are "great, and enduring," and that it is in them "that the best of him is to be found."

Dutton, Richard. *William Shakespeare: A Literary Life.* New York: St. Martin's Press, 1989.

Not a biography in the traditional sense, Dutton's very readable work nevertheless "follows the contours of Shakespeare's life" as it examines Shakespeare's career as playwright and poet, with consideration of his patrons, theatrical associations, and audience.

Honan, Park. *Shakespeare: A Life.* New York: Oxford University Press, 1998.

Honan's accessible biography focuses on the various contexts of Shakespeare's life—physical, social, political, and cultural—to place the dramatist within a lucidly described world. The biography includes detailed examinations of, for example, Stratford schooling, theatrical politics of 1590s London, and the careers of Shakespeare's associates. The author draws on a wealth of established knowledge and on interesting new research into local records and documents; he also engages in speculation about, for example, the possibilities that Shakespeare was a tutor in a Catholic household in the north of England in the 1580s and that he acted particular roles in his own plays, areas that reflect new, but unproven and debatable, data—though Honan is usually careful to note where a particular narrative "has not been capable of proof or disproof."

Potter, Lois. *The Life of William Shakespeare: A Critical Biography.* Malden, Mass.: Wiley-Blackwell, 2012.

This critical biography of Shakespeare takes the playwright from cradle to grave, paying primary attention to his literary and theatrical milieu. The chapters "follow a chronological sequence," each focusing on a handful of years in the playwright's life. In the chapters that cover his playwriting years (5–17), each chapter focuses on events in Stratford-upon-Avon and in London (especially in the commercial theaters) while giving equal space to discussions of the plays and/or poems Shakespeare wrote during those years. Filled with information from Shakespeare's literary and theatrical worlds, the biography also shares frequent insights into how modern productions of a given play can shed light on the play, especially in scenes that Shakespeare's text presents ambiguously.

Schoenbaum, S. *William Shakespeare: A Compact Documentary Life.* New York: Oxford University Press, 1977.

Schoenbaum's evidence-based biography of Shakespeare is a compact version of his magisterial folio-size *Shakespeare: A Documentary Life* (New York: Oxford University Press, 1975). Schoenbaum structures his readable "compact" narrative around the documents that still exist which chronicle Shakespeare's familial, theatrical, legal, and financial existence. These documents, along with those discovered since the 1970s, form the basis of almost all Shakespeare biographies written since Schoenbaum's books appeared.

Shakespeare's Theater

Bentley, G. E. *The Profession of Player in Shakespeare's Time, 1590–1642.* Princeton: Princeton University Press, 1984.

Bentley readably sets forth a wealth of evidence about performance in Shakespeare's time, with special attention to the relations between player and company, and the business of casting, managing, and touring.

Berry, Herbert. *Shakespeare's Playhouses.* New York: AMS Press, 1987.

Berry's six essays collected here discuss (with illustrations) varying aspects of the four playhouses in which Shakespeare had a financial stake: the Theatre in Shoreditch, the Blackfriars, and the first and second Globe.

Berry, Herbert, William Ingram, and Glynne Wickham, eds. *English Professional Theatre, 1530–1660*. Cambridge: Cambridge University Press, 2000.

Wickham presents the government documents designed to control professional players, their plays, and playing places. Ingram handles the professional actors, giving as representative a life of the actor Augustine Phillips, and discussing, among other topics, patrons, acting companies, costumes, props, playbooks, provincial playing, and child actors. Berry treats the twenty-three different London playhouses from 1560 to 1660 for which there are records, including four inns.

Cook, Ann Jennalie. *The Privileged Playgoers of Shakespeare's London*. Princeton: Princeton University Press, 1981.

Cook's work argues, on the basis of sociological, economic, and documentary evidence, that Shakespeare's audience—and the audience for English Renaissance drama generally—consisted mainly of the "privileged."

Dutton, Richard, ed. *The Oxford Handbook of Early Modern Theatre*. Oxford: Oxford University Press, 2011.

Dutton divides his study of the theatrical industry of Shakespeare's time into the following sections: "Theatre Companies," "London Playhouses," "Other Playing Spaces," "Social Practices," and "Evidence of Theatrical Practices." Each of these sections is further subdivided, with subdivisions assigned to individual experts. W. R. Streitberger treats the "Adult Playing Companies to 1583"; Sally-Beth MacLean those from

1583 to 1593; Roslyn L. Knutson, 1593–1603; Tom
Rutter, 1603–1613; James J. Marino, 1613–1625; and
Martin Butler, the "Adult and Boy Playing Companies
1625–1642." Michael Shapiro is responsible for the
"Early (Pre-1590) Boy Companies and Their Acting
Venues," while Mary Bly writes of "The Boy Compa-
nies 1599–1613." David Kathman handles "Inn-Yard
Playhouses"; Gabriel Egan, "The Theatre in Shoreditch
1576–1599"; Andrew Gurr, "Why the Globe Is Famous";
Ralph Alan Cohen, "The Most Convenient Place: The
Second Blackfriars Theater and Its Appeal"; Mark
Bayer, "The Red Bull Playhouse"; and Frances Teague,
"The Phoenix and the Cockpit-in-Court Playhouses."
Turning to "Other Playing Spaces," Suzanne Westfall
describes how " 'He who pays the piper calls the tune':
Household Entertainments"; Alan H. Nelson, "The
Universities and the Inns of Court"; Peter Greenfield,
"Touring"; John H. Astington, "Court Theatre"; and
Anne Lancashire, "London Street Theater." For "Social
Practices," Alan Somerset writes of "Not Just Sir Oliver
Owlet: From Patrons to 'Patronage' of Early Modern
Theatre," Dutton himself of "The Court, the Master of
the Revels, and the Players," S. P. Cerasano of "The-
ater Entrepreneurs and Theatrical Economics," Ian W.
Archer of "The City of London and the Theatre," David
Kathman of "Players, Livery Companies, and Appren-
tices," Kathleen E. McLuskie of "Materiality and the
Market: The Lady Elizabeth's Men and the Challenge
of Theatre History," Heather Hirschfield of " 'For the
author's credit': Issues of Authorship in English Renaissance Drama," and Natasha Korda of "Women in the
Theater." On "Theatrical Practices," Jacalyn Royce discusses "Early Modern Naturalistic Acting: The Role of
the Globe in the Development of Personation"; Tiffany
Stern, "Actors' Parts"; Alan Dessen, "Stage Directions
and the Theater Historian"; R. B. Graves, "Lighting";

Lucy Munro, "Music and Sound"; Dutton himself, "Properties"; Thomas Postlewait, "Eyewitnesses to History: Visual Evidence for Theater in Early Modern England"; and Eva Griffith, "Christopher Beeston: His Property and Properties."

Greg, W. W. *Dramatic Documents from the Elizabethan Playhouses*. 2 vols. Oxford: Clarendon Press, 1931.

Greg itemizes and briefly describes almost all the play manuscripts that survive from the period 1590 to around 1660, including, among other things, players' parts. His second volume offers facsimiles of selected manuscripts.

Harbage, Alfred. *Shakespeare's Audience*. New York: Columbia University Press, 1941.

Harbage investigates the fragmentary surviving evidence to interpret the size, composition, and behavior of Shakespeare's audience.

Keenan, Siobhan. *Acting Companies and Their Plays in Shakespeare's London*. London: Bloomsbury Arden Shakespeare, 2014.

Keenan "explores how the needs, practices, resources and pressures on acting companies and playwrights informed not only the performance and publication of contemporary dramas but playwrights' writing practices." Each chapter focuses on one important factor that influenced Renaissance playwrights and players. The initial focus is on how "the nature and composition of the acting companies" influenced the playwrights who wrote for them. Then, using "the Diary of theatre manager Philip Henslowe and manuscript playbooks showing signs of theatrical use," Keenan examines the relations between acting companies and playwrights. Other influences include "the physical design and facilities of London's outdoor and indoor theatrical spaces" and the diverse audiences for plays, including royal and noble patrons.

Shapiro, Michael. *Children of the Revels: The Boy Companies of Shakespeare's Time and Their Plays.* New York: Columbia University Press, 1977.

Shapiro chronicles the history of the amateur and quasi-professional child companies that flourished in London at the end of Elizabeth's reign and the beginning of James's.

The Publication of Shakespeare's Plays

Blayney, Peter W. M. *The First Folio of Shakespeare.* Hanover, Md.: Folger, 1991.

Blayney's accessible account of the printing and later life of the First Folio—an amply illustrated catalogue to a 1991 Folger Shakespeare Library exhibition—analyzes the mechanical production of the First Folio, describing how the Folio was made, by whom and for whom, how much it cost, and its ups and downs (or, rather, downs and ups) since its printing in 1623.

Hinman, Charlton. *The Norton Facsimile: The First Folio of Shakespeare.* 2nd ed. New York: W. W. Norton, 1996.

This facsimile presents a photographic reproduction of an "ideal" copy of the First Folio of Shakespeare; Hinman attempts to represent each page in its most fully corrected state. This second edition includes an important new introduction by Peter W. M. Blayney.

Hinman, Charlton. *The Printing and Proof-Reading of the First Folio of Shakespeare.* 2 vols. Oxford: Clarendon Press, 1963.

In the most arduous study of a single book ever

undertaken, Hinman attempts to reconstruct how the Shakespeare First Folio of 1623 was set into type and run off the press, sheet by sheet. He also provides almost all the known variations in readings from copy to copy.

Werstine, Paul. *Early Modern Playhouse Manuscripts and the Editing of Shakespeare.* Cambridge: Cambridge University Press, 2012.
Werstine examines in detail nearly two dozen texts associated with the playhouses in and around Shakespeare's time, conducting the examination against the background of the two idealized forms of manuscript that have governed the editing of Shakespeare from the twentieth into the twenty-first century—Shakespeare's so-called foul papers and the so-called promptbooks of his plays. By comparing the two extant texts of John Fletcher's *Bonduca,* one in manuscript and the other printed in 1647, Werstine shows that the term "foul papers" that is found in a note in the *Bonduca* manuscript does not refer, as editors have believed, to a species of messy authorial manuscript but is instead simply a designation for a manuscript, whatever its features, that has served as the copy from which another manuscript has been made. By surveying twenty-one texts with theatrical markup, he demonstrates that the playhouses used a wide variety of different kinds of manuscripts and printed texts but did not use the highly regularized promptbooks of the eighteenth-century theaters and later. His presentation of the peculiarities of playhouse texts provides an empirical basis for inferring the nature of the manuscripts that lie behind printed Shakespeare plays.